REBEL TALENT

Francesca Gino is an award-winning researcher and the Tandon Family Professor of Business Administration at Harvard Business School. Her consulting and speaking clients include Bacardi, Akamai, Disney, Goldman Sachs, Honeywell, Novartis, P&G, and the US Air Force, Army, and Navy. She has been honoured as one of the world's top 40 business professors under 40 by Poets & Quants and one of the world's 50 most influential management thinkers by Thinkers50. Her work has been featured on CNN and NPR, as well as in the *Economist*, *Financial Times*, *New York Times*, *Newsweek*, *Scientific American*, and *Psychology Today*.

REBEL
TALENT

Why It Pays to
BREAK THE RULES
at Work and in Life

FRANCESCA GINO

PAN BOOKS

First published 2018 by Dey Books,
an imprint of HarperCollins Publishers, New York

First published in the UK 2018 by Macmillan

This edition first published 2019 by Pan Books
an imprint of Pan Macmillan
20 New Wharf Road, London N1 9RR
Associated companies throughout the world
www.panmacmillan.com

ISBN 978-1-5098-6063-0

1 3 5 7 9 8 6 4 2

A CIP catalogue record for this book is available from the British Library.

Printed and bound by CPI Group (UK) Ltd, Croydon, CR0 4YY

Visit www.panmacmillan.com to read more about all our books
and to buy them. You will also find features, author interviews and
news of any author events, and you can sign up for e-newsletters
so that you're always first to hear about our new releases.

To Alexander, Olivia, and Emma

*In the real-life version of my favorite improv
comedy game, you are the "Three Things!"
that make life really matter.*

CONTENTS

INTRODUCTION

MARCIA!

You don't let tradition bind you. You let it set you free.
—MASSIMO BOTTURA, OWNER AND CHEF, OSTERIA FRANCESCANA

"*Marcia!*" Upon hearing this command, which means "Gear up!" in Italian, I hustled from the hushed dining room back to the bright, boisterous kitchen to pick up the next dish—called, of all things, "The Crunchy Part of the Lasagna" (*La parte croccante della lasagna*). Spoonfuls of ragù and béchamel rested under a sheet of pasta that looked like the corner piece of a lasagna—all carefully assembled to take on the appearance of a lightly scorched Italian flag. I followed the lead of another waiter, Pino, as he picked up his dish and then walked to the dining room. My hand trembled as, in unison, Pino and I placed our plates in front of a famous Italian couple who were celebrating their wedding anniversary. On the walls, painted light blue and gray, hung a world-class collection of contemporary art, one of many unusual touches at Osteria Francescana, a restaurant in Modena, Italy, that holds three Michelin stars and took first place in the World's 50 Best Restaurant awards in 2016. It was the first Italian restaurant in history to reach the top of the list.

Back in the kitchen, Pino and I picked up another signature

dish, *"Bollito non bollito"*—quite literally "Boiled Meats, Not Boiled." Bollito misto is a classic northern Italian stew largely composed of boiled meat. Traditionally, the dish consists of various parts of the cow, such as the tongue and other off cuts, served with the broth and a *salsa verde* (green sauce) and sometimes a few other piquant condiments. Although the dish is comforting on a winter day, it is not very pleasing to the eye, and the process of boiling the meat strips it of its flavor and color. Yet this is simply how the dish is done. Italian cooking follows an extremely stringent set of rules: Short pasta goes with meat sauces, while long pasta goes with seafood sauces. Time-honored recipes are not to be polluted with substitutions. From cooking and folk dances to festivals celebrating saints and a day off for La Befana, a night in January when a good witch on a broomstick delivers candy, Italian culture cherishes its traditions.

Massimo Bottura, the owner and chef behind Osteria Francescana, wanted to challenge the traditional way bollito misto is cooked. After much experimentation with his team, Bottura discovered that the taste and texture of the meat were far superior if he used *sous vide*, a cooking technique where food is placed in a vacuum-sealed plastic pouch and immersed in heated water to be cooked at a precise, consistent temperature for hours. In *Bollito non bollito*, six different cuts of meat are cooked *sous vide* and then shaped into cubes. Each block is then placed on the plate in a line, alongside a second line of bright green parsley, smoked red and yellow gelatin made with peppers, a few capers and anchovies, onion marmalade, and some apple mustard. The dish, I learn, is inspired by New York City, where Bottura worked when he was a young man. In a nod to Central Park, the meat cubes rise like little skyscrapers above green foam trees, and the red and yellow gelatin makes a lawn with little anchovy people mingling on it. *Bollito non bollito* leaves you speechless; the cubes melt in your mouth like anxiety after a first kiss, bursting with waves of intense flavor: meaty, fatty, and sumptuous, yet buffeted by the light herbaceous foam and the gelatin.

Two orders of *Bollito non bollito* for Table 8 were ready in the kitchen. I carefully adjusted my plate until it matched Pino's, watching for his approval. I followed him out of the kitchen, matching his movements, and taking care to protect the delicate dish.

What was I, a Harvard Business School professor, doing in the heart of Italy's Emilia Romagna, serving food in one of the world's top restaurants? I was as surprised as anyone to have ended up there. But I had written two Harvard Business School case studies of fast-food chains, and I decided that it would be interesting to see how restaurants work at the other end of the spectrum. I contacted Bottura, and he told me that to understand his business, I would have to spend a full day in the kitchen and another in the dining room. No problem, I told him: On-site visits are a typical part of HBS case studies. Plus, being a native Italian, I always take any excuse I can to visit Italy.

I showed up early on the morning of my first day. As I entered one of the restaurant's three dining rooms, I saw a tall man chatting with the staff—Giuseppe Palmieri, the restaurant's longtime maître d' (called "Il Direttore" at the Osteria) and sommelier. Seeing a new face, he welcomed me with a smile. Everyone calls him "Beppe." Beppe introduced me to Pino, who was apparently going to try to keep me out of trouble. Just a few minutes later, I was polishing dishes and glasses with Pino. Next, we took care of the silverware and then the *mise en place*—getting the tables ready. A few other activities followed, including checking that there were flowers in all the appropriate places, and helping to set the table for the staff meal. As we prepared for our first customers at noon, it dawned on me that Bottura planned to have me do everything, including serve customers, during my time there. I had worked in various low-key restaurants in Italy and in the UK when I was younger, but Bottura did not know this. Putting a novice out in the dining room of a top restaurant—my hands trembling as I placed dishes on the table—seemed a rather odd move, and not one I imagine other owners of fancy restaurants would make.

It was classic Bottura. Many of Bottura's management decisions can seem impulsive. In 2005, two head chefs had joined Osteria Francescana: Kondo Takahiko, known as Taka, had lunch as a customer and, not long after, was cooking in the kitchen; Davide di Fabio had just started the process of sending out applications when he received a phone call from Bottura, offering him a job without even an interview. Bottura first met Beppe while he was working at a big two-Michelin-star restaurant close to Bologna, a place where Bottura and his wife used to dine. On his way home from dinner the first night they met, Bottura called Beppe with a job offer. Many of Bottura's hires happened this way: fast, almost as if by accident.

The second youngest of five children, Bottura grew up in Modena, not far from Osteria Francescana. His mother spent most of the day cooking, alongside her own mother, to feed the children, her husband, a sister-in-law and a brother-in-law who were living with them, and everybody's friends. As a five-year-old boy, Bottura often watched his mother and grandmother cook, curious about the rolling pins they used to make pasta and the interesting tortellini shapes. When his brothers got home from school, they would chase him around the kitchen, using any makeshift weapons they could find. Bottura would hide in his safe spot under the kitchen table, ready to eat the bits of pasta dough that ended up on the floor.

Bottura didn't go to culinary school. His career as a chef was an act of defiance. He had gone to law school to please his father but dropped out after two uninspiring years. In 1986, the Campazzo, a trattoria on the outskirts of Modena, came up for sale. The restaurant was falling apart, and Bottura, twenty-three at the time, had no restaurant experience. But he thought—*why not?* After all, he had done plenty of cooking. When he was still in high school, he and his friends would often find themselves back at Bottura's house after a late night of studying or partying, and he was always the one at the stove. He remembers taking a beach vacation near Salerno, in southern Italy, when he was eighteen. He would use a megaphone to call down to the water, asking what kind of pasta his friends wanted for dinner, carbonara or amatriciana.

Bottura is in his fifties, thin and bearded, with graying hair. He wears chunky, modern, black glasses and comfortable jeans, cuffed at the bottom. His hands are in constant motion. I was with him when a supplier dropped off fresh *mozzarella di bufala*, and he immediately opened the box, carefully lifting out a large, white, creamy ball of mozzarella. A staff member came in with a fork and knife so that he could taste it, but Bottura was already taking big chunks off with his bare hands. "This is simply divine," he said, handing me a piece. "You've got to taste it."

I once asked Bottura who inspired him, and he named the Chinese conceptual artist Ai Weiwei. Trained in the West, Ai combines different traditions, particularly minimalist and conceptual art. One of Ai's performance pieces was *Dropping a Han Dynasty Urn*, in which the artist smashed a two-thousand-year-old historic vase. "Why break thousands of years of history in an instant?" Bottura asked me. "You see, as I came to understand later, Ai's destructive gesture was actually a constructive one. A beginning. Break, transform, create."

MOST BUSINESSES ARE ALL ABOUT FOLLOWING THE RULES, NOT BREAKING THEM. Whether they are standard procedures on how a job needs to be done, a detailed chain of command, or even the dress code on the job, rules can be found everywhere in organizations. Disregard the rules and it will lead to trouble. Even chaos. Rebels are grudgingly tolerated, or, if they become too annoying, they are shown the door.

Bottura was different. In a context where rules had been cemented by centuries of tradition, he could seem utterly reckless—yet, somehow, it all worked in his restaurant, and spectacularly well. In fifteen years of studying businesses, spending time in the environments where people do their work, and talking to executives, I have occasionally run across characters like Bottura: People who are not afraid to break the rules when the rules are holding them back. People who question their own assumptions and strongest beliefs, as well as the widely accepted norms around them, to identify more creative, effective ways of doing transcendent work. People who are "deviants," but in a positive and constructive way.

For years, my academic work led me to study why people cheat on exams or tax forms, or tell lies on speed-dating websites, or don't stop at red lights. I had become an expert on people who break the rules and, rightly so, end up in trouble. But over the years, I also saw how much rule breaking is associated with innovation. I followed stories of corporate corruption and misconduct, yes, but also stories of courage. These were stories of rule breaking that brought about positive change and, in ways big and small, made the world a better place. I found myself wondering, what might we all learn from these people? What are their secrets?

At around the same time that I became curious about these questions, I had also begun to explore another phenomenon. At many of the companies I studied, work was not something that most people enjoyed. I saw the same pattern again and again: Employees would become disengaged after a certain amount of time at a job and would use more and more of their time unproductively—and in ways that made them unhappy and frustrated. Why was this the case? Or, to put it another way: Why does work suck?

On a visit to the Harvard Coop, a local store in Cambridge,

these two ideas came together for me. I was browsing the book-shelves, a cup of coffee in my hand, when a book caught my eye. Its appearance was somewhat unusual (it was large, and merlot in color, with thick gold lettering on its cover), and so was its title: *Never Trust a Skinny Italian Chef*. It was a cookbook, but not a typical one. It was filled with beautiful color photos of unusual, playful dishes, like *La parte croccante della lasagna*, and each was accompanied by the unusual tale of its origin. This is where I first learned the story of Massimo Bottura and how he had sought "to break with tradition and make way for a new Italian kitchen." I know well how Italians value their traditions, and so it was im-mediately clear to me that Bottura was a rebel. But I also recog-nized how much he loved his work. This connection—between rule breaking and passion for one's work—was not one I had made before, and yet it seemed powerful. The two so often go together.

I teach at Harvard Business School, but my work is grounded in psychology. Across borders, and between industries, organiza-tions differ in so many respects. And yet they all share one thing: *People* work in them. The confluence between organizations and psychology is fascinating because it allows me to make sense of behaviors that, on the surface, seem to make little or no sense at all. Looking inside an organization raises all sorts of questions—from why we avoid difficult conversations to how we work effectively in teams. To answer them, at a basic level, we need to understand how our minds work—the psychology behind our decisions. This psychological perspective was essential as I sought to understand rebels and the organizations in which they work.

I have found rebels in many places over the last few years, from a Ducati Corse motorcycle racetrack to call centers in remote, ru-ral parts of India. I've traveled the streets of Milan, raced through the desert in the Middle East on quads, and walked the floors of various manufacturing plants. I've talked to musicians, magicians, surgeons, sport coaches, CEOs, and pilots. I've gone behind the scenes of improv theaters and sat through welcoming and training sessions at a professional services firm. I traveled to Pixar in San Francisco, to Valve Software in Seattle, to Goldman Sachs in New York, and to Morning Star in California.

The rebels I met in these organizations came from all walks of life, and each struck me as unique. But all of them have the quality that I have come to call *rebel talent*. In my observations, I have also come to identify five core elements of rebel talent. The first is *novelty*, seeking out challenge and the new. The second is *curiosity*, the impulse we all had as children to constantly ask "why"? The third is *perspective*, the ability rebels have to constantly broaden their view of the world and see it as others do. The fourth is *diversity*, the tendency to challenge predetermined social roles and reach out to those who may appear different. And the fifth is *authenticity*, which rebels embrace in all that they do, remaining open and vulnerable in order to connect with others and learn from them.

As this book progresses, I will explore each of the five elements of rebel talent in more depth, and I will show you how to combine them successfully, like executing a great recipe. Rebellion, as you'll see, is an approach to life and work that we can all embrace. Rule breaking does not have to get us into trouble, if done correctly and in the right doses—in fact, it can help us get ahead. To see this in action, we'll journey to some surprising stages of rebellion, from a Tennessee drive-through of a fast-food chain with a giant hot dog on its roof to Italy's first typewriter factory in the foothills of the Italian Alps. We'll visit rebels at work in high-end hotels, tomato fields, consulting firms, and a Hollywood movie studio. We'll learn from rebels who are willing to be their most vulnerable in front of twenty thousand–plus basketball fans. And I'll ultimately share the eight principles rebels live by, and how we can all be agents of positive change by embracing them. Every one of us, no matter our innate personality or where we are in our career, can be a rebel.

One of the biggest surprises in my research has been the discovery of how important, and meaningful, rebel talent can be in one's personal life. I began this project by trying to understand rule breaking in the workplace. But breaking rules, as I discovered along the way, enriches every aspect of our lives. Living life like a rebel is energizing. I've tried it myself, and it's opened me up to a world of new experiences. As a result, I now drink milk in all sorts of colors for breakfast, wear red sneakers on formal occasions, and am always on the lookout for positive ways of being in the world that may at first feel wrong, or possibly even destructive. My hope is that this book will help you discover your own rebel talent and allow you to help others to do the same. There are strong habits that pull us toward the familiar and comfortable. We need to learn to "break" these habits, like so many Han dynasty urns. Only then will we be ready to transform them—and, ultimately, to create our own success.

1

NAPOLEON AND THE HOODIE

THE PARADOX OF REBEL STATUS

It's not rebels that make trouble, but trouble that makes rebels.
—RUTH MESSINGER

"Forward! Remember that from those monuments yonder, 40 centuries look down upon you." The French soldiers, despite being tired, thirsty, and hungry after marching for twelve hours under the hot Egyptian sun, felt energized by these words from their leader. The Great Pyramids were faintly visible on the horizon, some ten miles away. More clearly visible was the enemy army, waiting for them on the left bank of the Nile.

It was July 21, 1798. Under General Napoleon Bonaparte, the French army was approaching the fortified village of Embabeh, eighteen miles northwest of Cairo. Earlier that year, Bonaparte had proposed invading Egypt, knowing it would provide a new source of income for France and deal a blow to his nation's main European opponent, Britain: Controlling Egypt meant blocking the Red Sea, a major British access route to India. A French invasion might even benefit the Egyptians themselves. The country was ruled by the Mamelukes, descendants of Muslim slave soldiers. The Egyptians had endured the Mamelukes' oppressive rules for centuries and believed the French could save them. Having already secured Alexandria, Bonaparte hoped to next capture Cairo, which would decisively claim the prize of Egypt.

On the enemy side, an estimated six thousand mounted Mameluke soldiers, supported by forty cannons and a small Turkish contingent, were ready for battle. The soldiers' horses pranced and snorted in the heat of the day. Riders were armed with muskets and pistols; javelins made of sharpened palm branches; whatever battle-axes, maces, and daggers they could attach to themselves or their saddles; and short, curved swords made of black Damascus steel. Soldiers had dressed in turbans and caftans for the glory of battle and carried precious jewels and coins. Closer to the Nile and the Embabeh village, some fifteen thousand fellaheen-peasant levies stood, armed mostly with clubs and spears or long-barreled muskets. On the Nile's east bank was a force led by Ibrahim Bey, who, along with Murad Bey, was one of the two Mameluke chieftains. (*Bey* translates as "chieftain.") Under Ibrahim Bey's command were thousands more Mamelukes and about eighteen thousand fellaheen-peasant infantry. On the Nile itself waited a small Mameluke flotilla manned by Greek mercenary sailors. All told, the enemy had over forty thousand troops.

The Mameluke forces clearly outnumbered the French, who had deployed about twenty-five thousand men in five divisions, supported by artillery and a few cavalry troopers. But because of the Mamelukes' position, Bonaparte believed he had an advantage. By placing his troops on the left bank of the Nile, Murad had made a strategic mistake: He saved the French from having to cross the river under fire to attack him. Ibrahim Bey would have to cross the Nile to help Murad Bey if something went wrong. Given this advantage, Bonaparte decided to engage in a decisive battle. After allowing his troops just an hour to rest, he sent orders for each of his divisions to advance on Murad's army.

This wasn't the only advantage Bonaparte saw. He had witnessed the Mamelukes' primary tactic, a cavalry charge, in other battles. After trying to intimidate the enemy with parade maneuvers, the Mameluke cavalry would rush the enemy en masse, often repeatedly, attacking from the flanks or from the rear. The horsemen in these mass cavalry charges, known to be highly skilled in close fighting, approached very close to one another, like a moving wall.

Bonaparte had created what he thought would be an effective countermeasure: the massive divisional square. The square was actually a rectangle—the front and rear faces of it consisted of the division's first and second demi-brigades, while the two sides consisted of the third demi-brigade. The French soldiers lined up in a hollow formation with the artillery and supplies in the center. The army could rotate as the Mamelukes attacked, picking off enemy fighters. An hour into the battle, the French emerged victorious. The Mamelukes had lost about six thousand men; the French, only thirty.

The victory had many legacies: the eviction of the Mamelukes, the liberation of the Egyptians, further expansion of the French empire into the East, and increased French domination of mainland Europe. And thanks to the 150-plus scientists, engineers, and artists that Bonaparte brought on the journey, the victory spurred an exploration of Egypt's past and present. The birth of Egyptology revealed the secrets of the pyramids and the society that built them. In addition, Egypt was influenced by its new relationship with France and its culture, as seen in its later adoption of the Napoleonic Code.

Bonaparte's brilliant strategies have formed the basis of military education throughout the Western world. When planning a campaign, determined to be thoroughly prepared and to avoid the errors of previous generals, he would read books about his opponent's history, geography, and culture. Always, he strived for surprise. Sometimes that meant striking a decisive blow when the enemy was off guard. In an era when armies tended to march against each other in an orderly, gentlemanly formation, Bonaparte led his troops into position at a very fast speed, surrounding the enemy before they even realized he was there.

Bonaparte revolutionized warfare by introducing the corps system, which rendered the tactics of other countries virtually obsolete. The corps system organized troops into mini-armies, allowing them to separate when marching, but always to come together when it was time to fight. The corps would move within a day's march of each other; each changed into the rearguard, vanguard, or reserve quickly, depending on what the situation demanded and on the enemy's movement. Since France's defeat in the Seven Years' War in 1763, military strategists and theorists had been struggling with how the country could improve, and Napoleon was France's new savior. The military expedition to Egypt that he led in 1798 cemented the growing belief in his abilities and would serve as a springboard to power for him. Thanks to a coup he engineered in 1799, at just thirty years of age, he became First Consul of the Republic. Even as his political career advanced, Bonaparte continued to carefully study the works of successful generals, tacticians, and officers and put their ideas to practical use on the battlefield. For instance, the core idea behind Bonaparte's strategy of the central position came from Pierre de Bourcet, a chief of staff who was part of the royal armies in various wars, including the Seven Years' War. The strategy involved splitting numerically superior enemy armies into parts so that each could be attacked separately. Another tactic Bonaparte often used was the *ordre mixte* formation: He mixed line and column formations so that a battalion in line was supported on each wing by an infantry battalion column. Though Bonaparte did not invent these concepts, he perfected them, and his radical, strategic mind heralded the birth of modern warfare.

Bonaparte also fought in the trenches alongside the troops, which was highly unusual. Historians believe that his men nicknamed him "the little corporal" during the Battle of Lodi in May 1796, after he took over the sighting of one of the cannons himself, a job typically performed by a corporal. When his army faced direct fire, he was usually in the thick of it. At a critical moment on the first day of the Battle of Arcole in November 1796, for instance, Bonaparte rallied his troops by seizing the colors of one of his battalions and exposing himself to intense Austrian fire until one of his officers dragged him away. When the fighting was over and the enemy's guns fell silent, Bonaparte would generally rise up sweaty, dirty, and covered in gunpowder. He also made an effort to remember his soldiers' names and visited their campfires before battle, chatting with them about home and expressing confidence that they would triumph over the enemy. In Bonaparte's army, soldiers from humble backgrounds could rise through the ranks to become officers, as Bonaparte himself had done.

This same spirit guided his political reforms. At the time of the French Revolution, laws were often not applied equally to all people, and they were not even codified. By introducing the Napoleonic Code, Bonaparte created a legal system based on the idea that everyone was equal before the law. The code forbade birthright privilege, granted freedom of religion, and indicated that government jobs should be awarded based on merit, not rank. Dozens of nations around the world later adopted the code. Bonaparte ensured that the tax system applied equally to everyone. And, recognizing the importance of education, he introduced reforms that served as the foundation of the educational system in France and much of Europe today. He also implemented various liberal reforms to civil affairs, from abolishing feudalism and establishing legal equality to codifying religious tolerance and legalizing divorce. Bonaparte's contributions to the institutions of France and to Europe were large and long lasting.

Historians have often portrayed Bonaparte as power hungry and driven by hubris. But British historian Andrew Roberts in the biography *Napoleon: A Life* makes a compelling case for why this interpretation of Bonaparte's story is misguided, arguing that his downfall was caused not by a big ego, but by a few mistakes that led to significant defeats. Others disagree with this interpretation. There is no doubt, though, that when it came to battle strategy, Bonaparte was an outlier. Europe's other monarchs adhered to a strict military hierarchy in which recruitment and promotion were based on wealth and noble titles rather than qualifications and skills. Many of Bonaparte's contemporaries kept their distance from the troops, sending their generals out to lead while they spared themselves the fight. Bonaparte did things differently: He threw himself into the fray.

ON A COLD FEBRUARY MORNING IN BOSTON, I STRUGGLED THROUGH A HEAVY SNOW-storm on my walk to work. In my classroom at Harvard Business School, 110 eager executives, all with quite remarkable résumés, were unbundling themselves and taking their seats, ready for a session on "Managing Talent." I'd be teaching them about Morning Star, the largest tomato-processing company in the world and the subject of a case study—a ten- to fifteen-page article based on intensive research and interviews—I had written. The case focused on the company's unorthodox operations. There are no bosses or job titles at Morning Star. The company's employees decide for themselves how their skills can best help the company and then develop their own mission statements, which they discuss with colleagues before making them final.

Morning Star employees do not need to run upgrades by managers. Instead they go to the experts: the employees who would be working with the new equipment. Though the company has no R&D department, strong incentives exist to encourage innovation. Employees who successfully innovate earn the respect of coworkers, in addition to financial compensation. One of the dilemmas presented in the case was the decision to introduce a new compensation system, and whether it was consistent with the core philosophy the company was founded on.

Class began, and though case discussions generally open with a question about the challenge a protagonist is facing, I instead led the executives in a short free-association exercise. What comes to mind, I asked, when you hear the phrase "rule breaking"?

"Chaos," said the CEO of a global restaurant chain. "Disorder," shouted another student. I wrote these words on the blackboard. Some of the students' answers were positive: innovation, creativity, flexibility. Most, however, were negative: crime, rebellion, rejection, loss of reputation, misconduct, illegality, dissonance, penalty, punishment, fights, and deviance.

Terms like *rule breaker*, *nonconformity*, and *deviance* make us think of subversive, even dangerous, individuals. One student brought up Wells Fargo, where employees had created millions of fake savings and checking accounts in the names of real customers. After clients discovered they'd been charged unanticipated fees and issued credit and debit cards and lines of credit they hadn't asked for, regulatory bodies had fined the bank $185 million and the bank had fired more than 5,300 employees.

Another student mentioned Bernie Madoff, the financier who had persuaded thousands of investors to trust him with their savings. With his creative rule breaking, Madoff had made more than $20 billion disappear in a Ponzi scheme that presented itself as a hedge fund. He's now serving a 150-year prison sentence for running one of the biggest frauds in U.S. history.

Most of our decisions are governed by well-defined institutional arrangements with pre-specified obligations and rights. Some of these arrangements are relatively straightforward, like signing an apartment lease or hiring a babysitter. Others are more complex, like our relationships with government and corporations, which come with explicit rules. For instance, organizations use company handbooks to establish policies ranging from vacation time to codes of conduct. We generally expect people to obey these rules and codes of conduct. But this was not the case at Wells Fargo, where employees had betrayed their duty to act in the best interest of customers, or with Madoff, who had filed false regulatory reports and lied to his clients.

We also adhere to social norms—unwritten rules about how to behave in a particular culture, society, or social group, ranging from a friendship to a work team to a nation. For example, we expect students to arrive to class on time and complete their work. We expect people to be silent in libraries, to not interrupt us when we are talking, and (at least in most groups) to wear clothes in public. Social norms provide order and predictability in society and have played a critical role in the evolution and maintenance of cooperation and culture over centuries. Children as young as two or three years old understand the rules governing many social interactions. Usually, we internalize social norms so effectively that we don't even consider the possibility of violating them. To do so would be embarrassing or distasteful. Violators tend to be punished with gossip, derision, and rumors—all of which are powerful corrective measures that influence how we behave. In colonial America, a person caught breaking social norms, such as stealing or committing adultery, was confined to the stocks or pillory in the center of town. These long confinements were uncomfortable, but even worse was the realization that everyone you cared about would know what you did.

Shared rules make society run smoothly. In the military, recruits are taught from day one to follow orders, immediately and without question. In fact, those who enlist in the U.S. military, active duty or reserve, solemnly swear to obey the orders of their officers. For thousands of years, military leaders across the globe have maintained a strict hierarchy to keep order under the stress of battle.

Bonaparte ran things a little differently. In 1793, as a twenty-four-year-old captain, he was given the opportunity to take control of the artillery during the Battle of Toulon. The city was a key port, occupied at the time by antirevolutionary British forces. If the French revolutionaries did not triumph, they would not be able to build a navy to defy Britain's dominance of the sea. Suffocation of the French Revolution would follow.

One battery in particular was critical to the bombardment due to its elevated terrain. But it was also the most vulnerable to counterattack, thus making it the most dangerous to operate. Bonaparte's superiors informed him that no soldier would volunteer to man the battery. Walking through camp in contemplation, he spotted a printing machine, which gave him an idea. He created a sign to hang near the battery: "The battery of the men without fear." When the other soldiers saw it the next morning, they clamored to earn the honor of operating that cannon. Bonaparte himself wielded a ramrod alongside his gunners. The cannon was manned day and night. The French won the battle; Bonaparte won acclaim.

To break the rules is not necessarily to become an outcast. Madoff, of course, deserves to be in jail. Wells Fargo deserves its fines. But Bonaparte broke the rules and, rightly, earned status and respect. He is a prime example of how a rebel can be a hero.

BACK IN THE NINETEENTH CENTURY, THE WEALTHY POPULATIONS OF EUROPE AND the United States typically adorned themselves in diamond-studded jewelry and overindulged in rich foods and potent drinks. In the United States at the time, middle-class extravagance often went even further, including things like bathtubs cut from solid marble, waterfalls installed in dining rooms, and garden trees decorated with artificial fruit made of fourteen-karat gold. From an economic perspective, this behavior made little sense. People in the middle class were spending as if they were rich.

The behavior caught the attention of the Norwegian-American sociologist and economist Thorstein Veblen, who is known for challenging many of the economic theories of the era. Veblen concluded that this kind of spending demonstrated that the buyer was able to "waste" money and that the real point of it was to enhance status. The lavish spending of the rich "redounded to their glory, and now the middle class was using its newfound wealth to purchase elite status." Veblen famously dubbed this phenomenon "conspicuous consumption": choosing and displaying obviously expensive products—such as sports cars, expensive watches, and luxury clothes—rather than their cheaper, functional equivalents. Conspicuous consumption signals to the world our financial success, even if the success is mostly on loan.

As it turns out, we engage in this kind of costly signaling all the time. Many of the personal qualities that we want to convey to others are not directly observable, such as commitment, dedication, cooperativeness, or persistence. As a result, you may spend hours in yoga classes not because you really take pleasure in yoga, but because you want to show your partner that you are a disciplined person. Similarly, you might choose to attend an expensive business school to communicate your prestige, smarts, and persistence to future employers.

Signals such as fast cars, fancy suits, and jewelry share an important feature: They aren't cheap. And even absent financial burden, those yoga classes we secretly dread rob time and effort from activities we actually enjoy. Signals can also involve personal risk. Wearing expensive jewelry can attract thieves as well as admirers, and signaling toughness through gang tattoos might catch the eye of the police.

This type of public grandstanding is common in the animal world, too. Israeli ethologist Amotz Zahavi noted that animals often engage in showy and even dangerous displays of courage to attract mates and raise their status. Male peacocks show off their gorgeous plumage in part to demonstrate to females that they can support the heavy weight, an evolutionary disadvantage. (Large tail feathers translate into slower running and a reduced ability to hide from predators.) Antelopes often engage in *slotting*: They leap acrobatically straight into the air when hungry cheetahs are pursuing them, even though sprinting straight for the horizon is the better move. The animals' dangerous waste of energy conveys strength, telling the cheetah, "Don't even bother trying." Similarly, guppies swim right under their predators' noses before darting away. In evolution, it seems, survival of the fittest only captures part of the story.

From one perspective, Bonaparte's decision to join "the battery of men without fear" seems foolish. He was, by the social rules of the time, working beneath his level. He was also risking his life. But by taking these burdens on himself, for all to see, he was sending a costly signal—that his talent allowed him to break the rules, to serve, and to lead his charges to victory. This is an important insight of the rebel mindset.

ON MAY 7, 2012, A CROWD OF PAPARAZZI GREETED A BLACK SUV AS IT ARRIVED AT the Sheraton hotel in Manhattan's Times Square just before one p.m. Facebook's cofounder and CEO, Mark Zuckerberg, stepped from the car and was escorted into the hotel by security guards. For Zuckerberg, it was the kick-off event of a cross-country initial public offering roadshow: a presentation to potential institutional investors, a prelude to any IPO. CFO David Ebersman and COO Sheryl Sandberg joined him onstage to discuss the deal. About 50 bankers and 550 investors, most dressed in suits, packed the hotel and formed a snaking line around the block, watched by police, clipboard-carrying staffers, and members of the press. The stern-looking security guards ensured that only invitees would hear the presentation.

Facebook's was perhaps the most anticipated IPO in the history of the tech industry. The company had experienced rapid growth in recent years. In 2012, it was responsible for 56 percent of all shared content online, far surpassing email, which ranked a distant second with 15 percent. By taking the company public, Zuckerberg would cement his place in history, reward the investors who had backed him, and firmly establish that, among the many failed social networking sites of the era, he alone had found the right formula to create a lasting online powerhouse.

The meeting lived up to expectations, introducing what turned out to be the biggest technology IPO to date, with a peak market capitalization of over $104 billion. Interestingly, though, one of the big headlines from that day concerned Zuckerberg's attire. Like Steve Jobs and Albert Einstein before him, Zuckerberg didn't waste any mental energy on the trappings of fashion. Instead, he appeared onstage in the casual, fashionless uniform of the typical software engineer: gray T-shirt, black hoodie, comfortable blue jeans, and simple black sneakers. The entire ensemble had probably cost less than $150.

"Mark and his signature hoodie: He's actually showing investors he doesn't care that much; he's going to be him," Michael Pachter, an analyst with Wedbush Securities, told Bloomberg TV. "I think that's a mark of immaturity. I think that he has to realize he's bringing investors in as a new constituency right now, and I think he's got to show them the respect that they deserve because he's asking them for their money."

In fact, Zuckerberg was not the first tech whiz whose wardrobe choices at key business meetings raised eyebrows. When a young Bill Gates was about to take Microsoft public back in 1986, the story goes, a PR consultant nearly wrestled him to the ground to force him to swap his patented floppy sweater for a tailored suit. Steve Jobs initially made concessions to sartorial tradition, but after Apple made so many people rich, he went back to his trademark black mock turtlenecks. For these leaders, dressing down meant flouting social norms for proper business attire. They weren't oblivious to corporate dress codes, but they intentionally decided to defy convention.

We generally have a clear sense of how to match behavior with context. For example, we expect the audience to be quiet at the symphony and loud at rock concerts, for executives to wear relatively formal clothing at meetings, and so on. Rules and norms in organizations and, more broadly, in society instill order and predictability. But as with conspicuous consumption and public generosity, something very powerful happens when we act in ways that are unconventional or unexpected.

If you were to stroll down New York's Fifth Avenue from one luxury boutique to the next, you'd expect to see well-dressed shoppers carrying bags filled with thousands of dollars' worth of merchandise. This would fit your expectations of relevant social norms. But, as it turns out, those who subvert these expectations may be more likely to attract our admiration, my research shows.

Rome is the capital of Italy, but Milan is the country's fashion capital. Postcards of the northern city generally depict its classic Gothic cathedral, the impressive shopping mall Galleria Vittorio Emanuele II (the oldest in the world), and the well-known opera house Teatro alla Scala. But when I visit the city, I always like to take a stroll down the "fashion quadrilateral," which consists of Via Manzoni, Via Monte Napoleone, Via della Spiga, and Corso Venezia. Along these four streets you can find luxurious boutiques, both

Italian and foreign, from Bottega Veneta, Armani, Valentino, and Prada to Chanel, Burberry, Dior, Kenzo, and Hermès. No matter what you are wearing, it is easy to feel underdressed as you pass the store windows. Nearby, imposing houses with high, ivy-covered walls, lattice doors, miniature fountains, and beautiful courtyards help make this one of the noblest areas in the city.

In 2012, when I traveled with colleagues to Milan to conduct an experiment, we homed in on the fashion quadrilateral, knowing we were in the perfect place to learn more about the signals that clothing sends. For our research, we asked shop assistants working in luxury-brand boutiques to respond to a survey. Each read one of two versions of a vignette in which a woman about thirty-five years old entered the boutique. In one version, she had a dress on and a fur coat; in the other, she wore gym clothes. The shop assistants rated the woman's promise as a client by answering questions about how likely it was that she would make a purchase. They were also asked to rate the likelihood that the woman was a celebrity or a VIP. We used these surveys as measures of the potential customer's perceived status.

Contrary to what you might expect, the elegant woman in fur projected less status than the woman in gym clothes. The shop assistants had the strong suspicion that the dressed-down customer was intentionally deviating from the norms of appropriate behavior. "Wealthy people sometimes dress very badly to demonstrate superiority," one shop assistant said. "If you dare to enter these boutiques so underdressed, you are definitely going to buy something." Context is everything. When we presented a similar scenario to people at Milan's central train station, they said the dressed-up woman, not the dressed-down one, had higher status.

This is not just a high-fashion phenomenon. We surveyed American college students and asked them to react to a description of a professor teaching at a top-tier school. For some students, we described the forty-five-year-old professor as wearing a T-shirt and having a beard. For others, we described him as clean-shaven and wearing a tie. The students rated the professor in a T-shirt as having higher status. The perception that an individual is consciously *choosing not to conform* is critical.

To signal status, deviations from the norm must demonstrate one's autonomy to behave consistently with one's own inclinations and to pay for the cost of nonconformity. In another study, we found that participants perceived a guest wearing a red bow tie at a black-tie party at a country club as having higher status—and even being a better golfer—than a conforming club member wearing a black bow tie. The man in the red bow tie was not seen as clueless, but as a master of his domain—a rebel.

A FEW YEARS AGO, I WAS ASKED TO TEACH TWO BACK-TO-BACK, NINETY-MINUTE executive education classes at Harvard Business School for ICIC, the Initiative for a Competitive Inner City. I was intrigued by the opportunity. Founded in 1994 by HBS professor Michael Porter, ICIC is a national nonprofit organization that conducts research and advisory work on the economies and businesses of inner-city neighborhoods in the United States. The organization focuses on neighborhoods with poverty rates of 20 percent or higher, and with unemployment rates greater than those found in metropolitan areas. About a hundred business, government, and philanthropic leaders from more than a dozen cities would participate in each of the two sessions, hoping to refine their negotiation and influence skills. This is a topic I regularly teach at the executive level, and one that participants generally find valuable, as the applications to real-world settings are easy to see.

For those teaching executive-level classes at HBS, expectations are always high. As a professor, you are well aware of the students' time being especially precious, and you certainly don't want to waste it. Often, they are a tough crowd to please, clock-conscious and deeply experienced. In addition to wanting my students to learn, I also want their respect; after all, if they see me as influential and high in status, they will be more likely to listen closely and remember what I teach. The class I was about to lead typically requires hours of preparation. I needed to be clear, professional, direct—and properly dressed. Not being a big fan of skirts, my dress code for executive teaching consists of a conservative suit over a blouse or dress shirt, and a pair of dressy leather shoes.

But the back-to-back sessions I would be teaching to two sets of ICIC students were exactly the same, so I decided to use the day as an opportunity for a little experiment on the effects of attire on status determinations. Specifically, during the break after the first class, I slipped off my leather shoes and laced up a pair of red Converse sneakers. Just imagine: I was wearing a dark blue Hugo Boss suit, a white silk blouse, and a pair of very red, very non-dressy shoes. Colleagues gave me strange looks as I made my way back to the classroom.

It is often difficult to tell whether students are engaging with the material and enjoying your classes. But I could sense a tangible difference between the two classes that day: The red-sneakers class seemed more attentive and thoughtful, and they laughed more. Part of the difference, I realized, was likely due not only to the sneakers, but to the effect they had on me. I didn't feel more self-conscious, despite the reaction of my colleagues. Rather, I felt more confident. Even though I was teaching brand-new material, I felt more certain about its effectiveness, more poised when leading discussions, and more adept when making transitions.

At the end of each session that day, I asked the students to complete a short survey assessing my professional status and competence. For instance, I asked them to guess at my status within the school and how likely my research was to be featured in the *Harvard Business Review*. Interestingly, the students viewed me as having greater status when I wore the red shoes. They also thought my consulting rate was higher. All thanks to a pair of red sneakers.

After the second session, I bounced back to my office thinking the red-sneakers test was worth expanding on. So I devised an experiment in which I invited college students to complete a task that most of us would view as stressful (at least, without a few beers): singing the Journey song "Don't Stop Believin'" in front of an audience of peers. Before the performance, I asked half the students to wear something that they agreed would make them feel uncomfortable—namely, a bandanna wrapped around their heads. (The bandanna, I expected, would serve as the nonconforming behavior—the headgear version of my red sneakers.) The other group did not wear a bandanna. With help from the karaoke machine, I measured note-hitting accuracy, as well as heart rate and confidence. The bandanna-wearing students sang better, had significantly lower heart rates, and also reported feeling more confident.

We all have opportunities to boost our confidence through nonconforming behaviors. In another study, I recruited a few hundred employees from different companies and asked some of them to behave in nonconforming ways at work over the next three weeks, such as voicing their disagreements with their colleagues' decisions, expressing their true ideas or feelings rather than those they were expected to have, or proposing ideas that colleagues might find unconventional. I asked others to behave in conforming ways for three weeks, such as staying quiet and nodding along even when they disagreed with a colleague's decision. And then I asked another set of individuals, the control group, to behave as usual during this time. After the three weeks had passed, members of the first group indicated that they felt more confident and engaged in their jobs than members of the other two groups. They were also more creative when completing a task I gave them as part of a three-week follow-up survey, and their supervisors rated them higher on both innovativeness and performance.

Nonconformity can enhance not only our professional lives, but our personal lives as well. When hanging out with friends, we've all found ourselves nodding along during a discussion, even when we seriously disagree with the argument being made. And at times, we may express emotions we don't feel just to please those close to us. Or we might dress to fit in with a group, or order the same dish as our date even if we'd rather have something different. In research similar to my field study on employees and conformity, I asked a large group of college and MBA students to behave in ways that were conforming or nonconforming in their personal lives outside of work for a few weeks. The results of engaging in nonconforming behaviors were equally beneficial in the students' personal lives. Nonconforming behaviors (such as expressing true preferences in social circles rather than going along with the majority opinion) improved their happiness in their day-to-day interactions. Interestingly, the participants had predicted just the opposite.

Despite our differences, we all share the desire to be happy. What my research suggests is that we can actually bring more joy into our lives by being rebels: by behaving in ways that defy conformity. And something as simple as a pair of red sneakers might make all the difference.

A MAN, LIKELY IN HIS THIRTIES, SITS AT A SMALL TABLE OUTSIDE A CAFÉ IN AM-sterdam. Behind him, two picture windows reveal some of the life inside the café—menus on the walls, a large espresso machine, and waiters bustling to bring drinks and food to customers. This man is the protagonist of a short video clip that University of Amsterdam psychologist Gerben Van Kleef and his colleagues created for an experiment. Two versions of the video were shot. In the first version, the man violates what we would all probably agree are norms of proper public behavior: He puts his feet on another chair and flicks his cigarette ash to the ground. After consulting the menu, he doesn't return it to its stand. And when the waitress asks for his order, he brusquely answers, "Bring me a vegetarian sandwich and a sweet coffee." He does not reply when the waitress says, "Right away." In the second version of the video, he behaves politely, crossing his legs and using the ashtray on the table. He also carefully returns the menu to the stand. And when the waitress asks for his order, he replies with a much more polite, "May I have a vegetarian sandwich and a sweet coffee, please?" and then thanks her when she says, "Right away."

Imagine how you'd feel if you were waiting on the man in the first video. Having worked as a waitress when I was younger, I can say with confidence that he would have annoyed me. After all, being polite and respectful doesn't require very much effort. Nor does sitting properly in a chair. Unfortunately, all of us encounter such irritating rule-breaking behavior on a regular basis. Someone puts their package on the only vacant train seat, so that you have to ask them to move it to sit down. Your boss walks abruptly into your office without knocking, interrupting your private phone call. A loud conversation in the movie theater distracts you from the film. A friend looks at her cell phone constantly during dinner. In these cases, rule breaking has gone too far, from the realm of the admirable to the realm of the annoying. But even if these norm violators drive us crazy, we still view them as powerful, research says.

In Van Kleef's experiment, participants were divided into two groups, with half being asked to watch the first version of the video and the other half being asked to watch the second version. After watching, each participant answered a few questions about their reactions to the man depicted, including how powerful they viewed him to be. The result? Participants who watched the man violate norms in the first video were more likely to see him as powerful than those who watched him conform in the second video.

Power is typically associated with lack of constraint, and we think of powerful people as generally having the freedom to behave as they wish. Indeed, as you may have noticed in your own professional and personal life, people *in* powerful positions and those who *feel* powerful often act without fear of negative consequences. In one study, people who felt powerful were more likely than those who felt less powerful to switch off an annoying fan while working on a task that required concentration—they were less concerned about what the experimenter might think. Whether power is real or simply perceived, it leads us to take more risks, express stronger emotions and views, act based on our natural inclinations and impulses, and ignore situational pressure.

We perceive people who interrupt others as more assertive than those who don't interrupt, and those who express anger as mightier than those who express sadness, a more socially acceptable emotion. As people gain power, they feel greater freedom to defy conventions. Paradoxically, these violations may not undermine their power but instead augment it, thus fueling a self-perpetuating cycle of power and rule breaking that can go too far, as with people like Bernie Madoff. The link between nonconformity, power, and status leads us to a deeper question: How should we use the power and status that we gain throughout our careers?

IT'S EARLY MORNING AT VIA STELLA, 22, ON A PICTURESQUE COBBLED STREET IN the center of Modena, Italy. There is a discreet coral-colored façade, and the only indication that one has arrived at Osteria Francescana is a small brass sign bearing its name. The scene gets more lively around nine a.m., when the staff starts showing up for work. Noise from the engine of a black Ducati motorcycle fills the street: Bottura arriving not long after his team. Within minutes, he has put on his white chef's coat and grabbed a broom to start sweeping the pavement outside the restaurant.

Bottura regularly takes on tasks that other chefs couldn't be bothered with. It's Bottura who waits for the cargos of fresh produce, fish, and meat. He is the one who jumps onto the back of the truck, opening up the big boxes to inspect the produce and ask the deliverymen about it. When his questions are answered, he helps unload the truck. This is part of the excitement of working at Osteria Francescana. Everyone at the restaurant knows that there are no pre-defined roles that will box them in. Everyone is free to work on tasks that in other restaurants would be assigned to a particular individual. At most places, only the delivery person unloads the produce from the truck, and only the pastry chef prepares the desserts, but at Osteria Francescana this is not the case. Everyone is free to experiment with ideas and to challenge their "leader" with a unique perspective. And Bottura himself shows little regard, maybe even contempt, for the idea of tradition-bound roles. Right before service, he joins his staff for a meal. In between services, he is either helping with cleanup or playing soccer with the staff outside of the restaurant. None of this is typical chef behavior. Bottura's troops are so devoted because they have seen him on the front line, and they are inspired to greatness.

2

THE DOG NAMED "HOT"

A TALENT FOR NOVELTY

The first kiss is magic. The second is intimate. The third is routine.
—RAYMOND CHANDLER

A man steps to the center of a small stage, pulls up a brown leather chair, and sits down. He is wearing a sleeveless white shirt and loose-fitting jeans. I'm sitting offstage with my husband, Greg, and a group of about a dozen other people. We're in a large room, used by a local public school during the day, and in one section there are different areas set up for children's activities—drawing and painting, reading, LEGOs. The lights are dim.

The man extends his hands, as if gripping an imaginary steering wheel, and starts to drive. I rise from my seat and step onto the stage, pull up another chair, and sit next to him. "Welcome to the *Enterprise*," he says. "Did you hear about the new uniform-making machine?"

"Yeah," I say. "I was disappointed when I heard about it. After our last meeting, I was hoping that we would focus on another product to launch our business. Didn't we think striped underpants would be the next big thing?"

Laughter.

Another woman, Rachel, rises from the audience and taps my shoulder. I return to my seat, and the scene continues. "I wasn't sure what to say," I whisper to my husband, "but somehow people found it funny."

Greg smiles. "You didn't get it? You totally missed the reference. That was *Star Trek*. Eric was doing Captain Kirk. So you took the scene in a pretty different direction." Eric wasn't driving a car—he was commanding the USS *Enterprise*.

Greg and I were in Central Square, Cambridge, not far from where we were living at the time, at a beginner's improv comedy class I had signed us up for—two-hour sessions across ten consecutive Mondays. That night we were playing an improv game called "actor switch," in which one player starts a scene and is soon joined by another. New players step in one at a time, tapping the shoulder of someone already onstage to replace him or her, building on the original story and characters. Nothing is decided in advance, but after only a few seconds, the group has cooperatively established a basic dramatic frame. By the end of the scene, we've managed to develop a rather complex (and pretty funny) scene.

In improv, you go with the flow. Maybe you're not crazy about the choices of the person who came before you, but you accept the terms of the scene and then add to it, rather than contradicting it. So, if the first player says "This is an apple," you shouldn't reply "No, it is a rather small melon." That might buy you a laugh, but it would kill the scene. It's much better to follow the "yes, and" principle that lies at the heart of improv: "Yes, and we can fill it with poison before we offer it to the queen." The story I've just told wasn't the first (or last) time I completely missed a classmate's cultural reference. (I have yet to watch *Star Trek*.) But if I hadn't been willing to miss these cues and go with it, I wouldn't have had as much fun.

Improv is all about performing without preparation and without a script—responding to others in the moment, listening to your inner voice, and bursting out with whatever comes to mind. The British-Canadian director, playwright, actor, and improv pioneer Keith Johnstone once noted that improvisation is like steering a car by looking through the rearview mirror: You don't know where you're going; you can only see where you've been.

The improv experiment was a Christmas present I gave to Greg in 2011, before parenthood made it harder to go out on weeknights. I thought it would be a good gift since we would spend some time together on a regular basis, involved in a totally new activity—one that consisted, in my mind, of just making fun of ourselves and laughing a lot. But that wasn't my only motive. Recent research suggests that if we inject novelty into our romantic relationships, we'll stay more engaged in them and experience greater satisfaction in the long run. Greg and I were happy. From the first time we met, in the security line at Logan International Airport, our relationship had always felt natural and easy, even when our different cultures—I'm Italian, and he was born in Warner Robins, Georgia—introduced differences of perspective. But I knew how easy it is for marriages to suffer the grind of routine. What, I wondered, would happen if we had a weekly date with the unexpected?

IT HAD ALL BEEN DECIDED: ON JUNE 27, 2009, GREG AND I WOULD GET MARRIED IN Tione di Trento, my hometown of three thousand people in the mountains of northern Italy. Picture a warm summer afternoon, the perfume from daisies and roses hanging in the air as a gentle fresh breeze dances between the vaulted ceilings of an old church, its main door open, waiting for the guests to enter. A little orchestra of clarinets, trombones, and flutes plays softly as the groom waits nervously for his bride . . .

We were excited. Maybe even more excited was my mum, who

would finally see a church wedding for one of her three children, complete with all the important traditions. My brother had decided against marriage, though he had settled down with his partner and two children. My sister and her husband had tied the knot at City Hall.

Months before the wedding, I bought my white wedding dress. I also bought a garter, following a tradition that dates to the fourteenth century, when it was thought that the guest who departed with a piece of the bridal trousseau would be blessed with good luck. The groom had his own rituals to honor, including supplying the bridal bouquet as a final gift to his girlfriend before she became his wife. And then there would be the *bomboniere* with *confetti*: wedding favors with sugared almonds for the guests. For a traditional Italian wedding, the almonds must be coated in white sugar, and the number given must always be odd. Why? Because marriage unites two people, and the amount must never be divisible by two. With the wedding over, we would go on a *luna di miele*, or honeymoon—so named because in ancient Rome, newlyweds would spend an entire phase of the moon eating a portion of honey at every mealtime.

Of course, respect for tradition is about as uniquely Italian as a bride in a white dress. In Indian weddings, couples recite seven vows and aren't considered legally married until they've taken seven steps around a holy fire, after which seven married women greet them. In Vietnam, families of the bride and groom avoid the number seven at all costs because it brings bad luck. Throughout Latin American, a *quinceañera*, the coming-of-age celebration for a girl's fifteenth birthday, often involves fathers changing their daughters' shoes from flats to high heels. In Japan, during the traditional coming-of-age day, Seijin no Hi, parents present their daughters with a pair of flat zori sandals.

From celebrating religious beliefs to mobilizing political action, rituals and traditions have a long history across societies. Today they are ubiquitous forces, from our family lives to the workplace to the locker room. Notre Dame football players walk an identical route from the university basilica to the stadium before kickoff, while employees at companies such as Walmart and New Balance begin the day with chants and stretches. Such rituals, my research shows, improve group performance. For instance, in a scavenger hunt that my colleagues and I organized through the streets of Boston, groups who practiced rituals together during the event performed better than those who didn't. Another study, this one of over two hundred people working in many different types of jobs across industries, found that they were more satisfied by their jobs when they regularly engaged in meaningful workplace rituals— including playing their own version of Bingo with their colleagues and, when they worked on a Saturday, regularly shouting out "half time" about halfway through the day and doing a "happy dance."

One of the main purposes of rituals and traditions is to impart and nourish values. At home, daily family prayers emphasize the importance of faith; nightly bedtime stories affirm the value of education, reading, and lifelong learning; and regular family dinners or activities strengthen our most cherished bonds. In time, shared values gain the power of treasured memories. On the flipside, given the meaning and closeness that traditions reinforce, broken traditions can give rise to disappointment.

Nearly a year before our perfect Italian wedding, Greg and I learned this lesson firsthand. It was a sunny morning in early September in 2008, when we were living in Chapel Hill, North Carolina. While sipping coffee on our porch, we finally agreed that it was time to call my family. Almost two weeks earlier, on August 20, Greg and I had gotten married at City Hall to address some of the legal issues related to an Italian marrying an American in the United States. I still hadn't told my mum. I knew she'd be very upset at the news, even furious. She would probably yell at me for breaking from such an important tradition.

"It's not a big deal," Greg reassured me. Our real wedding—the traditional one we had so carefully planned—was still set to take place in Italy the following summer. I dialed my mum's phone number. As soon as she picked up, I said: "Mum, I have some wonderful news to share."

"You are pregnant?"

"No," I said. "Greg and I got married!"

Click. She had hung up.

When I finally got her on the line again, days later, she did yell at me, as I'd expected. She was furious that there hadn't been a single family member present to celebrate one of the most meaningful moments in her child's life. There were no wedding-themed pictures of the family, no memories she could cherish. In time, though, she got over it; I had my Italian wedding with my family all around us, and all turned out well.

Rituals can bring us together and imbue life with deeper meaning, but often they also rob us of something equally valuable—the experience that comes with making difficult decisions. Planning my Italian wedding was rather easy, as most of my choices were already made for me. (The hardest decision we faced was picking a date.) But the process was also short on opportunities to challenge and surprise myself. In the grip of tradition, we miss out on novelty—and therefore the excitement of working without a script. Boredom, or something worse—any kind of mindless complacency—can creep up on us. The rebel—always trying new things, the way Greg and I did with improv—fares better.

We stick to traditions and old ways of doing things because, at least in part, we figure there must be a good reason for them. In one study, for instance, a team of Yale researchers found that children model themselves after adults so faithfully that they even copy their mistakes. In one of the study's exercises, a group of three- to five-year-old children could see a dinosaur toy that had been placed in a clear plastic container. A researcher followed different steps to retrieve the toy, some of which were useful, such as unscrewing the lid, and some of which were not, such as tapping the side of the container with a feather before removing it. The children had to indicate which steps were silly and which made sense, winning praise when they identified the former. This was done to show that the adult could not be trusted and that the unnecessary steps he had used could be safely ignored. Later, the children watched adults as they took a toy turtle out of a container using needless steps. When they performed the task themselves, the children still over-imitated, squandering time and effort in the same way that the adults had. In fact, when children see an adult taking a prize from a container by a method that both adults and chimpanzees can easily identify as both inefficient and clumsy, they seem to lose the ability to figure out how to open the container "correctly." In other words, watching an adult do something wrong prevents kids from figuring out how to do it right.

Experience would seem to be the cure, but on the contrary, studies show that over-imitation actually increases as we age, with adults performing irrelevant actions with higher levels of fidelity than preschoolers. Hard to believe? Ask yourself the following: When trying to understand some new, complicated device, like a computer, how often have you followed on faith the instructions of an expert? If you're like me, the answer is very often, as you may (or may not) find out later when someone else points out a simpler way to operate the device. Much of what we "know" is really only trust in someone else's knowledge. After all, we conclude, if a practice has been around for a long time, there must be a very good reason for it, right?

In one study examining this phenomenon, I brought groups of four participants into a room where a team of paid actors was folding T-shirts. Some groups saw teams using an efficient process to fold T-shirts, while other groups saw teams adding a few irrelevant actions to the process, such as stacking the T-shirts in piles of three before folding them or folding and unfolding the sleeves. At the beginning of the study, when participants received information about the task they would complete, they were told that they would be paid based on the number of T-shirts they folded in the allotted time. (Adding unnecessary steps obviously slows down the process.) The participants watched the paid actors fold T-shirts for a couple of minutes and then took their spots. They folded T-shirts individually for ten minutes, until another group came to watch them for a few minutes before taking over the work. This pattern was repeated six times with groups of four participants.

Among the participants who watched teams fold inefficiently, 87 percent simply imitated the actions of the initial group of actors, and thus walked away with less money than those who were part of the groups that observed the efficient process. Those who watched an initial group of actors fold inefficiently for just a few minutes perpetuated this behavior across time to many other groups. Of the 336 people in the study, only three explicitly asked questions or raised concerns about inefficiency. As often happens in real life, most team members accepted the nonsensical process without protest.

The traditions and rituals you encounter in your organization and in society often endure out of routine, rather than as the result of thoughtful deliberation. Psychologists and economists alike have a name for this phenomenon: the status quo bias. William Samuelson and Richard Zeckhauser first demonstrated this bias back in 1988, in a study in which they presented participants with a series of decision-making problems that either included or did not include the choice of sticking with a status quo position. Participants tended to favor the status quo when it was offered to them, even as an objectively inferior choice.

Too often, we take deeply ingrained rituals and traditions for granted. When we become comfortable with the current state of affairs, we experience any diversion from the status quo as a loss, and we weigh these losses much more heavily than the idea of potential gains. In fact, when offered a bet with an equal probability of winning or losing, the average person requires a gain that's twice the value of the potential loss before accepting. If only we could put aside the fear of losing, we might jump at the chance to win. But instead, the fear holds us back, chaining us to the status quo even when change is clearly in our best interest.

STUDYING THE LONG HISTORY OF IMPROV LED ME HOME. THE MOST DIRECT ANCES-tor of the art form is thought to be the Italian Commedia dell'Arte. In Europe in the 1500s, performers would travel from town to town with their troupes, performing shows in public squares. Improvised dialogue within a set "scenario" would serve as the framework for these performances. From the beginning, their craft broke with the traditions of mainstream theater, demanding of players an unusual ability to react in the moment.

Long after the Commedia died off, improv was reinvented in the 1950s by British-Canadian playwright Keith Johnstone and American acting coach Viola Spolin. The two made separate, spontaneous contributions to improv. In their own ways, both brought novelty to the stage. Believing that live theater had become pretentious and catered only to intellectuals and the upper class, Johnstone—who was writing plays and teaching acting in London—wanted to create art for everyday people, those whose favorite forms of entertainment were ball games and boxing matches. His answer? A new acting method, "spontaneous improvisation," and a hybrid form of entertainment called Theatresports in which features of sports—like teams, judges, scores, and competitions—were adapted to improvisational theater. Teams would compete for points that judges would award them, and audiences would be encouraged to cheer for scenes they enjoyed and mock the judges ("Kill the umpire!").

When working with actors, Johnstone tried to help them be

more responsive and alive in their work. Informed by his own childhood, he had come to believe that the educational system was blunting creativity. Flipping the notion of children as immature adults, he viewed adults as atrophied children. Johnstone wrote down a list of "things teachers stopped me from doing" and told his own students they should do just the opposite. His unconventional approach and strategies were highly successful in helping actors become more spontaneous.

In her native Chicago in the 1920s and '30s, Spolin had the same passion as Johnstone: theater for the masses. Her approach to teaching adults was based on the insight that children enjoyed learning to act when lessons were presented as a series of games. She had instructed immigrant children in drama as part of a public works project and realized that the same techniques could be used to stimulate creative expression in adults. Spolin's son, Paul Sills, built on this insight in the mid-1950s, helping to spearhead an improv movement centered around the University of Chicago. The group that sprang from Sills's work, The Compass, eventually led to the development of the famous improv theater company Second City, where Tina Fey, Bill Murray, and many other comedy greats got their start.

In the third week of my improv adventure with Greg, the teacher asked all of us to sit in a circle on the floor. We were going to play the game "one-word story." The teacher would provide the title of the story and then pick a person to say the first word. The person to their left would say the next word, and so on, continuing around the circle. The point of the game is to tell a coherent, original story, one word at a time, as if a single narrator is speaking at a normal, conversational pace.

"Here is your title," the teacher began. "A furry dog sits on a stove."

And then we were off: "A—dog—named—Hot—enjoyed—sitting—on—a—red—and—yellow—stove.—One—day—he—

did—not—realize—the—stove—was—on—so—his—butt—felt—warmer—than—usual . . ."

The story kept going, ending with a parrot yelling "butt—on—fire!"

In improv, we are trading in the currency of unpredictability. We don't know what our partners will say next, how others will react, or even when a scene will end. The other players may bring up topics that we know nothing about. That's okay. The goal is to always react purely in the moment. Consider the strategies required in two popular games, chess and Ping-Pong. When you play chess, you need to think ahead. You focus on following your own strategy, as well as anticipating your opponent's. By contrast, when you play Ping-Pong, you need to react in a split second. You can try to anticipate the next volley, but a better bet is to focus on where the ball is moving in the moment. The same goes for improv: You can't "pong" until the other player has "pinged."

Even as it makes us anxious, this unpredictability fuels our need for novelty, which runs surprisingly deep. In the 1860s, German zoologist Alfred Brehm placed a covered box of snakes in a cage with several monkeys. When the monkeys lifted the lid, they were terrified, as any monkey (and most humans) would be. But then the monkeys did something rather odd: They lifted the lid again to get a second look at the snakes. Since Brehm published these findings, scientists have examined the reactions of more than a hundred species of reptiles and mammals to things they've never seen before. No matter how frightening the sight, the animals cannot resist the pull of novelty, and they take another peek.

Novelty compels both humans and animals to engage with the unfamiliar. Indeed, our strong desire for novelty has evolutionary roots, improving our survival odds by keeping us alert to both friends and threats in our environment. As new parents quickly learn, when given a choice, babies consistently look at, listen to, and play with unfamiliar things. One of my favorite moments from early parenthood was when I watched my infant son notice his hands for the first time. His discovery stands out as a metaphor for learning: His interest in what those strange, wonderful appendages could do was his first step toward controlling them. The preference for novelty is an efficient way for immature cognitive systems to process information, helping babies cope with changes to their environment before unleashing their inner explorer.

Interestingly, in human genetics, a preference for novelty has been linked to the migration of early humans to the far reaches of the earth. Recent studies have shown that human groups that migrated the farthest from Africa had more of the genes linked to novelty seeking. That is, the people who traveled the farthest from home may have had some biological propensity to experience mysterious new places. And yet, while we are born with a strong drive to seek novelty, this drive fades over time. As we grow older, other desires take over, like wanting more predictability. The organizations we build and join reflect this reality: paychecks at the same time each week or month, evaluations according to established processes, jobs that involve a known set of activities.

The thrill of novelty—running into an old friend in an unfamiliar city, buying a new car, accepting a promotion—can instill a sense of delight and wonder at our good fortune, but not for ever after. You and your friend eventually part; the car loses its new car smell and starts to seem ordinary; the promotion brings the stress of new responsibilities. In time, we grasp a difficult truth about emotional experiences: their intensity fades.

PAL'S SUDDEN SERVICE IS A FAST-FOOD CHAIN WITH TWENTY-NINE STORES IN northeast Tennessee and southwestern Virginia. Most are boxy, eleven-hundred-square-foot double-drive-thru restaurants topped with statues of burgers and fries. Speed is a key factor at Pal's, and employees are trained accordingly: A typical order of two sandwiches, two sides, and two drinks takes about forty-three seconds to fill. The work is highly standardized: Whether taking orders, grilling, toasting bread, or preparing hamburgers, employees learn to follow the process with zero errors, even during peak times. Responsibilities are split between fifteen different stations. Employees get to work on one of them only after taking a test, and the only passing score is 100 percent.

All businesses face the same conundrum: To stay profitable and competitive in the marketplace, they depend on the work of their people, but people always need new challenges. Pal's is the kind of place where tedium is a constant threat. But the owners have come up with a clever way to fight the tedium of highly standardized work: Not until employees arrive at work for their shifts do they learn the order in which they'll move through the stations. The first task on a Monday may be making shakes, followed by French fries; on Tuesday it may be biscuit production and order delivery. As a result, workers are less likely to shift into autopilot and more likely to up their game. Novelty is a stimulant.

Pal's has achieved impressive numbers: They average one drive-thru order filled every 18 seconds (competitors need minutes), one mistake in every 3,600 orders (the average in the industry is one every 15 orders), scores of 98 percent for customer satisfaction, and above 97 percent for health inspection. Turnover at the managerial level and on the front lines is very low. The sales numbers are similarly remarkable: about $2 million a year per store. In fact, despite operating in a highly competitive industry where global giants like McDonald's, Burger King, and Wendy's dominate the market, Pal's performs remarkably well financially. On most measures—from revenue per square foot and gross margins, to return on sales or on assets and customer satisfaction—Pal's beats the competition.

As this fast-food chain demonstrates, there's room for variety in even the most rote job. My colleague Brad Staats (of the University of North Carolina, Chapel Hill) and I analyzed two and a half years of data from transactions of employees who processed applications for home loans at a Japanese bank. The mortgage line required each employee to engage in seventeen different tasks, activities like scanning applications, comparing the scanned document to the original, inputting application data, comparing that data to underwriting standards, and conducting credit checks. After a worker completed a task, the system automatically assigned him or her a new one. We found that when workers were assigned a greater variety of tasks across a few days, their productivity (as measured by processing time) improved. Variety acted as a motivator.

Novelty increases our job satisfaction, our creativity, and our overall performance. It also increases how much we grow in both confidence and ability. In research conducted by psychologists Brent Mattingly (Ashland University) and Gary Lewandowski (Monmouth University), participants were asked to read a list of facts. Some participants were provided with facts that came across as interesting, novel, and exciting ("Butterflies taste with their feet"), while others were given information that was duller ("Butterflies begin life as a caterpillar"). Reading interesting facts made participants believe they were more knowledgeable than reading mundane ones did. All of a sudden, they felt more like masters— and more confident in their ability to accomplish new things in the future. When presented with new tasks, they worked harder on them.

Part of the explanation is that, in our brains, novelty and pleasure are deeply entwined: Novelty generates surprises, and surprises lead to pleasure. In a series of studies led by Tim Wilson at the University of Virginia, the happiness people experienced after an unexpected kindness (such as a gift) lasted longest when the act was anonymous. In another study, researchers had participants watch an uplifting film based on a true story. They were then given two passages describing what happened to the main character after the events depicted in the film—one true, one fictional. Both passages told positive stories, but their details differed slightly. One group was told which story was true, the other group was kept in the dark. Members of the uncertain group stayed in a more positive mood for much longer after seeing the film. The uncertainty of the situation increased their pleasure rather than detracting from it.

Another factor serves as a powerful source of novelty: excitement. In a now-classic study published in 1993, psychologist Arthur Aron and his colleagues had fifty-three upper-middle-class, middle-aged couples fill out questionnaires asking them about the quality of their marriages. They were also given a list of sixty activities that couples could engage in together, such as dining out, going to a movie, attending concerts or plays, skiing, hiking, or dancing. For each activity, each member of the couple individually rated how exciting and how pleasant they thought the activity would be to share with their partner. In some cases, ratings varied widely. While one person may highly anticipate the new episode of a favorite show, the other may be bored by the prospect of another night in front of the TV. Similarly, one half of the couple may love to ride roller coasters, while the other person practically has a panic attack just contemplating the idea.

Next, couples were randomly assigned to one of three treatments. In the first condition, they were asked to engage in an activity they both had rated as "exciting" but only moderately pleasant, just once a week for ten weeks, for ninety minutes at a time. In the second condition, the couples chose a weekly activity they both had rated as "highly pleasant" but not as exciting. In the third condition, couples were not asked to engage in any special activities. The researchers found that engaging in highly exciting but only moderately pleasant activities dramatically improved relationship quality. But for the couples in the other two conditions (pleasant activities or no special activities), there was no change. For an experience to be exciting, psychologists have learned, it needs to be more than novel—it also needs to be challenging.

A more recent study of one hundred couples found that those who engaged in activities that both members deemed exciting for at least ninety minutes per week for four weeks reported higher levels of happiness and relationship satisfaction. The effect lasted at least four months. In fact, research that has followed couples through time has found remarkable benefits in novel activities—and dire consequences in their absence. Insufficient novelty makes us feel that the relationship is boring, which takes a toll. One longitudinal study found that among married couples, lack of novelty predicted especially strong declines in satisfaction nine years later.

Even very brief novel activities, such as reading through a new recipe to try, watching a movie trailer together, trying a tango move, or picking a subject at random to talk about—have been found to increase relationship quality. A study of 274 married people in the United States found that 40 percent of those who had been married more than ten years reported still being "very intensely in love," a state that was linked to the fact that they shared novel activities. Interestingly, when we engage in exciting activities together, we view both our partner *and* the relationship as exciting. What this research suggests is not that you and your spouse should learn hang-gliding. Seeking novelty may involve simple activities such as walking in a part of town you're not familiar with, checking out a new restaurant, or giving improv a try.

Surprisingly, novelty is even more important than stability. In a study I conducted with a group of three hundred new employees, I found that the more frequently they experienced novelty in their work in the weeks that followed (because they learned new skills, met new colleagues, or felt challenged in their tasks), the more they felt satisfied with and energized by their jobs, and the longer they were interested in staying with the organization. Stability, by contrast, did not seem to bring these benefits. When employees reported that their job felt "more or less the same every day," their satisfaction suffered, and they were more eager to move on.

In another study, I enlisted about five hundred workers across a wide range of U.S. organizations to take part in a six-week study inspired by Arthur Aron's research on novelty and romantic relationships. I randomly assigned each employee to one of three conditions. In the novelty condition, I asked participants to carve out some time at work (at least once a week) to engage in novel or challenging tasks, such as reaching out to a colleague in a different division, learning a new skill, or working on a project outside their comfort zone. I sent them a reminder once a week for five weeks. For participants in the pleasant condition, I asked them to make some time at work to engage in tasks they enjoyed, to the extent possible. In the control condition, participants did not receive any instructions.

At the end of week six, I asked everyone to complete an online survey on job satisfaction, engagement, commitment to the organization, and innovative behaviors. I also sought permission to ask their supervisors about their performance. Just as in the romantic relationships Aron studied, boosting novelty produced the highest scores on all the measures I assessed. I found the same results for employees in a large retail organization in India and for a large sample of European workers. The value of novelty at work (and in relationships) seems pretty universal.

At Pal's, managers regularly set up new challenges. One manager liked to make weekly deals with his employees, such as the following: He told a worker at the order window that if she could correctly predict the orders of one hundred drive-thru customers in the next hour, she would receive a $100 gift card. As the employee told me the story, she recalled thinking initially that the task seemed impossible. And I agreed. But then she told me that most of Pal's customers are repeat customers, people who drive in to get lunch or dinner three to five times a week. "After a while, you recognize their faces and the order they always seem to make, almost out of habit," she noted. She claimed her prize.

WHEN GREG FIRST OPENED THE BIG BOX TIED IN RED RIBBON THAT I HAD PUT UN-
der the Christmas tree for him in 2011, I could tell he was disappointed. Being a bit of a tech geek, he was probably expecting
me to get him some exciting new gadget. What he found instead
was a lot of empty space and a printed-out description of our improv class, something he'd never considered doing on his own and
clearly wasn't interested in. I was convinced he was wrong—that
he would love it as soon as we started. But after the first session, he
told me that he'd hated the class. He'd felt uncomfortable being
so vulnerable in front of strangers. Worse, he didn't think he was
funny.

The second class didn't do much to change his mind. I can per-
fectly picture his face during an exercise called "three things!" The
group stood in a circle chanting "three things!" while bouncing
our fists, as if pounding a table. The rules are simple: One person
starts the game by turning to a neighbor and naming a category:
"three things you'd find at the back of your closet!"; "three brands
of cereal!"; "three terrible excuses for showing up late!" As quickly
as possible, the neighbor has to call out three responses with authority. The group chant starts up again, and the next person gets
a category. Sometimes the answers fit the category "appropriately";
other times, they don't, but that's okay—whatever comes to mind
is the right answer. The idea is to generate and celebrate a quick
response.

I was standing right across from Greg in the circle. A person
in the group shouted, "Three things you could hide in your nose if
you had to!" while turning to Greg, who had no quick answer. After hesitating a few more seconds, and getting encouraging smiles
from others, he stopped biting his lips and said, "my finger, a raisin,
a penny." At the end of the class, as we walked out of the building,
"three things!" was still on his mind. "It was so awkward," he told
me. He was miserable.

But soon, things began to change. Greg learned to get the most out of class without worrying what others were thinking. He embraced being in the moment and surprised himself with his own reactions. He was fascinated, as I was, by the lessons and experience each exercise unlocked. He came to truly enjoy improv. Our delight in a particular session would carry into the next day, and the day after that. We started to share our enthusiasm with friends, describing the scenes or jokes we surprised ourselves with. And if Greg giggled after a cultural reference sailed right over my head, I usually joined in.

Another funny thing that eventually happened to both of us: we felt we were good at something new. We never became great actors, but we learned how to put ourselves out there, to be more comfortable with both our strong and weak points, and to support each other. We had no problem making fun of ourselves afterward. And when we played "three things!" again in later classes, the answers flowed with no hesitation. We'd become masters of producing answers in seconds, and the only safe prediction was that we'd end up laughing.

Psychologists call this kind of experience "self-expansion." When we engage in novel activities and acquire new skills, our sense of who we are expands, as does the number of traits we use to describe who we are. This, in turn, heightens our confidence that we can accomplish our goals, even when we're outside of our comfort zone, and it also increases our commitment to reaching our destination, no matter how tough the road. Aron initially wrote about self-expansion as a side effect of being in rewarding relationships. By getting closer to our partner, we learn something new from them, and we ourselves "expand," broadening our knowledge and interests.

Before we took our improv class, neither Greg nor I thought we were very good at being funny on the spot. And while we don't fool ourselves into thinking we're ready for *Saturday Night Live*, our sense of who we are has expanded: We now know that we are capable of being silly, and thus vulnerable, in front of strangers. We grew closer to each other by sharing in this sometimes frightening experience and seeing each other in a new light. Aron wrote about self-expansion as a natural desire to grow and change. When we challenge ourselves to move beyond what we know and can do well, we rebel against the comfortable cocoon of the status quo, improving ourselves and positioning ourselves to contribute more to our partners, coworkers, and organizations.

The third week of improv class, we warmed up with a game called "hot spot" that made me intensely uncomfortable. We all stood in a circle. One person entered the center and began singing a song. In no particular order, other players took turns singing in the center. The first time I sang, I felt huge discomfort. I've never been much of a singer, and my voice sounded soft and thin. But the beauty of the experience was that I didn't really have time to focus exclusively on my own discomfort. Rather, I needed to focus outward and support my classmates, helping them look good as they suffered through their own discomfort in the center of the circle. I learned that by smiling at them, singing along, or taking their place quickly when they were struggling, I could help. As I took the spotlight in the weeks that followed, my nerves dissolved and I found myself focusing on the excitement that came with singing new songs. My voice became stronger and more assured—even if I was still completely out of tune.

Improv teaches that it is OK to be uncomfortable. Comfort is overrated. It doesn't make us as happy as we think it will. With too much comfort, we miss out on the anticipation of what's going to happen next. It's so much better to go through life like a child dreaming of Santa Claus, wondering what gifts the future holds.

3

THE VANISHING ELEPHANT
A TALENT FOR CURIOSITY

Look at this life—all mystery and magic.
—HARRY HOUDINI

When New York City's Hippodrome Theater opened in 1905, its builders touted it as the largest and grandest theater in the world. Spires and American flags adorned the roof, giving the Hippodrome the appearance of a grand castle. Inside, seats for crowds of more than fifty-six hundred fanned the stage in a three-tiered semicircle. In popular magazines of the era, the theater was referred to as a "mammoth show-place on Sixth Avenue," "supreme in size and extravagance."

On January 7, 1918, the famed illusionist Harry Houdini walked across the stage, dressed all in black, with the eyes of the sold-out crowd upon him. For over two decades, the Hungarian-born escape artist and magician had been traveling the world, astonishing audiences with his death-defying escapes from handcuffs, ropes, straitjackets, and chains. He was particularly known for extricating himself from locked containers—from prison cells to milk cans to airtight coffins. One of his best-known escapes is called the "Chinese water torture cell." To perform the trick, Houdini began by dangling upside down with his ankles locked into a frame, before being lowered headfirst into a tank of water. If he couldn't escape within two minutes, an assistant standing by with an ax was prepared to break the glass—but that was never needed: Houdini broke free every time.

Houdini's exploits went beyond remarkable escapes. One of his tricks involved swallowing a hundred needles and twenty yards of thread with nothing more than a drink of water as a chaser. After showing the audience his empty mouth, Houdini would then reach in and pull out every single needle, fully threaded together and sometimes spanning the length of the stage. Often enough, his audiences were too dumbfounded to applaud right away.

At the Hippodrome that winter, the crowd was expecting him to perform the world's most incredible illusion. Houdini stood in the middle of the stage next to a giant wooden box on wheels, about eight feet square. "Ladies and gentlemen," he cried. "Allow me to introduce Jennie, the world's only vanishing elephant!" Jennie, a full-grown Asian elephant, came walking out onto the stage, standing eight feet tall and weighing over six thousand pounds. She raised her trunk in greeting, a baby blue ribbon tied around her neck. "She is all dressed up," Houdini said, "like a bride."

Twelve attendants turned the wooden box in a circle, opening all the doors to show the crowd that there was no way to escape. The doors were then closed, and the trainer marched the elephant slowly around the box before leading her inside. Houdini closed and sealed the doors, confident in his every movement.

He had been a trickster from the beginning. As a child, young Harry learned to open the locked cabinets in which his mother hid the pies and sweets she had baked. Growing up, he helped supplement his family's modest income by shining shoes and selling newspapers, but when he wasn't working, Houdini was drawn to athletics and practiced acrobatic stunts. He held his first performance at age nine, calling himself "the Prince of the Air"— wearing a pair of red socks his mother had made for him, he would swing on a trapeze hung from a tree. He launched his professional career when he was seventeen, performing magic shows in front of civic groups, at sideshows, inside music halls, and at the amusement park on New York's Coney Island, where he had as many as twenty shows a day. Fascinated by locks and handcuffs, he became an expert on them. Whenever he traveled to a new town, Houdini would offer $100 to anyone who could produce a pair of handcuffs from which he could not escape—but he never had to pay.

At the Hippodrome, a loud, dramatic drum roll filled the air, followed by the firing of a stage pistol. Then, the stagehands flung open the doors of the box at both ends. Poof: the giant pachyderm had vanished. "You can plainly see, the animal is completely gone," Houdini announced to rapturous applause. And for over ninety years, long after Houdini's death, the trick's secret remained a puzzle that even other magicians could not solve.

THE EIGHTEENTH-CENTURY SCOTTISH ECONOMIST AND MORAL PHILOSOPHER ADAM Smith is commonly regarded as the father of modern economics for having articulated the tenets of capitalism. However, Smith also made some interesting, lesser-known observations about the experience of wonder, writing that it arises "when something quite new and singular is presented . . . [and] memory cannot, from all its stores, cast up any image that nearly resembles this strange appearance." According to Smith, wonder is associated with a specific bodily feeling: "that staring, and sometimes that rolling of the eyes, that suspension of the breath, and that swelling of the heart."

In ancient times, people felt a sense of wonder and awe when the sun was blacked out by a solar eclipse. And even in the modern era, when we know what causes an eclipse, when to expect it, and exactly how long it will last, the phenomenon continues to beguile. For the total eclipse that crossed North America on August 17, 2017, many thousands of people traveled to spots within the "path of totality" to see the moon completely cover the sun and briefly instill darkness during the day. The sight drove some to tears and left many speechless. The natural world is a common source of wonder: the birth of a child, the sight of lions and elephants on a safari, or even watching the progression of an inchworm across one's finger.

Infants and children, who are experiencing everything for the first time, are likely the creatures most filled with a sense of wonder—as I'm reminded whenever I'm with my four-and-a-half-year-old son, Alexander. Lately, one of his favorite words is "Why?" As in: "Why is the sky blue?" "Why do you get receipts when you pay for things?" "Why can't we keep on playing?" and "Why do we wear clothes most of the time?" Every time I am confident I've given him a thoroughly satisfying answer, he pelts me with another string of queries. Like most other young children, he doesn't assume he has everything figured out or feel embarrassed about not knowing something. He takes time to puzzle over issues and doesn't dismiss ideas that might be outlandish.

This youthful sense of wonder was a central part of Houdini's personality, and it remained so throughout his life. When Houdini was seven, a traveling street circus passed through his hometown of Appleton, Wisconsin. What most captured his attention was not the clowns and acrobats, but the man in tights who climbed twenty feet into the air to a small platform and then walked across a taut wire stretched between two poles. As the crowd cheered, Houdini wondered: Why was the man risking his life? How long did he have to train to be able to walk the wire? When the man suspended himself from the high wire by his teeth, Houdini asked himself, How did he do it? How many times had he performed the trick before? What if he failed? Did his teeth hurt?

All these questions needed answers. Houdini rushed home that afternoon and found some rope to tie between two trees. Balancing on the rope was not easy: the first time he tried, he fell to the ground. But with perseverance, he learned to walk the tightrope. As for his attempt to replicate hanging by his teeth, it failed, as he did not realize that the man from the circus had used a mouthpiece. "Out came a couple of front teeth," Houdini remembered. Curiosity has its costs.

IN THE EARLY 1900S, HENRY FORD, FOUNDER OF FORD MOTOR COMPANY, WAS DEtermined to find a way to lower his production costs in order to create a car for the masses. On October 1, 1908, Ford realized that vision by rolling out the first Model T. The car had a twenty-two-horsepower, four-cylinder lightweight engine, could drive as fast as forty miles per hour, and ran on either hemp-based fuel or gasoline. The company's engineers had developed a system of interchangeable components, which not only saved time and reduced waste, but also made it easy for workers to assemble the cars, no matter how skilled (or unskilled) they were. This approach was far ahead of the rest of the auto industry. Ford's single-minded focus on efficiency and minimizing costs for the Model T turned out to be a remarkable success, and by 1921, the Ford Motor Company was responsible for 56 percent of all the passenger cars produced in the United States.

But in the late 1920s, as the U.S. economy rose to new heights, consumers began to thirst for greater variety in cars, not to mention a closed-body design (that is, a roof!). Competitors like General Motors saw an opportunity. In 1924, Alfred Sloan Jr., GM's president at the time, came up with a new market strategy: He divided the U.S. car market into different segments by price range and by what he called "purpose." Cars in the different segments would have different features and looks, depending on what consumers wanted and how deep their pockets were. Ford, instead, remained fixated on improving the Model T. Ford's competitors surged ahead while the Motel T started running out of gas. By the late 1920s, Ford had lost its lead position and GM had the largest share of the market. In the years that followed, Ford continued to lose market share to GM and was criticized for not understanding what customers wanted in a car. "The old master," GM's Sloan was happy to observe, "has failed to master change." Ford remained a follower in terms of the look and style of his cars, even when launching new models such as the Mustang, Maverick, and the Pinto. Despite some successes along the way, Ford ultimately lost in head-on competition with GM, and to this day, Ford has not regained its former position.

This brings us back to Harry Houdini. If you are trying to run a company efficiently, someone like Houdini might not be your first choice for an employee. But when we look closer, we see that unlike Ford, but like Ford's competitors, Houdini allowed his sense of wonder to guide his thinking. He may have lost a few teeth in the process, but he was always elevating his craft.

Even as I criticize Henry Ford, I'll admit that I personally often have the same inclination. Take a common early morning at my house. It's 6:30. The sun rose not long ago, but my fifteen-month-old daughter, Olivia, rose before it. I am half-asleep and still in my pajamas, making coffee. Meanwhile, Olivia is full of energy. She opens one of the cabinets in the kitchen and finds the colander; soon she's wearing it as a hat, then as a mask. Before I know it she's on the other side of the kitchen, opening another cabinet and moving jars of spices to a new location. Next, she fixates on a tall plastic canister containing rice. She sits on the floor and shakes it. "How can I get these small white pieces out of this container?" she seems to be asking. Next, my son, Alex, is up and ready to join in. The kids are both giggling as they find buttons to press and drawers to open.

I have to stop myself from picking Olivia up and putting an end to all this opening and closing of cabinets, all this fun exploration. Children absorb information like sponges, and they learn at a rapid pace. But as they grow, they become more aware of how others—adults in particular—see them, and they begin to rein in their curiosity. Curiosity, research suggests, typically peaks around age four or five. With age, self-consciousness increases, and so does our desire to make a show of expertise. But rebels learn to hold on to this childlike curiosity, and they never stop asking "why."

One recent morning, Greg poured Alex some cereal and milk for breakfast. Alex was sitting on his stool at the kitchen counter, and he seemed to be thinking hard about something. "Daddy, remember the food coloring we bought for Easter? When we colored eggs? Do we still have it?" Greg went over to the cabinet with the baking supplies, fished out the food coloring, and put the box next to Alex's bowl. "Here it is," Greg said. "What are you going to do with it?" Alex informed us that he was going to use the food coloring in his breakfast. Greg looked at him, confused. "Alex, we don't use food coloring in our milk."

"Why not, Daddy?"

Greg turned to me. "We just don't do that. Right, Mommy?" Meanwhile, Alex had taken the cap off the little red bottle, and soon his cereal swam happily in pink milk. Greg frowned. As he sipped his coffee and kept quiet, he seemed to be struggling with the same urge I'd felt seeing Olivia exploring the kitchen. He was resisting the impulse to put the cap back on the bottle of food coloring and pour our son a fresh bowl of cereal. While at the same time asking himself, Why, really, *shouldn't* the milk be pink? And, perhaps, what other colors could breakfast be?

IN 2000, THE BRITISH BROADCASTING CORPORATION, KNOWN ACROSS THE GLOBE
as the BBC, was facing challenges on many fronts. Established in
1922 as a private company, it initially broadcasted programs to radio owners. Its first director-general, John Reith, had a clear vision
for the BBC: "to educate, inform, and entertain" British people.
In the years that followed, the BBC grew and developed television broadcasting. It also entered the news business and, later on,
it started offering digital services like the twenty-four-hour BBC
news service and the BBC Online. The company became one of
Britain's best-known global brands.

But in the late 1980s and 1990s, the marketplace started to
change, and the media industry went through a seismic shift.
The nineties saw the arrival of a new digital broadcast technology
known as cable, which gave consumers many more choices—twice
as many channels as compared to analog technology, better quality
of services, and Internet access. The commercial channels risked
losing audiences and, with that, advertising revenues. Yet the BBC
had no clear vision or strategy for how to adapt. To compound the
problem, the BBC itself was going through some tough struggles
internally. It had lost its vitality, and the quality of its content was
suffering. There were 168 different business units all operating
within the BBC, and complexity and confusion had taken over
what had once been a well-organized workplace. A group of employees had come up with a three-word description for the BBC:
"despondent, down, and dismayed."

In 2000, the company brought in a man named Greg Dyke to
be its new director-general. Dyke had begun his career as a journalist, eventually entered broadcasting and became director of programs for London Weekend Television in 1987, and then served as
the company's group chief executive. In 1995, he joined Pearson
Television as CEO. Over the years, Dyke developed a reputation
for being a charismatic leader with a remarkable track record in

television. Early on in his career, for example, while working as program director of a new morning TV franchise at London Weekend Television called TV-am, Dyke rescued the channel by promoting a puppet called Roland Rat to a regular slot every morning and introducing cartoons for younger viewers. If children liked Roland and watched the show, Dyke predicted, then their mothers would keep the channel on. The ratings went up, and so did the number of people who watched the channel, from about 200,000 when Dyke started to 400,000 people just one month after his arrival, to 1.5 million by the end of his first year in charge.

The BBC presented a different kind of challenge for Dyke. It was much larger than his previous employers and had a deep connection to the public sector. Though the BBC operated independently from the British government, there were strong ties between the two entities: the government signed off on the BBC's long-term charter, and it also appointed the chairman of the BBC Trust. Dyke came up with an interesting transition plan. He overlapped with his predecessor, John Birt, by five months, and spent that time getting to know the BBC. Birt had developed a reputation for leading the BBC from his office in London. Dyke, instead, began traveling all around the United Kingdom, from Wales to Northern Ireland to Scotland, from the well-known BBC facilities to the most remote ones. He visited every major location and traveled to offices that had never received a visit from a director-general in the past. At each location, he met with the entire staff. Confounding employees' expectations, he didn't give a lengthy presentation about what he planned to change. Instead, he asked a simple question: "What is the one thing I should do to make things better for you?" Then Dyke would sit down and listen to the responses. After that, he asked a follow-up question: "What is the one thing I should do to make things better for our viewers and listeners?"

Dyke's first move in one of the most powerful jobs in Brit-

ish broadcasting was remarkable. People generally fear that asking questions will make them look foolish, especially when they
are asking for help with large problems that have been around for
some time. Aren't leaders supposed to provide answers? Management books are filled with guidelines on how leaders can make
long-lasting first impressions by communicating their vision right
from the start: Make clear who's in charge, for example, and del-
egate when appropriate. CEOs joining organizations are expected
to start implementing their vision, not to spend time asking others
how they can be most helpful to them. Many leaders in Dyke's
position, brought in to fix the problems of a deeply troubled organization, would have *talked* rather than ask questions. And most of
us would have the same impulse.

When Dyke made his visits, he didn't have lunch in the executive dining room. Rather, he'd often grab a tray in the cafeteria
with the staff and keep asking them questions. Dyke learned that
employees were frustrated by the many top-down changes Birt had
put in place without asking for input. They felt unmotivated and
disempowered. Many believed the BCC had lost its creative spark;
they also complained that facilities were badly in need of updating.

By Dyke's first official day in the job, when he formally ad-
dressed the staff, they were eager to hear his plans for the future
and to work with him to implement them. Dyke explained that
he wanted to shift the BBC's goal from being "the best-managed
organization in the public sector," as his predecessor had suggested,
to being the "most innovative and risk-taking place there is." As a
signal for the change he wanted to create, Dyke distributed yellow
cards that looked like the penalty cards that soccer referees hold up
when they're cautioning a player. He encouraged the staff to use
the cards to "cut the crap and make it happen." If anyone saw or
heard someone trying to block a good idea, they should wave the
yellow card in the air and state their case.

Dyke's unconventional approach paid off. Within a year of his arrival at the BBC, ratings increased for both BBC1 and BBC2, and audience satisfaction with the BBC increased overall from a 6 out of 10, just before Dyke arrived, to a 6.8. In July 2002, ratings for the flagship station BBC1 surpassed those of its main competitor, ITV, for the first time in many years. BBC radio reached record audiences. The BBC also dramatically reduced its overhead, allowing it to put an additional 270 million pounds into new broadcasting programs. And the upgrades that the employees wanted were also put in place.

The way that we typically think about the effect of asking questions—especially when we are in leadership positions—is just plain wrong. We fear that others will judge us negatively for not having all the answers, when in truth it's just the opposite. When we interact with others by asking questions, our relationships grow stronger, because we are showing genuine interest in learning about them, hearing their ideas, and getting to know them more personally. As a result, we gain their trust, and our relationship becomes more interesting and intimate. If you are worried that by asking a question you may come across as incompetent, you have that wrong also: People think of us as being smarter when we ask questions than when we don't.

To demonstrate the value of asking questions, my colleagues and I recruited a group of 170 students. We sat them down in front of computers and told them that they would be matched with another person taking the study, who would remain anonymous. What they did not know was that their partner was a computer-simulated actor. As a cover story, participants were told that the study was about understanding how instant messaging influences performance on a brain teaser. Participants then had to solve the task under time pressure, and they learned that their partner would also be completing it later in the study. They were told that their performance mattered, as they would be paid a bonus for each of the five problems in the brain teaser that they solved correctly.

To make sure the participants had no doubts that their partner was a real person, we gave them the opportunity to send an instant message to their partner at the beginning of the study. The computer-simulated actor did not provide a direct response to the message but simply sent one to them that said: "Hey, good luck." Once they had completed the brain teaser, the participants received another message from their partner. Depending on the condition they had been randomly assigned to, they received one of two messages: "I hope it went well" or "I hope it went well. Do you have any advice?" Participants could respond to this message after they received it knowing they would not hear back. They then evaluated how competent they thought their partner was and reported on how likely they would be to ask their partner for advice on a similar task in the future.

Participants who had a partner who asked them for advice rated the advice seeker higher on competence. They also indicated that they would be more likely to turn to their partner for advice. Thus, contrary to what we tend to believe, asking for advice *increases* rather than decreases how competent we are perceived to be. We underestimate how flattering it is to be asked for advice. By asking questions, we give others the opportunity to share their personal experience and wisdom, thus stroking their ego. Curiosity is a way of being rebellious in the world. Rebels fight their fears and are willing to push past the discomfort of showing others that they need their help. It may feel scary, but it brings about all sorts of benefits.

Curiosity is related to both greater positive emotions and greater closeness when we interact with strangers for the first time. In one study my colleagues and I conducted, we had college students engage in conversations with a peer where they were instructed to ask many questions or just a few. Students liked their partner more when they received more questions, we found, simply because that gave them the opportunity to talk and disclose information about themselves. People who ask more questions are better liked, our research shows, and speed daters who ask more questions get more second dates. In another study, undergraduates who didn't know each other were instructed to either engage in a conversation with a peer designed to generate intimacy, asking questions like "For what in your life do you feel most grateful?" or they engaged in casual small talk. Those who had an intimate conversation reported feeling closer to their partner and happier than those who engaged in small talk. Yet we are usually reluctant to ask more probing questions like this, believing we're getting too personal and that we should mind our own business instead.

Research has also found curiosity to be associated with greater satisfaction and a greater sense of social support in existing relationships. When arriving home after a day of work, you'll feel more connected to your partner if you show you are curious about how their day went. In a newer relationship, you'll have a more enjoyable date, and you'll be more excited to have another, if your partner asks questions that lead you to share more about yourself. When you show curiosity by asking questions, others share more, and they return the favor, asking questions of you. This sets up a spiral of give and take that fosters intimacy.

When we open ourselves to curiosity, we are more apt to reframe situations in a positive way. Curiosity makes us much more likely to view a tough problem at work as an interesting challenge to take on. A stressful meeting with our boss becomes an opportunity to learn. A nerve-racking first date becomes an exciting night out with a new person. A colander becomes a hat. In general, curiosity motivates us to view stressful situations as challenges rather than threats, to talk about difficulties more openly and to try new approaches to solving problems. In fact, curiosity is associated with a less defensive reaction to stress and, as a result, less aggression when we respond to a provocation. In a diary study conducted each day over four weeks, people who had higher tolerance for uncertainty indicated that they had conflicts with friends less often, fewer passive-aggressive reactions, and were more willing to excuse transgressions. Curiosity, in short, translates into greater engagement with others and with the world, thanks to the exploratory behavior and learning that it inspires.

How we express our curiosity has its roots in childhood and can be shaped by the lessons we are taught as we grow up. In one study, researchers showed eight- and nine-year-olds a school science project called "The Bouncing Raisins," which involves adding raisins to a mixture of vinegar and baking soda and watching them bounce up to the top of the glass. After the activity, the experimenter responded to the children differently. For half the children, she asked, "I wonder what would happen if we dropped one of these [picking up a Skittles candy from the table] into the liquid instead of a raisin?" To the other half of the children, she simply said, "I'm just going to tidy up a bit. I'll put these materials over here," as she cleaned up the work area.

In both scenarios, the experimenter then left the room, saying, "Feel free to do whatever you want while you are waiting for me. You can use the materials more, or draw with these crayons, or just wait. Whatever you want to do is fine." Children in the first group, who had seen their guide deviate from the task so that she could satisfy her own curiosity, tended to play with the materials much more, dropping raisins, Skittles, and other items into the liquid. Children who instead had seen her tidy up were more likely to simply do nothing. A teacher's behavior has a powerful effect on a child's disposition to explore. Similarly, a manager's actions can influence the curiosity and creativity of those in their organization. At Intuit, when curiosity results in innovations that are particularly creative, it is recognized with a Scott Cook Innovation Award. But there is also the "Greatest Failure Award," which celebrates curiosity that did not lead to a good result but still offered an important learning opportunity. The award comes with a "failure party."

The same researchers then flipped the Bouncing Raisins study to measure how teachers would respond to children's displays of curiosity and exploration. The teachers who volunteered were asked to do the same experiment with a student, whom the experimenters had instructed to behave in a certain way (unbeknownst to the teachers). Half of the teachers were told that the focus of the lesson was to learn about science. The other half were told that the focus of the lesson was filling out a worksheet. The teachers began by showing the children the Bouncing Raisins experiment, as before; this time, the students were instructed to stray from the instructions and put a Skittle into the glass. If the teacher asked the child what she was doing, the student was trained to reply, "I just wanted to see what would happen."

The results were striking. Teachers who believed that the goal of the lesson was learning about science responded to the diversion with interest and encouragement, saying things like, "Oh, what are you trying?" or "Maybe we should see what this will do." But those teachers who had been encouraged to focus on completing the worksheet said things like, "Oh, wait a second, that's not on the instruction sheet" or "Whoops, that doesn't go in there." How we react to the exploration and experimentation of our colleagues or subordinates is likely to directly influence whether they feel comfortable exploring their curiosity. A workplace with failure parties is going to yield a lot more creativity than one where efficiency is celebrated above all else.

As in the case of the production of Model Ts at Ford Motor, or the urge we feel as parents when we want to stop our children in their messy explorations of the world, I fear that schools may be too focused on perfecting skills or preparing for tests in ways that are detrimental to curiosity. While checking out schools for Alex's pre-K year, I saw a teacher in one of the classes teaching children how to draw perfect triangles, squares, and circles and then color them. She seemed particularly interested in having the shapes be "properly" drawn, and when the children colored, she continually reminded them "NOT to color outside the lines!" Focusing on teaching students to avoid making mistakes, to perform well on standardized tests, or to be well behaved may lead teachers to forget what education is about, at least in my mind: the beauty of fueling and nurturing their natural curiosity so that they will keep asking questions about the world. I also fear that workplaces are not that different in their approach to curiosity: By following rules and orders in executing the work, employees lose the sense of wonder that could lead them to approach the job differently.

Massimiliano (Max) Zanardi is a manager who knows how to tap into his employees' curiosity, and his own, to run a better business. He likes to introduce himself as "100 percent Italian, and 50 percent Turkish." He was born in Italy but spent many years living in Turkey. Like many Italians, Zanardi talks in an animated fashion and uses lots of hand gestures. He was the general manager of the Ritz-Carlton in Istanbul for several years, playing a key role in the hotel's opening and working hard to improve customers' experiences. In 2015, the hotel was voted Turkey's Best Luxury Hotel in the prestigious *Business Destinations* Travel Awards, and *Business Destinations* magazine praised the hotel as standing out for its innovation, unparalleled facilities, and the passion of its employees for the work they do. Standing in the lobby, you will enjoy the subtle fragrance of the hotel's bespoke perfume, and throughout public areas in the hotel, carefully selected contemporary music inspires you to smile or even do a little dance.

The hotel's employees attribute their passion to the way that Zanardi encouraged them to always ask questions. As general manager, Zanardi regularly challenged employees to redefine luxury by asking "Why?" and "What if?" For example, each year employees were used to planting flowers on the terrace right outside the hotel's restaurant. One day, when it was time to fill the pots and choose what to plant, Zanardi asked staff members, "*Why* do we always plant flowers? How about vegetables? What about herbs?" This conversation eventually led to a terrace garden full of herbs and heirloom tomatoes that were used in the hotel's acclaimed restaurant, Atelier Real Food. All of this from asking a few simple questions.

ON OCTOBER 29, 1908, IN A SMALL PICTURESQUE TOWN IN THE FOOTHILLS OF THE Italian Alps, Camillo Olivetti founded Italy's first typewriter factory as a family business. A gifted and eclectic engineer, Olivetti had been inspired by a visit to the United States to import typewriters to Italy, and then, later, to manufacture them. Olivetti started with twenty employees, who assembled about twenty machines per week. Under its founder's direction, the company, called simply Olivetti, grew rapidly; by the early 1920s, it had 250 employees and was producing more than 2,000 machines a year.

In 1924, Camillo's son, Adriano, joined the family business after graduating from college. He started as a production worker on the factory floor. Adriano noticed the monotony of many of the tasks employees completed day after day and the tough working conditions—there was not enough light inside the factory, nor enough time for breaks. Workers were also too isolated from one another, he thought, with each person handling a different step of the production process, and their hours were too long. Adriano was struck by the fact that, as workers completed routinized and simplified tasks in the style of Fordism, they stopped thinking. Work, Adriano believed, should not be passive or negative. Rather, it should provide joy and have a noble purpose, leading people to a better life. In Adriano's mind, companies have a moral obligation toward their workers; after all, it is through workers' physical and intellectual contributions that companies grow. Adriano believed that companies should not only provide their employees with economic rewards, but also promote cultural and social initiatives that would help them and their families flourish alongside the firm.

The management scholar James March first wrote about this trade-off between efficiency and innovation in 1991, highlighting the contrast between "exploitation" and "exploration" in organizations. Exploration, or looking for and identifying new ideas and ways of doing things, involves risk taking, experimentation, flexibility, play, discovery, and innovation. Exploitation, in contrast, involves improving and refining existing products and processes through efficiency, selection, implementation, and execution. These two activities, March argued, require substantially different capabilities, processes, and cultures. Groups organized around exploration tend to have flexible structures and are associated with improvisation, autonomy, chaos, and emerging businesses and technologies. Meanwhile, those organized for exploitation are more often associated with routine processes, control and bureaucracy, and stable markets and technology. Exploitation, March noted, often crowds out exploration.

Departing from the single-minded focus on efficient processes that characterized Ford's methods, Adriano Olivetti was able to get the balance between exploration and exploitation just right. He became the company's general manager in 1932 and its president in 1938. Under Adriano's leadership, the firm adopted a much more efficient production system, thus following in Ford's footsteps. But unlike Ford, the company also invested in its workforce—in ways that were rather unusual, especially at that time. In the northwest Italian town of Ivrea, new factory buildings were built almost entirely of glass, so that the workers could see the mountains and valleys, and those outside could see what was happening inside. Cultured, sophisticated, and community-minded, Adriano was an engineer fascinated by art, design, and architecture, and he drew on these interests in his corporate role. Under Adriano, Olivetti's design strategy became integrated into the product-development process. In fact, in 1937, the company was one of the first to integrate a graphic design department into its corporate structure. Rather than limiting designers to fashioning the appearance of products only after engineers had developed them, Olivetti's designers were equal partners from the start.

In the 1940s, Olivetti launched creative new products into the market, like its Divisumma electric calculator (launched in 1948), a ten-key printing machine capable of division, which became very popular. In 1969, Olivetti's Valentine typewriter turned what was once a utilitarian machine into a must-have of the day. Using modern materials, a new manufacturing process, and a clever design, the portable Valentine typewriter created a new mass-market product category. The company also started to diversify—specifically, into the production of the first mechanical calculators and a highly innovative electronics division. Thanks to the fact that designers were so involved in the process, Olivetti's products became known for being highly functional but also aesthetically unique. For instance, the Valentine typewriter had smooth lines and punchy colors—it came in red, white, green, and blue—making it fun, and adding personality to an area that had long taken itself too seriously: the office. At the same time, Olivetti expanded internationally, opening subsidiaries across Latin America and Europe. The company grew from a factory with fewer than nine hundred employees in its early years to a multinational firm with about eighty thousand workers at ten establishments in Italy and eleven abroad. By the 1970s, Olivetti had become "an undisputed leader in industrial design," a phrase Steve Jobs would use a decade later when talking about what he wanted his company Apple to be.

Though initially impressed by the production efficiencies he saw at Ford, Adriano believed the intensive work schedules overly stressed employees and could, in the long term, alienate them. He not only paid Olivetti workers more than other companies did at the time, but he went to great lengths to ensure that they remained engaged, curious, and exposed to knowledge and culture from different disciplines. Under Adriano, new factories included playgrounds for workers' children, libraries filled with tens of thousands of books and magazines, and rooms for film screenings and debates. (Tech companies like Google and Facebook offer similar perks these days, but they were rather uncommon at the time.) He also hired writers, poets, and other intellectuals. During the 1950s, for example, the novelist and psychologist Ottiero Ottieri oversaw recruitment, and the poet Giovanni Giudici ran the firm's library (which Adriano referred to as the "factory of the culture"). Workers were given a two-hour break for lunch: one hour to eat food, the other to "eat" culture—by reading books from the library, or attending concerts and talks by famous intellectuals Olivetti had invited. Mechanical engineers received lessons on the history of music or the French Revolution. For Christmas, management gave employees special editions of books that were considered classics, or custom-made calendars with reproductions of famous artworks or illustrations made by emerging artists. The company also sponsored the renovation of various masterpieces, including Leonardo da Vinci's *The Last Supper*.

Adriano had no data to support his approach to management, and other executives often thought he was "wasting time" with all these activities and initiatives for his employees. But he was clearly spot-on with his intuition: By investing in workers' well-being and curiosity, his company kept innovating and putting successful products on the market. In addition to the traditional typewriter, Olivetti developed products that allowed the company to expand into new markets, including, eventually, the first personal computer in the world, Programma 101 (P101), in 1964.

By making innovation the core of his company's production strategy, Adriano Olivetti fostered a highly creative environment for his staff. He believed that the success of Olivetti products was about much more than the processes; it was about what he did for his people. He gave workers much more ownership over the manufacturing process, invested in their well-being, and encouraged them to be curious. Olivetti is the oldest technology company in Italy, and it has also become the largest. In the mid-1990s, it was the second-largest computer maker in Europe. Its great design and innovation are the key sources of that success, together with the company's vast range of products, from the first mass-produced personal computer and typewriters, to fax machines, cash registers, and inkjet printers.

In a similar manner today, design and consulting company IDEO seeks to hire what are known as "T-shaped" employees. (This terminology apparently originated at the management consulting firm McKinsey & Company in internal hiring conversations.) The vertical stroke of the "T" in "T-shaped" employee refers to the depth of knowledge and skill an employee relies on to add her contribution to the creative process. The horizontal stroke of the "T" refers to an employee's inclination for collaboration across functions, which consists of two aspects: empathy and curiosity. Empathy is what allows people to take another person's perspective when considering problems and to listen actively. Curiosity refers to an interest in other people's activities and disciplines, an interest so strong that an employee may start to practice them. Adriano hired prestigious designers to design Olivetti's typewriters—people who clearly had deep skills—but he also assured that the workplace was structured to nurture their empathy and curiosity. Like IDEO's leaders, he believed that people perform at their best not because they're specialists, but rather because their depth of skill is accompanied by an intellectual curiosity that leads them to keep exploring.

Research evidence for a link between curiosity and innovation abounds. Spencer Harrison, of the INSEAD business school in France, and his colleagues examined this relationship in the context of an e-commerce website where people sell handmade goods. Over a two-week period, the artisans answered questions about the level of curiosity they experienced at work. Their productivity was then assessed by counting the number of new items each artisan listed over a two-week period. Curiosity was associated with a greater creative productivity; a one-unit increase in curiosity (e.g., moving from a score of 5 to 6 on a 7-point scale) was associated with a 34 percent increase in productivity.

Curiosity produces performance benefits in all kinds of jobs. Take the case of call centers, where jobs are heavily structured. As a result, turnover is generally high. To make matters worse, calls are often monitored, and employees' performance is evaluated based on the speed at which they handle each call. Harrison and his colleagues asked new employees from ten different call-center organizations to complete a survey that measured their curiosity before they started working in their company's call center. Four weeks into the job, the same employees reported on different aspects of their job, such as how well they were learning and whether they were seeking information by reaching out to other colleagues. The most curious people the company had hired were those who sought the most information from coworkers, and they were the best able to use that information in a way that allowed them to be creative and perform at higher levels. Some of them, the researchers learned in follow-up interviews, saw their jobs less as "an assembly line in your brain," in the words of one employee, and more like a puzzle in which they had to figure out new ways to use the prescribed system to benefit customers. It was these people who became the highest performers.

My own research finds that curious people often end up being star performers in their organizations for several reasons: they have larger networks; they're more comfortable asking questions; and they more easily create and nurture ties with others at work—ties that are critical to their career development and success. The organization also benefits, as these curious employees are more connected to others who can help them overcome work challenges and are more motivated to go the extra mile.

When Adriano was the CEO of Olivetti, one of his workers was caught leaving the factory with a bag full of iron pieces and machinery. The colleagues who caught him accused him of being a thief and suggested the company fire him. The employee protested that he wasn't stealing, but rather taking the parts home to work on a project over the weekend because he didn't have enough time to do it at work. When Adriano heard the story, he asked to speak with the worker directly. At their meeting, the worker explained that he had a plan to build a new machine, a calculator. Intrigued, Adriano put him in charge of the production process for the new machine. Not long after, the new electrical calculating machine was built—the first of its type on the market. The Divisumma offered automatic calculation with all four basic mathematical operations. In the 1950s and 1960s, Divisumma became a popular product across the globe and was a dramatic, lucrative success for Olivetti. Adriano promoted the worker to the position of technical director. Rather than firing the employee, Adriano gave him the opportunity to play with his curiosity, with astounding results.

HIGHWAY 101 RUNS FOR OVER FIFTEEN HUNDRED MILES ON THE WEST COAST OF the United States, through the states of California, Oregon, and Washington. Back in 2004, an anonymous billboard made its appearance on the highway south of San Francisco, in the heart of the Silicon Valley. The billboard had a strange ad on it: "{first 10-digit prime found in consecutive digits of e}.com." Across the country, in Cambridge, Massachusetts, a similar mysterious banner appeared at the Harvard Square subway stop.

The message contains a challenging math puzzle. As I found out after a bit of searching online (since I couldn't remember this from my math classes), e, the base of the natural system of logarithms, has a numerical value of 2.71828. The number actually goes on forever, but eventually you will get to the first ten-digit prime found consecutively within it. (The correct answer is 7427466391 .com.) If you were curious enough to solve the problem and then go to the website, you would have found another equation to solve, an even harder problem. Eventually, if you were a determined enough problem-solver, you would have found yourself at a Google webpage asking you to upload your résumé. From there, the few remaining contestants landed an interview at Google headquarters.

Tech companies have relied on mathematical and logical puzzles for quite some time, at least since the 1950s, in their attempts to recruit the most curious candidates. For instance, Microsoft, which popularized this hiring method, posed the following problem to candidates in first-round interviews: "Imagine an old-fashioned clock with two hands on it. When it is at twelve o'clock, the minute hand is directly on top of the hour hand. The question is, how many times a day does it happen that the minute hand is right over the hour hand, and how would you determine the exact times of the day that this occurs?" (You can find the answer in the Notes section of this book.) Other companies use more obvious methods to find curious employees, from explicitly encouraging curious people to apply in job postings to asking candidates about their interests and hobbies outside of work.

With its billboard recruitment plan, Google was looking for people who are "geeky enough to be annoyed at the very existence of a math problem they haven't solved, and smart enough to rectify the situation," according to an official blog post written by Googlers in 2004. If engineers were curious enough to pursue answers to the problem, they had a quality the company was looking for. Curiosity encourages new ways of thinking, challenges long-held assumptions, and fuels transformative change. As Google

CEO Eric Schmidt has commented, "We run this company on questions, not answers."

Recruiting creative people is certainly important, and finding them can be challenging. But by far the biggest challenge that organizations and their leaders face comes after an employee is hired: How do we keep people creative? The curiosity we all naturally had as children does not express itself as easily when we become adults. And as we enter new relationships, whether at work or in life, we all face the risk of seeing our creativity decline because we stop asking questions. In one survey, I asked about 250 people who had recently started new jobs with various companies about their level of curiosity when they started. Although they started off at different levels, after six months passed, their curiosity level had dropped by more than 20 percent, on average. Why? We ask too few questions when approaching problems. We work to finish assigned tasks without questioning the process or asking about overall goals. And, rather than celebrating curiosity, our leaders often discourage it. They see its value, but their actions often tell an alarmingly different story.

In another survey, I asked over three thousand employees from several industries to answer a few questions about curiosity. Most of them (92 percent) credited curious people for bringing new ideas into teams and organizations, and viewed curiosity as a catalyst to job satisfaction, innovation, and high performance. Yet only a minority, about 24 percent, reported feeling curious in their jobs on a regular basis. And about 70 percent reported facing barriers to asking more questions at work, like the pressure to execute their work at a rapid pace, the reluctance to take risks, fearing some sort of punishment in the case of failure, and the unwillingness to question existing procedures.

We all differ in how curious we are by nature. But no matter our natural level of curiosity, in organizations, curiosity can be fostered. Leaders can encourage it throughout their company by first being more inquisitive and curious themselves. Curiosity needs champions, and that needs to start at the top. Whether in brainstorming sessions or in regular firm meetings, leaders can set a good example by asking "Why?" and "What if?"—just as Zanardi did at Ritz-Carlton and Greg Dyke did at the BBC— and by encouraging others to do the same. As the sense of curiosity grows in a workplace, some good answers will likely follow. Outside of company meetings, leaders can stress the importance of curiosity in other ways. For instance, Facebook CEO Mark Zuckerberg publicly sets new personal learning goals for himself each year, inspiring others inside the firm to do the same. In the last few years, Zuckerberg's goals included learning Mandarin, reading a book every other week, meeting a new person every day who doesn't work at Facebook, and visiting and meeting people in every state in the United States.

Organizations can also foster curiosity by encouraging their employees to explore their interests. When Adriano Olivetti was presented with a "thief," he recognized a talent who needed the time and resources to explore a great idea. Other successful leaders and organizations have done the same kind of thing. Since 1996, the manufacturing conglomerate United Technologies (UTC) has provided up to $12,000 in tuition per year to employees seeking advanced degrees on a part-time basis, no strings attached. Employers are often not in favor of training staff, fearing they might find a job with a competitor and leave the firm with their expensively acquired skills. But Gail Jackson, UTC's vice president of human resources, thinks differently about this. "We want people who are intellectually curious," she notes. "It is better to train and have them leave than not to train and have them stay."

Another way leaders can foster curiosity in employees is by acknowledging the limits of their own knowledge with a simple "I don't know—let's find out," or by highlighting the inherent ambiguity of a decision the company is facing. At one company I visited, employees were asked to come up with "What if . . . ?" and "How might we . . . ?" questions about the firm's goals and its plans. As a sign that questioning was not only encouraged but also supported and rewarded, employees and management chose the best of these questions to display on banners on the company's walls. Maintaining this sense of curiosity is crucial to creativity and innovation in an organization. Think of the story behind Polaroid: The inspiration that led to the instant camera was born out of a question that the three-year-old daughter of its inventor, Edwin H. Land, asked in the mid-1940s. When her father snapped a photo, she found herself waiting impatiently to see it. She learned that the film had to be processed first, but as her father explained this to her, she wondered aloud, "Why do we have to wait for the picture?"

There's a good management lesson to learn in the way parents respond when their baby comes across something new. First a baby will express surprise, and then look at the parent: If the parent makes a sad face or a face that evokes negative emotions, then the child's surprised expression turns negative. If the parent expresses pleasant excitement, on the other hand, then the child does as well. Similarly, at work, we'll continue questioning and exploring only if we are part of a group or organization characterized by what researchers refer to as "psychological safety"—a shared belief that members can take risks. If a workplace does not feel safe, a person is reluctant to ask questions or even to bring up problems that would clearly make the group better off. When Harvard Business School management scholar Amy Edmondson studied medical teams in various hospitals, she discovered that the best teams were the ones that were psychologically safe: Team members were not afraid to admit to errors and discussed them openly with their colleagues. In a group that is psychologically safe, you would not fear being embarrassed about raising unorthodox questions, ideas, or doubts.

Think of one of the most beloved characters in children's literature: Curious George. The little high-energy monkey who lives with the Man with the Yellow Hat dives into every experience he comes across, eager to explore and experiment. The Man with the Yellow Hat is always ready to bail George out of the sticky situations he gets himself into (for instance, flying by in a helicopter just when George floats too high on a bunch of balloons). Fortunately for George, he benefits from his curiosity, enjoying new experiences and discoveries, because he's never punished for getting into trouble. Too often, there is no room for Curious George characters in the workplace. People who explore and end up with unsuccessful experiments or, even worse, create a messy situation, are usually punished for it. Rarely are they praised for championing the value of experimentation regardless of outcome.

There are many ways that leaders can let employees know they value curiosity. When Satya Nadella joined Microsoft in 2014 as the new CEO, for instance, he changed the criteria in the firm's performance review so that they would include an evaluation of how well employees learn from their colleagues, share ideas, and apply their new knowledge. Ed Catmull, who cofounded Pixar Animation Studios and is now its president, worried that Pixar's success would lead new hires to be in awe, to the point that they would not challenge existing practices. To address his worry, during onboarding sessions when new employees are welcomed to the firm and get socialized into it, he shares examples of how the company has made certain bad choices in the past. He stresses the simple but often overlooked fact that we all make mistakes and that Pixar is not perfect. His unusual candor gives new recruits the license they need to be curious.

Training can also foster healthy questioning. Recently, an organization approached INSEAD's Spencer Harrison for advice on encouraging curiosity in its employees. With his colleagues, he created two versions of an online training program for the firm. Half of the company's employees were taught what the researchers called "the grow method," which explained that success would come from following existing processes. The other half received a modified version, called the "go back method," which asked employees to go back and question the common assumptions we all tend to hold about goals, roles, and the organization as a whole. As an example, employees learning the "go back method" were told the story of a scientist who was trying to help people with diseases that caused their extremities to shake, which made it difficult for them to complete certain activities, such as eating cereal for breakfast. Initially, the scientist was focused on the idea of creating a drug that would stop the shaking. But as he thought more about the goal of stopping the tremors, he came up with a mechanical solution: attaching a gyroscope to a spoon so that the spoon would absorb the tremors.

Weeks later, managers at the company rated the employees who went through the "go back" training as more creative and innovative than those who received the more traditional training (without knowing who had engaged in which program). Harrison and his colleagues also examined the type of connections people created at work by looking at the emails they exchanged with one another. They found that people who went through the "go back" training changed how they engaged with their colleagues: they expanded their networks, sent more emails, and, as a result, gathered more information, which allowed them to be more creative in their jobs. When we ask questions about aspects of our job and organization that we generally take for granted, we build relationships with colleagues more easily, and our ideas get more interesting.

ARE YOU STILL WONDERING ABOUT HOW HOUDINI MADE THE ELEPHANT DISAPPEAR? Researchers often use the Vanishing Elephant trick to trigger curiosity and study its effects on people's behavior. For instance, doctoral student Lydia Hagtvedt of Boston College and her colleagues divided participants into two groups, and asked them to read different versions of a news article on the Vanishing Elephant trick. For one group, the article described the Vanishing Elephant trick as an industry standard and included an explanation of exactly how Houdini accomplished it. Participants were asked to describe how they would feel if they were watching in the audience and how they thought Houdini did the trick, which had already been explained to them. They submitted their responses via computer. After a short delay, they were informed that their answer regarding the solution to the trick was correct.

For the second group, the experiment's "curiosity condition," the article did not include any clues about how the trick worked. After reading the article, the participants had to describe how they would feel if they were in the audience watching and how they thought Houdini did the trick, and, as with the other group, they submitted their responses via computer. But in this case, it appeared as if their answer to the question about how the trick worked was being compared to a correct answer in a database; in reality, this was simply a time delay in the program. After a few seconds, participants were told that their answer was close but not fully correct. In this way, participants in the second group remained curious about how the trick was accomplished, while those in the control group were led to feel confident that they knew the nature of the trick.

Next, all participants moved on to a different task: generating additional ideas for magic tricks. They had to imagine that they were Houdini and were hoping to perform a trick better than the elephant one. Professional magicians with over twenty years of experience evaluated the creativity of the participants' responses. In addition, independent coders read participants' answers and rated the degree to which their magic-trick ideas moved beyond the core aspects of the original Vanishing Elephant trick. So, for instance, a response such as, "I would put the curtain over the box with the elephant in it and then make the box disappear leaving just the elephant," received a low score because the idea involved the three core aspects of the Vanishing Elephant trick: disappearing, elephants, and boxes. But a response like "I would perform a trick where it looked like I was levitating" received the highest possible score because it did not contain any of the core aspects of the original trick.

Participants in the curiosity condition generated ideas that the professional magicians evaluated as creative significantly more often (69 percent of the time) than those in the control condition (34 percent of the time). Their ideas were also less fixated on core aspects of the Vanishing Elephant trick. Curiosity led participants to generate ideas that experts judged as more creative and that diverged more dramatically from the status quo.

Throughout his career, once Houdini had mastered one escape, like freeing himself from locked handcuffs, he would quickly move on to mastering a new challenge, like having the local police in a town he visited restrain him, and managing to escape. Once he'd mastered each of these situations, he decided to try jumping into rivers while handcuffed and chained. Houdini was constantly looking for new ways to challenge himself. He pushed himself relentlessly and trained hard for his various difficult feats. When we realize that we don't have an immediate answer to a puzzle or problem that confronts us, our mind fills with creative ideas, if we let it. Every single day we can choose between focusing on what we know or what we don't know. When we do the latter, we engage our curiosity and are more likely to see the world as Houdini did.

Houdini inspired awe in his audiences through his magic, Greg Dyke took the helm at the BBC by asking questions rather than providing answers, Google found rare talent by making potential job candidates wonder, and Adriano Olivetti created an almost magical workplace where he used various tricks to broaden his employees' interests. Although tough and competitive at different times and in different contexts, all these players were able to instill curiosity in those they interacted with, and remained curious themselves. Their inquisitive nature and sense of wonder was contagious.

As it turns out, the vanishing trick was not actually invented by Houdini. The credit for it goes to Charles Morritt, a hypnotist and illusionist from Yorkshire, England, whose trick the Disappearing Donkey was a precursor to Houdini's Vanishing Elephant. For the donkey trick, Morritt would usher the uncooperative animal into a wooden chamber on wheels, and the audience could see that there were no trapdoors being used. As Morritt closed up the sides, the audience could hear the sound of the donkey's hooves pounding the wood of the chamber that held him prisoner. Unbeknownst to those in the audience, the chamber had been specially designed, and when Morritt opened it up again, the donkey had "disappeared." Audiences loved the act, which eventually brought Morritt to Houdini's attention.

Despite his inventive genius, Morritt's ability and charisma as a performer were lacking. Morritt also needed money, so he sold Houdini the secrets to many of his best and most carefully guarded illusions, including the Disappearing Donkey. The switch from donkey to elephant was Morritt's idea as well, a suggestion he made to Houdini to make the stunt even more memorable. Here is how the Vanishing Elephant trick actually worked: When Jennie entered the box, her trainer hid the elephant behind a large mirror that extended on a diagonal from the corner of the box that was closest to the audience to the center of the doors at the back of the box. When the doors were reopened, the audience saw a seemingly empty box, not realizing that they were actually viewing only one half of the box's interior and its reflection.

Though Houdini did not invent the trick, he brought his amazing showmanship to it, and he constantly pushed to make it better. The fact that audiences remained amazed by the trick for decades, and that no one could figure it out until one of Houdini's prop engineers divulged the secret to *Modern Mechanix* magazine in 1929, was due in large part to how well Houdini performed and perfected it. For the stunned audience, Houdini's Vanishing Elephant magic trick raised a question with no clear answer—and it inspired the curiosity of generations.

4

THE HUDSON RIVER
IS A RUNWAY

A TALENT FOR PERSPECTIVE

*There's a literal freedom you feel when you're at the controls, gliding
above the surface on the earth, no longer bound by gravity . . .
Even at a few thousand feet, you get a wider perspective.*
—CAPTAIN CHESLEY SULLENBERGER

On a January afternoon in 2009, US Airways flight 1549 took
off from LaGuardia Airport in New York, headed for Charlotte,
North Carolina. The weather in New York was cold, about 21 degrees Fahrenheit. The winds coming out of the north were not too
strong, and the sky was mostly clear with only scattered clouds—it
had stopped snowing earlier that morning. The plane carried 150
passengers and five crew members; only one seat was empty. For
the crew, this was the final leg of a four-day trip. Captain Chesley Sullenberger, an experienced pilot known as "Sully," shared
the cockpit with Jeff Skiles, a first officer with whom he'd never
worked before.

Less than two minutes into the flight, Sully looked out of the cockpit's front windows to see birds—massive ones, their long wings extended horizontally—flying headlong toward the plane. The plane was climbing above 3,000 feet, the engines whining with the effort, at just over 230 miles an hour. "Birds!" Sully shouted.

At the same moment, the sound of something similar to a very bad storm filled the cockpit and cabin, as if the plane were being pelted by hail or heavy rain. The birds began to hit the plane just below the windshield, smashing against the nose, the wings, and the engines with a series of thuds. Then a loud screeching noise came from the engines, followed by severe vibrations, as if the engines were protesting the sudden disruption. A pungent charred smell entered the cabin, and then the engine noises subsided—an eerie quiet. Everyone heard a "rhythmic rumbling and rattling, like a stick being held against moving bicycle spokes. It was a strange windmilling sound from broken engines," Sully said. The Airbus A320-214 has two engines, and both had failed.

With so little altitude and both engines destroyed, there was little time to act. If the plane had lost one engine rather than two, the pilot and first officer would have been able to maintain control of the aircraft. They would have declared an emergency and, with the air traffic controller's help, found a nearby airport where they could likely land safely. But without any working engines, the plane had become a very heavy glider, loaded with fuel.

"My aircraft," Sully said, and took control of the plane. "Your aircraft," Skiles responded. He pulled out the aircraft's Quick Reference Handbook, found the checklist for loss of thrust in both engines, and got to work. "Mayday, mayday, mayday," Sully called out to Air Traffic Control. Patrick Harten, the air traffic controller sitting at his radar position at the New York Terminal Radar Approach Control located on Long Island, didn't hear the mayday call. At the same moment Sully was calling out for help, Harten was making a transmission of his own—to Sully himself, giving him routine direction for the flight. When Harten released his transmit button, he caught part of Sully's emergency message: ". . . hit birds. We've lost thrust in both engines. We're turning back toward La-Guardia."

In his ten years on the job, Harten had worked many thousands of flights and had never failed to help a plane in distress get safely to a runway. He had worked in many emergency situations in the past, from assisting jets with failures of one engine to helping airplanes hit by birds. Controllers guide pilots to runways: that's their job. Harten offered Sully LaGuardia's runway 13, which was the closest to the plane's current position. He immediately contacted the tower at LaGuardia, asking them to clear all runaways. "Cactus fifteen twenty-nine, if we can get it for you, do you want to try to land runway one three?" he asked, getting the flight number wrong in the stress of the moment.

Looking out the window, it was clear to Sully that there were few good options. The 150,000-pound plane was gliding at a low altitude, at low speed, with no engines, and it was descending rapidly. The jagged architecture of the nation's largest metropolis was all too clear through the windshield. There was no major interstate nearby without heavy traffic. Nor were there any long, level farmer's fields. Turning back for the airport they had left just minutes earlier would eliminate all other options. Given how densely populated the area surrounding LaGuardia is, choosing to turn back needed to be a sure thing rather than a probable bet. Even if they made it back—which wasn't looking likely to Sully—missing the runway by just a few feet would mean a torn-open airplane, engulfed in flames.

"All right, Cactus fifteen forty-nine, it's gonna be left traffic for runway three one," Harten said to Sully.

"Unable," Sully responded. He had made the decision: LaGuardia was not an option. As the plane kept dropping, the synthetic voice of the Traffic Collision Avoidance System issued a warning inside the cockpit: "Traffic. Traffic."

Harten offered another runway at LaGuardia.

"I'm not sure we can make any runway," Sully responded. "What's over to our right? . . . anything in New Jersey, maybe Teterboro?"

On his radar screen, Harten could see that the plane was now about nine hundred feet above the Manhattan side of the George Washington Bridge, which stretches across the Hudson River from New York City to New Jersey. Teterboro was no closer than La-Guardia, but Sully was considering all possibilities. Working with the Teterboro controller, Harten quickly arranged for the plane to land on the arrival runway—the one easiest to clear of traffic. But Sully could see the area around the airport moving up in the windscreen—Teterboro, he realized, was also going to be too far away. That left the Hudson River.

Sully had been flying airplanes for forty-two years, since he was in high school in Denison, Texas. He'd gone on to attend the Air Force Academy and began his career flying a Vietnam War–era fighter, the F-4 Phantom. In his many years of flying, he had never experienced an engine failure. Nor had he ever tried to land in a body of water. But from his perspective, the river was long enough, wide enough, and smooth enough to serve as a landing spot. Outside, it was just 21 degrees, the wind-chill factor was 11, and the water was about 36 degrees. Rescue boats or helicopters would take at least a few minutes to arrive at the scene to help. Hypothermia posed a serious risk to passengers even if the plane made it into the river intact. But the choice seemed to be the best option, for the simple reason that there were no buildings on the Hudson.

Sully made a cabin announcement: "Brace for impact."

Skiles had tried multiple times to relight the engines with the standard clicking igniters, but it hadn't worked: The engines had banged and flamed and lost thrust on the right and almost completely on the left. They had both swallowed dozens of Canada geese, but they hadn't exploded or thrown shrapnel into the fuselage. They were simply not restarting. Skiles stopped trying and focused instead on helping Sully as they were heading into the Hudson.

Without any thrust, the only control Sully had over the plane's vertical path was the raising and lowering of its nose—that is, the pitch. His goal was to maintain a pitch that would give the airplane an appropriate glide speed, not too fast, not too slow, so as to land in the water as gently as possible. The airspeed indicator was still working, so every time Sully thought he was slower than he needed to be, he lowered the nose of the plane slightly. And when he felt the plane was traveling too fast, he raised the nose.

". . . turn right two eight zero," Harten told Sully. "You can land runway one at Teterboro."

"We can't do it."

"OK, which runway would you like at Teterboro?" Sully was the one inside the plane, Harten knew, and had a better sense for the situation.

"We're going to be in the Hudson," Sully responded.

"I'm sorry," Harten said, ". . . say again?"

He continued to offer options to Sully, trying to find a solution that would keep the plane out of the water, but there was no answer. "Uh," he said, "you still on?"

Sully was focusing on the task at hand. The plane was less than twenty-two seconds away from impact. From the cockpit, the water was moving faster and faster toward the plane.

"Brace, brace! Heads down, stay down!" the flight attendants shouted. They had no eye-level windows, but some of the passengers could tell that the plane was headed into the water. One passenger called out from the back of the plane, "Exit row people, get ready!" A man sitting mid-plane asked the woman sitting next to him if he could brace her baby boy for her. She gave the child to him. Other passengers began to pray.

Back in the cockpit, the automated ground-warning alarm

kept going off: "Too low. Terrain. Caution, terrain." Another automated callout from a different warning system kept repeating the same message: "Terrain, terrain. Pull up. Pull up," as if it were hoping someone could change how the event was unfolding. Sully and Skiles worked to slow the plane by extending the flaps on the plane's wings. At 200 feet, flying at about 180 miles an hour, the plane was still on its glide.

Sully lowered the nose slightly in the last few seconds before the plane touched the water. This put the aircraft at a more favorable angle and at a speed of less than 140 miles an hour. The impact tore away the left engine and ripped open the plane's belly toward the rear. The plane skimmed to a stop. The Hudson's dark green heavy spray made the passengers sitting near the windows think they had gone underwater.

The plane was floating on the river, but there was no time to waste. Water rushed in from the tail of the plane, making the rear exit doors unusable. The doors at the front of the aircraft and those over the wings, all of them still above the waterline, were opened, and emergency rafts inflated when they did. One after the other, the passengers evacuated the airplane, climbing onto the wing and entering escape slides. Sully and Skiles helped the flight attendants assist passengers and hand out life vests. At the rear, the floor had buckled, and a beam from the plane had broken through, causing water to rise almost as high as the chests of the passengers and crew waiting to evacuate. As they made their way out, some were disoriented, stunned to realize they had landed in the Hudson.

In just three-and-a-half minutes, everyone had evacuated the plane. Sully and Skiles, with the help of some young male passengers, gathered blankets, coats, jackets, and life vests from inside to hand to those standing on the plane wings, shivering from the cold. Water rose to the ankles of some and almost up to the waists of others. One passenger jumped into the river and began swimming toward New York but, deterred by the frigid water, swam back to the plane; other passengers helped him get into a raft. One passenger slipped off the wing and into the water, and two others pulled her back, risking falling into the river themselves. On the plane's wings, on inflated slides, and in the emergency rafts, passengers and crew members awaited rescue.

Within four minutes, the first of the rescue boats arrived. Sully was the last to exit the plane and board a boat: He walked in the deep water of the cabin multiple times to make sure that no one had been left behind. There were no casualties. From the moment the flock of migratory Canada geese hit the plane to the moment Flight 1549 touched down onto the Hudson River, only 208 seconds had passed.

FOR MANY PILOTS, FLYING CAN BECOME A FAMILIAR ROUTINE, WHICH INCLUDES sticking to a scripted series of steps like checking the flight plan and fuel volume before departure, or working through the pre-flight checklists. Even in the case of an extreme emergency, pilots are trained to carefully follow standard operating procedures. After all, as any experienced pilot will tell you, it is much safer to work through a checklist than it is to frantically do the first things that come to mind.

Flight 1549 was no different. Captain Sully called for the Quick Reference Handbook (QRH) about thirteen seconds after the bird strike. First officer Skiles already had the QRH out and open to the appropriate page—the "Dual Engine Failure Checklist," which identifies steps to follow when both engines of an Airbus fail. The handbook is full of technical shorthand (e.g., FAC 1, OFF then ON; ENG MODE Selector, IGN) and directions that only experienced pilots would understand ("Add 1° of nose up for each 22,000 lbs above 111,000 lbs . . .").

Airbus designed its checklist under the assumption that dual-engine failures would only happen at cruising altitude and that the crew would have plenty of time to run the multipage list. But those were not the conditions that Skiles and Sully found themselves in. Nonetheless, they started to follow the plan. Various decision paths were built into the QRH. For instance, Step 1 concerns fuel. "If no fuel remaining . . ." has eight sub-steps to complete before going on to Step 2. "If fuel remaining . . ." is even more complicated, with guidance based on type of aircraft, ability to reach Air Traffic Control, and the results of trying to relight the engines. The longest path in the QRH has fifteen sub-steps. The crew of Flight 1549 worked through much of the checklist, including an attempt to relight the engines, but ran out of time and could not execute Step 3: preparing for ditching—that is, an emergency water landing.

When you face a stressful situation—a car veering into your lane, your boss asking you to speak up in a meeting on a topic you know little about, your partner lashing out after you forgot to do something important—your body responds by making sure you've registered the threat. Your heart pounds. Your palms get clammy. And your mind is affected as well: You focus on the immediate threat, to the exclusion of the world around you. Your thinking and attention narrow. Although this evolutionary trait, known as "fight-or-flight response," served humans well when they were facing threats in the wild, it leads to poor decision-making in the modern world. Under stress, we tend to scan a few alternatives quickly and overlook the bigger picture.

In a crisis, when we think about what we *should* do, we focus on the most apparent courses of action, often those we relied on when making similar decisions in the past, whether we are following a checklist or not. Paradoxically, though, it is at these moments of extreme stress that taking a step back would be most helpful. When we think about what we *could* do, our thinking becomes much broader: We imagine and explore a much larger set of possibilities before making a final decision. Considering what we *could* do shifts us from analyzing and weighing options that we assume to be fixed to generating more creative options.

The different outcomes of "should" and "could" thinking apply beyond our reactions to extreme emergencies. In all aspects of our lives, whenever we face an important decision, we naturally ask ourselves "What should I do?" But this framing constricts the answers we will come up with. When we instead ask ourselves "What could I do?" we broaden our perspective.

Imagine how easy it would be to fall into "should" thinking when you are flying a modern jet, with all of its automation and strict procedures. Sully avoided this fate, thanks in large part to his commitment to lifelong learning. For him, as he told me during an interview, that meant making each flight a learning experience and each one better than the previous one. By considering what he could learn every time he entered the cockpit, Sully remained open to the possibility that the flight would provide some new knowledge or insight he had not considered before. It's also essential, Sully told me, to be aware of the tunnel vision that threatens to engulf us in stressful situations, and to learn to broaden our perspective so that we are in a better position to evaluate a range of options, including novel ideas—such as landing in the Hudson River.

Once we get comfortable with a job, it is natural to perform many parts of it without much thought. By forcing himself to continuously learn, Sully was able to fight the tendency to succumb to routine and assume that every flight is the same as the previous one. This aspect of his rebel mindset kept him open to new perspectives, and saved the lives of everyone on the plane. In our own jobs, we might not be facing life-or-death situations, but we do face stressful situations.

Imagine you are on your way to be a top performer at B&B, a medium-sized investment bank. When it comes to organizational loyalty, B&B has an almost cult-like culture: Those who choose to stay there accept that company loyalty comes before their health, family, and friends. One of the main projects you have been working on involves orchestrating a leveraged buyout for one of B&B's clients, a company called Suntech. B&B provides short-term financing, put together bank financing for the deal, and it also acquired most of Suntech's assets. One of the banks that was involved in underwriting the loan for the senior debt was Universal, and you know one of the Universal team members who worked on the project well: She is your roommate, Sandy.

You come home one day after work and find Sandy in tears. She tells you that your conversation needs to be confidential, and you agree, assuming she's having a personal problem. But then she tells you that Universal is dissolving its capital finance group, which means that not only is Sandy out of a job, but the deal with B&B is now in jeopardy. Here's your dilemma: If you do not share this news with your boss at B&B right away, then the public might hear of it first, making potential investors in Suntech turn their attention to other opportunities and putting both B&B and the client at risk. But you also promised Sandy that you would not talk to anyone about this confidential situation. You face an almost impossible choice between breaching your loyalty to your friend and risking serious damage to your employer and one of its clients. This is a moral dilemma in which the competing principles of duty to your friend and to your firm and client are both important. There's no obvious "right" answer.

I framed this story as a fictional one, but it's based on the real-life experience of a former student in a leadership and accountability class taught by one of my Harvard Business School colleagues. This all transpired while this student was in my colleague's class, and he had reached out for advice. As part of a study, my colleagues and I presented a similar set of dilemmas to a group of study participants. We asked some of them, "What should you do?" We asked others, "What would you do?" And we asked yet another group to answer the question, "What could you do?" Approaching a dilemma with "could" thinking led participants to examine it from new and fresh perspectives, and to generate many more possible solutions. They realized that they did not have to concede one set of moral imperatives for another to resolve a dilemma. For example, one could-thinking participant wrote, "I would keep my promise to Sandy, but would line up alternative financing for the senior debt. If I could pull this off, I could spin the loss of Universal's role in the deal as a positive for other banks who would profit from Universal's defection." The solutions that "could" thinkers generated were more morally insightful than those of "should" or "would" thinkers: they went beyond choosing one side of the dilemma at the expense of the other. (In real life, following advice from my colleague, the former HBS student convinced his roommate to allow him to broker a meeting between the Universal and B&B team members, where the news inevitably came out, avoiding disaster.) When you open your mind to considering a seemingly impossible situation from a new perspective, a solution may come to you.

EVERY YEAR, CARDIOLOGISTS PERFORM HUNDREDS OF THOUSANDS OF ANGIOPLAS-ties, procedures that restore blood flow through the coronary artery, with the insertion of a small wire cage called a vascular stent. After being introduced in the 1990s, stents became the treatment of choice due to their ability to relieve pain and because they are a far less invasive (and cheaper) treatment than bypass surgery. Doctors and patients started to believe that stents also saved the lives of patients with stable angina (a painful condition caused by poor blood flow through the blood vessels in the heart), though there was no solid evidence of that. In the early 2000s, a new device called a drug-eluting stent came along, which slowly releases a drug to prevent the artery from closing again, something that could happen with the bare-metal stents. These stents were welcomed with much enthusiasm from both doctors and patients because they were more effective in keeping the blockage from coming back, but were considered just as safe, if not safer, than the bare-metal stents.

In late 2006, however, medical studies suggested that drug-eluting stents were being used in cases not approved by the U.S. Food and Drug Administration (FDA), including cases where patients had been diagnosed with more complex conditions, and that these "off-label" uses likely increased the risk of blood clotting and even death. As a result, in 2006, an emergency FDA advisory panel issued a warning about the dangers of such off-label use. In its announcement, the FDA advised physicians to use caution, particularly when treating off-label cases. Over the next several months, the market share of drug-eluting stents fell from over 90 percent to about 60 percent.

My colleagues and I wanted to understand how cardiologists reacted to the FDA's announcement and what role expertise might play. We gathered data on 147,010 angioplasty procedures performed by 399 cardiologists over a six-year period. There was a surprising pattern: Cardiologists with *more* experience were more likely to continue to use drug-eluting stents, despite the obvious dangers highlighted by the FDA. We saw the same thing with doctors who were surrounded by experienced cardiologists, independent of how long they'd been in the field. We all tend to modify our behavior as a result of pressure from those around us. For the doctors in our sample, this translated into following the choices of more experienced cardiologists, not realizing that the effect of experience was to obscure what was best for patients.

We generally think of experience as a good thing. With experience comes knowledge, skill, and expertise, after all. Sully, for example, wouldn't have been able to land his plane in the Hudson River without all those years of experience. When we face problems that we believe we've encountered in the past and that we have the proper knowledge to solve, we feel a sense of comfort and confidence. This feeling, psychology research tells us, often leads us to approach situations mindlessly rather than thoughtfully. Fighting this feeling was another way that Sully was exceptional.

Sully studied psychology at the Air Force Academy and then served as a fighter pilot for the U.S. Air Force for five years. "Flying a jet fighter is the pinnacle of tactical military aviation," he's said. "It's like driving a Formula One racer on steroids—in three dimensions, not just two." He often used his spare time to teach other cadets to fly airplanes and gliders on his weekends and after school. He went on to become a training officer and a flight leader after that, and then a commercial airline pilot—a position that led to thousands of additional hours of flying. Sully also enjoyed investigating past airline accidents and understanding the mistakes of other pilots as a pilot's union safety volunteer and accident investigator. He learned about cases where standard procedures did not produce the desired outcomes, and about cases where human judgment failed under pressure. To broaden his education, he completed two master's degrees: one in public administration from the University of Northern Colorado and one in industrial psychology from Purdue University. It's hard to imagine anyone having more expertise in the cockpit.

But Sully viewed expertise not as something to achieve, but as a process that must be kept alive. "I have been making small, regular deposits in this bank throughout my life of education, training, and experience," he told me. "When we were suddenly confronted with a tough situation that day, the balance in that account was sufficient that I could make a sudden withdrawal." He had never practiced a water landing before, as the simulators did not even allow it. But he had gained much experience from all sorts of different situations, which reminded him that there is always something more to learn and that every choice can be approached from more than just one perspective. And as he acquired more and more flying hours, Sully found a simple way to fight the feeling of knowing: Though flights are almost always routine, every time the plane pushed back from the gate, he reminded himself that he needed to be prepared for the unexpected. Before each flight, he would ask himself, "What can I learn?"

Our understanding of human psychology suggests that Sully's mindset was crucial. When we frame work around *learning* goals—such as developing our competence, acquiring new skills, and mastering new situations—we perform better than if we frame work around performance goals, such as hitting results targets. When we are motivated by learning rather than performance, we do better on tests, get higher grades, reach greater success in simulations and problem-solving tasks, and receive higher ratings after training. When Air Force–enlisted personnel received a challenging performance goal about the number of planes to be landed, the specific goal *decreased* rather than increased their performance landing planes. And in another study, sales professionals with a performance orientation performed worse than those who had learning goals.

The danger of the feeling of knowing is that it leads us to rationalize our prior views and decisions—and the urge gets stronger with more experience. "Like a totalitarian government," writes psychologist Joachim Krueger of Brown University, "the ego has been said to shape perception in such a way that it protects a sense of its own good will, its central place in the social world and its control over relevant outcomes." Experience should open our minds to the fact that the same decision or task can be approached differently. And yet, when the feeling of knowing intrudes unchecked, it closes us off instead. In one study, for instance, my colleagues and I asked participants to choose between two hypothetical investment options. Next, we made one group of decision makers, and not the other, feel like experts by having them answer an easy version of a general-knowledge test. The easy quiz had questions such as: "In what North American country is the city of Toronto located?" The quiz we gave to the other group included more challenging questions, such as, "Who is credited with inventing the wristwatch in 1904?" Once they completed the quiz, participants were shown the correct answers so that they could see how well they'd done.

We then presented everyone with bad news about the outcome of their investment choice and asked whether they wanted to change their decision. We wanted to see if those who felt like experts would be less open to a shift in strategy. And that is exactly what we found: As in the study of cardiologists, decision makers who felt a significant sense of expertise—even though it was founded on very little and unrelated to the area they were asked to judge—were unwilling to listen to important negative information.

Power aggravates the problem. As we climb the organizational ladder, our ego inflates, and we tend to feel even more threatened by information that proves us wrong. If we're not careful, being in charge can, over time, close us off to what others have to offer. When teaching the Harvard Business School cases I've written, I often invite the main protagonist to come in to class so that he or she can hear the class discussion and, during the last fifteen to twenty minutes of class, engage in a Q&A session with my students. A few years ago, I noticed an interesting pattern: the guests, usually high-level executives in the firm, typically said they were eager to learn from the students. But during the class, many would spend the time talking *at* the students, and in some cases even pontificating, rather than listening to the students' questions and being open to learning from them.

The gap between what many guests had told me they wanted to do in class and what they actually did was both puzzling and interesting, so I decided to investigate. My colleagues and I found that the executives in my classes were in fact exhibiting a more widespread behavior: When we (whether "we" are top executives or college students) feel powerful, we are less open to the perspectives of others. In one study, for instance, we induced some of our participants to feel powerful by asking them to write about a time when they had power over other people. When making decisions, those participants listened to their own opinions more than those of a more informed advisor. In another study, team leaders who were induced to feel powerful dominated the team discussion by taking most of the airtime. As a result, they missed out on learning critical information that other members of the team had. Their teams performed worse than those of leaders who were not induced to feel powerful, and team members enjoyed the experience less and felt less engaged. When Bob Nardelli was CEO at home retailer Home Depot, between 2000 and 2007, he used a brash communication style that didn't leave a lot of room for others' perspective. This lowered employees' morale, alienated workers, made stockholders angry, and led many executives to leave the company. After a few years at the helm, Nardelli came under fire and eventually resigned.

When we take too much "airtime," we demotivate those around us. In high-pressure environments, when leaders work with people who are highly talented and skilled, this lesson is especially critical. I saw this play out in a fascinating study I conducted while attending cardiac surgeries at a large teaching hospital in Boston. My colleagues and I observed fifty-eight operations and conducted thirty-four interviews with members of surgical teams, including surgeons, nurses, physician assistants, and anesthesiologists. The teams where everybody seemed to enjoy the work, in spite of challenges (from standing for hours on one's feet in a very cold room to the attention needed for coordination), were ones where the surgeons were approachable and not dictator-like in their style, inviting team members to contribute whenever appropriate. But other teams had a more difficult time working effectively together. The surgeons who led those teams, we found, had trouble trusting others. Their leadership style was more autocratic, and they especially struggled when they felt their authority was being threatened. Our observations supported other research on surgical teams, which has found that when a surgeon is inaccessible or has an autocratic style, the surgical team's performance suffers—often to the detriment of patients. Less autocratic surgery teams, by contrast, communicate and coordinate better, and achieve better outcomes for patients.

Rebels recognize that it is more important for the team to work well and get the job done than it is to display their power or respect some formal hierarchy. Once when Sully and his crew were preparing for a snowy flight out of Minneapolis, a baggage handler came up to the cockpit and told Sully that he had seen what looked like oil dripping from the right engine. Sully thanked him for his report. With the help of the first officer and a maintenance technician, Sully figured out that on the previous stop, a technician had put too much oil in the engine, and some of it had overflowed. But Sully wanted to thank the baggage handler for his effort, and rather than summoning him up to the cockpit again, Sully put on his overcoat and went down to find him. Even though there hadn't actually been a problem, Sully told the baggage handler, it was important to rule out this possibility. "You potentially saved us all a lot of trouble," Sully told the baggage handler. "I hope that, on another day, on another flight, if you notice something out of the ordinary, you will tell the crew again."

Too often, power is viewed as a license to raise one's voice without listening to the voices of others. When we feel powerful, research shows, we are more inclined to express our attitudes and opinions in groups, and we also come to devalue the perspectives, opinions, and contributions of others. As a result, we feel entitled to dominate these interactions. Leaders know all too well the power they have over their followers. In fact, "playing deaf" is a dysfunction I often observe in leaders: they disregard the views of others and pay attention only to their own. If they got to the top, they seem to think, it is because they know best.

At Osteria Francescana, with its three Michelin stars, there is always the risk that the fame that accompanies those stars can lead the whole team to become arrogant and inattentive to the needs of their customers. But as we were waiting to open the doors for dinner one night, maître d' Giuseppe Palmieri told me a story illustrating that this was anything but the case at the restaurant. A few months earlier, a family of four had booked a table for both Friday and Saturday nights. On Friday, all four family members—mother, father, and two sons, who were about eight and fourteen—ordered the thirteen-course tasting menu, called Sensations. On Saturday night, Palmieri and the rest of the front-of-the-house team welcomed them back. "We'll go with Tradition in Evolution for four," the father happily stated when it was time to order—another tasting menu, this one with ten courses. Palmieri smiled as he recounted the story to me. "I saw in the face of the kids a clear message, as if they were desperately thinking, 'Please, I don't want to eat that.' But they were being quiet about it. So I turned to the youngest boy and asked, 'What would *you* like to have?' And he told me, 'I would like to have a pizza.' "

Palmieri ran to the phone, called the best pizzeria in Modena, and ordered a pizza. It arrived not too long after, via taxi, for the kids to enjoy. "I am pretty sure those two children will never forget us for the happiness we brought to them that evening. It simply took a change of course, and one pizza."

WE ALL TEND TO PROCESS INFORMATION IN A SELF-SERVING MANNER. WE UNCRITI-cally accept evidence when it is consistent with what we want to believe and call for more data, or disregard the evidence, when it isn't. Harvard psychologist Dan Gilbert observed that the way we consider evidence resembles how we react to data from our bathroom scale when we weigh ourselves. If the scale gives us bad news, we get off and then step back on a second time, so that we can be sure there was not an error on the display, or that we weren't standing in a way that put unnecessary pressure on one foot. But when the display shows us good news, we proudly smile and then get into the shower. We get stuck in our own point of view and invested in just one type of thinking: our own.

Here's a more scientific example of how this tendency works. Two psychologists, Peter Ditto (of the University of California, Irvine) and David Lopez (founder and CEO of iAnalytics Statistical Consulting), told participants that they would take a test to determine whether they had a dangerous enzyme deficiency. For the test, participants had to put a drop of saliva on a strip and then wait for the results. Some learned that the test strip would turn green if they had the deficiency; others learned that green meant they did not have the deficiency. The strip wasn't a real test—it was simply a piece of paper that never changed its color. The result? Participants who hoped to see the test strip turn green as evidence that they didn't have the deficiency waited much longer than those who hoped not to see it turn green. That is, people waited more patiently for data when they believed the data would reassure them than when they believed it would scare them.

In another experiment, the two researchers asked participants to review information about a student one piece at a time so that they could evaluate his intelligence, the same way experts would during college admission decisions. The information was quite damning, and participants could stop examining it once they felt they had all the evidence they needed to reach a firm conclusion. Participants also received a picture of the student and some other information, allowing them to form a quick impression of the applicant. When participants liked the student, they kept turning over cards, searching for information that would allow them to evaluate him positively. But when they felt less fondly toward the student, they only turned over a few cards, enough to confirm the negative feelings they had for him.

Fortunately, there are ways to combat our self-serving tendencies. One powerful technique is suggested by the 1998 film *Sliding Doors*, in which Gwyneth Paltrow's character, Helen, rushes to catch a train in the London Underground. The film then follows two storylines: one in which Helen makes it through the sliding doors and onto the train, and one in which she misses the train. This seemingly minor moment ends up having a dramatic effect on Helen's life. The film prompts viewers to think about how events large and small might have changed how their lives have unfolded. Though we usually don't know how things might have gone differently if we'd made a train or caught an elevator, most of us, at different points in our lives, have probably found ourselves wondering, "What if I had . . . ?" Certain moments stand out to us as turning points that lead us to reflect on how life might have been different, for better or worse, if they hadn't occurred. For example, what if you had skipped the party where you met your romantic partner, accepted a different job, or approached a conflict with a coworker differently?

This "counterfactual thinking" is a powerful way to forget what you know and consider a situation from a fresh perspective. There are usually an infinite number of alternate worlds to all choices we make or problems we face, but most of the time we do not consider them unless we think counterfactually. When we do, we can feel more grateful for the jobs we have and happier in our relationships: we just need to think through alternatives that used to be available to us and that would have turned out to be quite undesirable.

When employees think counterfactually, their commitment to the organization and their coworkers rises, as does their happiness at work, research has found. In one study, for instance, a group of participants reflected upon the origins of their organization and then described how it might not have existed had certain events not occurred. Another group of participants also reflected upon the origins of their company, but then were asked to describe these events in more detail rather than thinking through counterfactual possibilities. Participants then indicated how committed they felt to the company and assessed whether its trajectory was positive or negative. Counterfactual reflection resulted in an increase in participants' commitment to the company as well as their optimism about its future. Recognizing that the organization might never have existed incited feelings of commitment that amplified what people liked about their organization.

Counterfactual thinking also prompts us to make positive changes. Thoughts such as "If I had worked harder, I would have performed better on the exam" or "If I were more patient, I would be more contented with my partner" make us more inclined to do better in the future.

Part of the reason we fall out of love with work and life is the common tendency to neglect information that contradicts our views or preferences and to instead focus on data that confirm them. Imagine that you change careers and aren't very happy at your new job. As a result, you feel regretful and think you made a mistake, even to the point of disregarding positive signs that things will get better. Counterfactual thinking should help you broaden your perspective: "What if staying in my old career ended up becoming a boring routine?" When we consider how things might have unfolded differently, we become more sensitive to the unpredictability of life. As a result, we consider decisions more systematically and approach life with a more open mind.

Counterfactual thinking can also instill a sense of meaning. In one study, a group of participants was asked to reflect upon an event that was pivotal in their lives. Some of the participants were also asked to consider how this event could have turned out differently. These participants, as compared to those who did not consider a different path, viewed the event as more meaningful. In another study, half of the participants were asked to reflect upon events that could have prevented them from ever meeting people who became their best friend. The other half, in the control group, instead were asked to reflect upon details of the time they first met their best friends. Participants who entertained counterfactual thoughts perceived their friendship as more meaningful.

Thinking counterfactually takes the focus away from just our own view, a troublesome tendency that is unfortunately compounded as we gain experience. One of the problems, it seems, is that we forget the experience of being *in*experienced. When we become experts, we have trouble remembering memories of our experiences as novices. We are also prone to the so-called hindsight bias: Having knowledge of an outcome leads us to assume that we knew the information all along.

This "curse of knowledge" leads us to overestimate the amount of knowledge that others have. If you've ever felt bewildered as a mechanic rattles off what's wrong with your car, or while a doctor rushes through an explanation of what's wrong with your body, the problem may not be your lack of expertise but rather the expert's failure to recognize what you probably don't know. When interacting with novices, people with more expertise often fail to account for the fact that novices don't have access to their specialized knowledge, and they also underestimate the amount of time it would take for novices to learn complex tasks.

Ting Zhang, a postdoctoral fellow at Columbia University, sought to determine whether experts can overcome the "curse of knowledge" and better communicate with and relate to novices by rediscovering the feeling of inexperience. In one study, she recruited expert guitarists with at least three years of experience playing. She asked some of them to flip their guitar around so that they were strumming using their nondominant hand (right hand for lefties, and vice versa); of course, the hand that they normally used for the fingerboard was reversed as well. She asked others, those in the control condition, to play as they normally would for a minute.

Next, all of these expert guitarists watched a video clip of a beginner guitarist who struggled to play a series of chords. The experts were asked to give advice to the beginner, to evaluate the beginner's potential, and to rate how similar they felt to the person. Zhang also recruited a separate group of guitarists who had played for less than one year to rate the experts' advice.

Playing with their guitars reversed proved difficult for the expert guitarists. They felt (and sounded) more like beginners than did those who played the instrument traditionally, suggesting that the change in how to hold the guitar was effective in allowing experts to rediscover inexperience. Guitarists who played nontraditionally also saw more potential in the novice than did guitarists who played traditionally. And, interestingly, novices rated the advice of experts who rediscovered the feeling of inexperience as more helpful than advice from those in the control condition. In this domain, at least, behaving like a beginner helped experts to more successfully take their perspective. Rediscovering the experience of inexperience is a way to counteract the misleading—and potentially life-threatening—feeling of knowing.

FOR DECADES, DIAMONDS WERE CUT USING MECHANICAL MEANS, LIKE SAWS. IN the 1970s, this started to change, thanks to the development of powerful, relatively cheap lasers. But this didn't necessarily simplify the process. When diamonds are cut, whether with a saw or a laser, this can create new fractures that are not visible to the naked eye, but which reduce the diamond's value. Diamond manufacturers wanted to come up with a technique for splitting diamonds along their natural fractures without creating new ones. They found a solution in a surprising source: food companies and the humble green pepper. When food companies need to deseed peppers, they place them in a special chamber and increase the air pressure, causing the peppers to shrink and fracture at the stem. Next, the pressure is dropped rapidly, which causes the peppers to burst at their weakest point, and the seed pod ejects. Diamond manufacturers figured out that they could submit diamonds to a similar process, which results in crystals splitting along their natural fracture lines with no additional damage to the stones.

At times, all of us face problems, whether at work or in our personal lives, that we're unable to solve on our own. Sometimes we can gain the knowledge we seek from an expert—a financial advisor for help managing our money or an experienced recruiter to help us jump-start a new career. Though experts can often help within their domain of expertise, there are times when we might try consulting someone who could offer a truly fresh perspective. Rebels understand that different perspectives can lead us away from stale assumptions toward deeper, more powerful thinking.

When a young man named Alph Bingham was attending Stanford as part of his PhD in organic chemistry, his chemistry professor assigned weekly projects. On the due date, the professor would start class by having five students stand up and defend their work on the project. Interestingly, Bingham noted, class after class, the students had very different solutions to any given problem. He concluded that the unique perspective we bring as students, by virtue of our different backgrounds and experiences, may be more important than what we're taught in class. Our freshest ideas and solutions come from our own unique approach, not from the tools we're given.

Bingham eventually became a scientist who worked for Eli Lilly. In Waltham, Massachusetts, in 1998, Bingham cofounded a start-up, InnoCentive Inc., with two other Lilly scientists, based on his insight from chemistry class: If a firm can't solve a problem on its own, it should make good use of the Internet and its reach to see if someone else has the solution. So InnoCentive works with companies called "seekers" that post their challenges on the company's website. "Solvers" are charged with coming up with answers and can win cash prizes the seekers offer. InnoCentive believes this approach of posting online challenges can work for problems in all types of fields, from engineering, chemistry, and computer science, to life sciences, business, and even economic development. Some challenges are narrowly focused, such as the request for a method for measuring the thickness of thin polymeric films, while others, such as increasing social and community acceptance of renewable energy, have a broad scope. Between 2001 and 2016, more than 1,600 challenges were posted on the InnoCentive website, with more than $40 million awarded to some of the over 300,000 registered solvers.

The problems posed on the InnoCentive site often seem to require deep domain expertise—yet winning ideas regularly come from outside the problem's domain. One challenge Bingham often talks about came from the field of polymer chemistry. The company that initially posted it was pleased with the variety of solutions that had been submitted and awarded five of them with cash prizes. The people who received those awards were an industrial chemist (no big surprise here), a veterinarian, a small agribusiness owner, a drug delivery system specialist, and an astrophysicist.

Harvard Business School professor Karim Lakhani and his colleagues analyzed four years of data from InnoCentive on 166 challenges successfully solved and found that people whose domain of expertise was six degrees removed from the domain of the problem were three times more likely to solve the problem than people whose domain of expertise was closer to the problem. Nonexperts were actually better problem-solvers than experts.

InnoCentive collaborated with another team of researchers, Oguz Ali Acar of King's College London and Jan van den Ende of Erasmus University, on another project. They collected data from 230 problem-solvers registered on the site. The researchers asked them to rate the degree to which they had chosen problems from their own field of expertise and how much they used a wide range of resources to figure out a solution. The respondents also indicated how many hours, in total, they'd spent on the project and how many people they'd contacted while developing an answer. Their analyses revealed that breakthrough solutions are more likely to be the result of investments of time and effort than of expertise in a field. Insiders, who already had quite a bit of knowledge about their own field, came up with solutions that were more creative when they used a more diverse set of outside resources. Meanwhile, the odds of outsiders developing a prize-winning solution were much higher when they dug deeply into the problem's field.

It can be easier to approach problems from fresh perspectives when we are *not* experts. Unfamiliar or unpleasant arguments, opposing views, information that disproves rather than affirms our beliefs, and counterintuitive findings—rather than familiar arguments and evidence that confirms our views—cause us to think more deeply and come to creative and complex conclusions. And that's where outsiders have an advantage over experts: They are less rooted in, and defensive of, existing viewpoints.

In 1500, Bayezid II, the Sultan of the Ottoman Empire, felt compelled to unite what today we know as "old Istanbul" with the nearby neighborhood of Karaköy. There was only one thing standing in his way: an estuary of the Alibeyköy and Kağıthane Rivers, which separated the two areas with twenty-five hundred feet of water and marshland. This inlet was better known as the Golden Horn, and it was thought to be impossible to build a bridge across it. Expert bridge builders struggled to come up with an effective design for a potential bridge, as its span and length posed some serious design challenges. The Sultan knew that a connection with Karaköy would only help both zones to flourish, and he needed the sort of bridge that even the Romans, despite their bridge-building prowess, had never attempted. He enlisted the help of Leonardo da Vinci, who at the time was much better known for his paintings than his engineering and seemed an unlikely source for a breakthrough. But the Sultan felt that Da Vinci's twenty-odd years of research into and study of self-supporting bridge designs might be exactly what was required. Despite the fact that Venice and the Ottoman Empire were at war, Da Vinci put his mind to the task, and using three well-known geometrical principles—the parabolic curve, the pressed-bow, and the keystone arch—he proposed a novel and elegant solution for the Golden Horn: a single-span 240-meter-long and 24-meter-wide bridge. Had Da Vinci's bridge been built, it would have been the longest at that time, and it would likely be the eighth wonder of our modern world today. But the Sultan studied Da Vinci's design carefully and, ultimately, rejected it as an impossibility. It could not possibly work, he believed.

Three hundred years passed before the engineering principles underlying Da Vinci's bridge became widely accepted. In 2001, engineers in Norway finally decided to build a bridge based on Da Vinci's design. The 328-feet-long, 26-feet-high wooden bridge was constructed in Aas Township, about twenty miles south of Norway's capital, Oslo. The bridge, which opened in 2001, is a pedestrian crossing, with railings made of stainless steel and teak. Outsiders can bring a fresh perspective to new and old problems. But it may take years, or even centuries, to recognize their brilliance since, as experts, we are often too focused on our own points of view.

TO WORK WITH CHEF BOTTURA IS TO BE CONSTANTLY REMINDED OF HOW DIFFER-ently people can see the world. For instance, he sometimes asks his staff to create dishes based on a piece of music. "I had been here for just a couple of months, and I was getting used to [Bottura's] style," Canadian-born chef de partie Jessica Rosval told me when we were cleaning up at the end of a day. "With all of his energy, he burst into the kitchen one day and said 'Okay, everybody: new project for today. Lou Reed, "Take a Walk on the Wild Side." Everybody make a dish.' And I was just like, 'Oh my gosh, where do I even start?'"

"We created a wide variety of dishes," Rosval said. "Some people focused on the bass line of the song. Some people focused on the lyrics. Some people focused on the era in which the song was written. We had this diverse array of different plates that were created from this one moment of inspiration when Massimo had been listening to the song in his car."

For Rosval and the rest of the staff, the assignment was challenging, but it also encouraged them to play in the kitchen, and that's unfortunately too rare in our jobs. Challenges like this one make work more playful and open our eyes to something we can easily forget: that our view of the world is incomplete. It's always good to be reminded that our knowledge and skill set can be expanded. This, in turn, increases our motivation as well as our humility. Tenelle Porter, a postdoctoral scholar in psychology at the University of California, Davis, writes about the importance of intellectual humility, or the ability to acknowledge that what we know is sharply limited. In Porter's research, higher levels of intellectual humility are associated with greater willingness to consider views that don't align with our own. People with higher intellectual humility also perform better, whether in school or at work. And intellectual humility makes us wiser: We are more apt to see that the world we live in is never still, that the future will likely be different from the present. Wisdom means rejecting the feeling of knowing.

With his Lou Reed challenge, Bottura also made his staff realize how the same problem can lead to a variety of solutions, similar to what Bingham saw in his Stanford chemistry class. Bottura's lifelong habit of thinking this way yields surprise after surprise. Take his dish *Camouflage: Hare in the Woods*, a rabbit stew that is served spread out on a plate like a canvas instead of in a pot: the bottom layer consists of cream of hare stew, toasted with dark brown Muscavado sugar, like a crème brûlée, which is then arranged in a camouflage design using variously colored mineral and root powders. The intensely savory hare liver morphs into a chocolaty, coffee-laced cream with the addition of crème royal. The dish was inspired by a story that Bottura heard about Gertrude Stein and Picasso back in 1914. While walking along Boulevard Raspail in Paris one evening, they encountered one of the first camouflaged military trucks. "We invented that!" Picasso reportedly burst out. "That is cubism!" As Bottura thought about this story, he had the idea of a hare wearing camouflage.

What we see in any situation—in a painting, in a three-Michelin star dish, or outside the cockpit window of a plane that's lost power—depends on our perspective.

5

UNCOMFORTABLE TRUTHS

A TALENT FOR DIVERSITY

*The difference between a lady and a flower girl isn't
how she behaves. It's how she's treated.*
—GEORGE BERNARD SHAW, *PYGMALION*

One evening in early February 2016, writer and filmmaker Ava DuVernay, forty-four, was sitting in the waiting area on the second floor of what is known as the Team Disney building, the company's 330,000-square-foot corporate offices in Burbank, California. Despite the imposing size of the building, it's hard not to smile when you see it: sculptures of the iconic Seven Dwarfs from *Snow White* stand tall on the façade, acting as de facto columns that hold up the roof. The nearly twenty-foot dwarfs are a whimsical reminder that the company is built on the magic of animated classics.

DuVernay, best known for her Oscar-nominated 2014 film *Selma*, was scheduled to meet with Sean Bailey, president of Motion Pictures Production at Walt Disney Studios, and Tendo Nagenda, Disney's executive VP of production. Bailey and Nagenda, who have worked together at the company for almost eight years, are tasked with keeping productions organized and on track, and choosing writers and directors for films that Disney is interested in producing.

The pair wanted to explore whether DuVernay would be the right person to direct an adaptation of *A Wrinkle in Time*, Madeleine L'Engle's beloved science fantasy novel. First published in 1963, L'Engle's book tells the story of thirteen-year-old Meg, who journeys with her younger brother and a close friend through time and space in search of her father, a gifted scientist who has disappeared. As a film project, it seemed daunting. *Wrinkle* is a science fiction story, but not the familiar Hollywood kind with lasers and spaceships. Meg travels to other dimensions by way of a tesseract, a cube that extends into the fourth dimension (time), which would have to be rendered visually. In both cost and scope, it promised to be a much larger film than anything DuVernay had done before. Also challenging was the very idea of a big-budget Hollywood movie whose protagonist was a cerebral thirteen-year-old girl wearing glasses.

There was a time when DuVernay could not have imagined such a meeting. She was raised in the city of Compton in Los Angeles County. Compton has a reputation for being a rough neighborhood, but for DuVernay it was a beautiful place where she was surrounded by family and friends. The oldest of five, DuVernay grew up watching her mother go to school at night, then move up from a job as a bank teller to a position in hospital administration to a role as the head of an HR department. Her aunt introduced her to films, taking her to the movies and talking with her about what they'd seen, and about the cinema more generally. As a child, she aspired to become a lawyer. In eighth grade, her grandmother Charlene bought her a briefcase, and she felt a few steps closer to her dream. DuVernay attended an all-girls Catholic school for twelve years, where she became the first black homecoming queen and student body president.

After graduating from UCLA, where she studied African-American history, DuVernay worked in journalism before starting her own film publicity company, and spending fourteen years as a Hollywood marketer and publicist. As someone who'd always been interested in movies, she relished having a role in the industry. She found herself on many sets and having long conversations with directors during plane rides to press junkets and premieres. "As a publicist, I was always around filmmakers," she told *Interview Magazine* in 2012. "I started thinking, 'They're just regular people, like me, with ideas. I've got ideas!'"

Even so, acting on these ideas would mean a delayed start in a field already overcrowded with extraordinary talent. At first, DuVernay hesitated. "But I started to realize that being so close to great filmmakers and watching them direct on set and the experiences that I did have, although different from film school, were still super valuable," she said in *Interview*. "I coupled that with some very intentional study and practice—picking up a camera—and just started making it." She was thirty-two when she directed her first short film.

On the path to Hollywood success, DuVernay faced several challenges as a woman in a male-dominated industry. Having men invade her personal space and question her leadership made her think carefully about her appearance on the set, including how she dressed. She often wore a hat to avoid unwanted "hair-touchers"—people interested in touching her locks—and glasses so that nobody would mistakenly get the impression that her eyes were welling up during a particularly moving scene, when in fact she was simply having trouble with her contact lenses. "You don't want to get caught up with the glistening," she told an audience at the LA Film Independent Forum. "Especially as a lady director, that's when the grip is going to walk by and say, 'She was crying.' It's just not worth it."

Her lack of industry connections, or, as she put it, "a rich uncle," increased the odds against DuVernay, and it sometimes stung to imagine where she might have gotten with some well-placed help. But then one day it hit her: "All of the time you're spending trying to get someone to mentor you, trying to have a coffee, all of the things we try to do to move ahead in the industry, is time that you're not spending working on your screenplay, strengthening your character arcs, setting up a table reading to hear the words, thinking about your rehearsal techniques, thinking about symbolism in your production design, your color palette . . . All of the so-called action that you're doing is hinging on someone doing something for you."

Her first two features were small-budget films, including one she financed with her own savings. Then came *Selma*, the story of the 1965 voting rights campaign that Martin Luther King Jr. led. The film was "bold and bracingly self-assured," according to A. O. Scott of the *New York Times*. "Even if you think you know what's coming, *Selma* hums with suspense and surprise," Scott wrote. "Packed with incident and overflowing with fascinating characters, it is a triumph of efficient, emphatic cinematic storytelling." *Washington Post* critic Ann Hornaday described DuVernay's film as "a stirring, often thrilling, uncannily timely drama that works on several levels at once . . . *Selma* carries viewers along on a tide of breathtaking events so assuredly that they never drown in the details or the despair, but instead are left buoyed: The civil rights movement and its heroes aren't artifacts from the distant past, but messengers sent on an urgent mission for today." In addition to the Oscar recognition—*Selma* was the first film helmed by an African-American woman to be nominated for best picture—DuVernay earned a Golden Globe nomination for best director.

After *Selma*, DuVernay showed no signs of slowing down. *Queen Sugar*, a series she created for the Oprah Winfrey Network, became a critical success, praised for its clever storytelling, strong sense of place, and thoughtful depictions of characters rarely glimpsed in pop culture—African-American farmers in the rural South. DuVernay decided to recruit only female directors for the series, thinking it would be "quite a radical statement." Instead of using typical Hollywood channels for hiring, she sought filmmakers whose work had inspired her over the years, in some cases connecting with them via Twitter. She also scouted independent films.

DuVernay was responding in part to challenges she herself had faced, some subtle. In interviews, journalists asked her about her background as an African-American, about being a woman in the film industry—about everything but making films. She was black, a black woman, a black director—but rarely just a director, seldom asked strictly about her vision for a film, or how she approached rehearsals. These were questions for white male directors. And so DuVernay fought back. Along with seeking out unsung talent, she hosts a podcast, *The Call-In*, in which she invites African-American filmmakers to discuss their writing, shooting, and editing in detail. Her questions skip over race and identity, and instead she asks her guests to zero in on the technical and creative process behind the work.

Arriving at Disney, DuVernay was able to put all these issues and frustrations out of her mind. She knew Bailey and Nagenda, who had already made clear how much they admired her work. "In that particular room, for the first time, I was able to walk in and tell my story," DuVernay said in an interview with *Vice*. She walked into the office, she said, "like a white man does." It did not take long for the Disney pair to realize that DuVernay was the right person to adapt *A Wrinkle in Time*. In follow-up discussions, DuVernay suggested that Meg could come from a mixed-race family, and that the film, in part, would be about how Meg became more comfortable in her own skin. Bailey and Nagenda thought the idea was brilliant, and the job was hers. A different studio might have pitched DuVernay another *Selma*-like project, but Bailey and Nagenda had a broader conception of her potential. They saw her for her talent, not her race, and DuVernay responded. When she sat down to talk with the Disney producers that February evening, she was just a filmmaker, ready to trade ideas about the work she was passionate about.

"All of the other stuff and baggage," she said, "was not there."

AT NINE O'CLOCK ON A SPRING MORNING IN CAMBRIDGE, MASSACHUSETTS, I WAS IN my office, anxiously checking my phone. Given where I was headed, I was cheered, at least, by the blue sky after days of heavy rain. I wasn't teaching, so I had dressed in business casual—blue cropped pants, a short-sleeved gray sweater, and flats. A colleague from Harvard Business School had offered to pick me up and take me to the Registry of Motor Vehicles, where I had finally scheduled a driving test after years of living in the United States without a license. I had passed a driver's test in Italy many years ago, but I was still a bundle of nerves. Failing in front of my colleague would be humiliating. Plus, he was lending me his car for the test, a BMW six-series. A little scratch could translate into a large bill.

My colleague's text pinged on my phone, and I zipped up my backpack and headed to our meeting point, where I found him dressed in a gray pinstriped suit. "The outfit is not to celebrate your American driving license," he said, smiling. "I'll be teaching later today." Soon we were in the parking lot of a Watertown mall, awaiting my turn behind the wheel. My friend listed common mistakes to avoid during the test, from rolling stops and improper lane changing to driving too slowly. He was interrupted by a tall DMV officer in dark sunglasses who called my last name.

"You can get into the driver's seat now," the officer told me as we approached the BMW, "and your dad can sit in the back and come with us, but he'll have to stay quiet."

I tried to stifle a laugh, while my colleague, who was only about fifteen years older than me, climbed in behind us. I was sure the officer didn't mean any offense; he'd just made a quick judgment based on our appearance—my colleague's suit, my backpack. After all, he must have been quite accustomed to dads riding along on driving tests.

Stereotypes, sets of attributes we associate with particular groups, are rooted in the fundamental mechanics of human thought. We make links and abide by them: thunder and rain; gray hair and old age; daughter and father showing up together for a driving test. In a world where the fittest survive, animals have evolved to make snap judgments about predators. Some chimpanzees instinctively attack chimps outside of their group. Certain fish go after their own kind simply because they weren't hatched in the same lake. We humans also distrust outsiders. To distinguish friend from foe, we have evolved to judge people using easily observed criteria, such as age, weight, skin color, and gender—as well as educational level, disability, accent, sexuality, social status, and job.

Stereotypes can help us make sense of the world. But because they are mere generalizations, they can also stir up a great deal of trouble. Irritating behavior, like the officer calling my colleague "your dad," is the least of the threat. When we buy into stereotypes, we can sometimes end up perpetrators of cruelty and discrimination, often without even being aware of it. Rebels, by contrast, realize that stereotypes are blinding and that fighting the tendency to stereotype produces a clearer picture of reality—and a competitive advantage. Rebels do not thoughtlessly accept the social roles and attitudes that society promotes. They challenge such roles and attitudes, never missing an opportunity to prove them wrong.

When we're not careful, stereotypes act like firewalls, blocking new information from penetrating our thoughts and preventing us from changing our minds unless something truly dramatic happens. In the 1999 film *Beautiful People*, which is set in London during the Bosnian War, there is a scene in which a young doctor brings home a Balkan War refugee who has recently arrived in the city—someone whom she, and the viewer, knows nothing about. At the dinner table, the doctor's conservative upper-class family comes across as a group of patronizing snobs, while the refugee appears to be unsophisticated and uneducated. And then the refugee sits down at the family's piano and starts to play *Souvenirs d'Andalousie for Piano*, a romantic piece by American composer Louis Gottschalk. He plays masterfully, and in the process catapults both the family and the viewer out of stereotypical assumptions so that we can view him, and maybe others like him, through a new lens.

Whenever I talk about stereotypes in the classroom, I give my students a little test. On a big screen, I flash words like "desk," "kitchen," and "computer" one after another, and I ask them to shout out whether each word belongs to a category shown at the top left of the screen (such as "career") or a category on the top right (such as "home"). My students always perform well when matching work-related words such as "desk" and "computer" to "career," and home-related words such as "kitchen" and "children" to "home." They also have no trouble matching typical male names like "Brian" to the category "male" and typical female names like "Katie" to the category "female." To make the task more difficult, I then have a round where the words flashing on the screen include both first names and words related to either career or home. The students need to shout out "left" or "right" to indicate whether the word that appeared on the screen belongs to one of the two categories "male" or "career" on the top left or to one of the two categories "female" or "home" on the top right of the screen. When this is what the task calls for, they rarely falter.

The trouble comes when I ask them to switch these orientations, having "female names" and "career" as the two categories listed on one side of the screen and "male names" and "home" as the two categories listed on the other. Now, all of a sudden, they stumble, performing half as fast. Right then, their bias sinks in: Men belong with work and the business world, and women at home. It hardly matters that the students, as they are quick to remind me, do not hold overt biases against working women—in fact, many of them *are* working women. We associate men with work more quickly because we are more used to seeing men in the workforce.

This kind of thinking surfaces early in life. By ten months, when shown faces of men and women, infants begin to make stereotypical associations with gender-typed objects such as a hammer or a scarf, telling us that even babies can form primitive stereotypes. By about age three, children exhibit a capacity to understand sex differences that have to do with adult possessions (shirt, skirt, tie), toys, roles, physical appearance, and activities. Children at about the same age also identify abstract associations related to gender (e.g., softness as female; hardness as male). When researchers examine the spontaneous associations children make regarding girls and boys, they find a consistent pattern in which children from preschool through fifth grade view girls as soft and nice, wearing skirts or dresses, and playing with dolls, and boys as being rough, having short hair, and enjoying active games.

Parents set the scene for gender stereotypes even before their children are born—decorating boys' rooms with airplanes and trucks, for instance, and girls' rooms with princesses and stuffed animals. And the fairy tales children hear at bedtime or watch on TV and in movies can affect how they see themselves and others. These stories often portray weak female characters who succeed only when a man intervenes. Think of Prince Eric providing Ariel with a life of luxury on land in *The Little Mermaid,* or Prince Charming helping Cinderella out of rags and into riches. Although Disney has lately strived to reduce stereotypical story lines in its films (as in *Frozen, Moana,* and *A Wrinkle in Time,* which feature strong female characters), most entertainment continues to conform to old ideas about gender.

Once learned, stereotypes and prejudices are hard to shed, even when evidence contradicts them. They are reinforced over time by the comfortable feelings we experience when interacting with others like us—people of the same gender, race, ethnicity, or political leaning. When we feel similar to others, we tend to think of them the same way we think about ourselves, and we also tend to assume we'll get along. Through adolescence and into adulthood, we continue to gravitate to people just like us. Conversation and cooperation feel easier when preferences, habits, and views are basically the same. Meanwhile, dealing with people who are dissimilar can cause friction, which feels unsettling or unproductive. Research on romantic relationships shows that, contrary to the old adage "opposites attract," we are attracted to people similar to us. And we feel more comfortable in groups in which we're surrounded by the like-minded, segregating ourselves accordingly from an early age.

Those who dare to violate stereotypes often experience a backlash, researchers have found. For women perceived as successful in masculine fields, the backlash can be especially strong. In a study in which women were portrayed as competent employees in a stereotypically masculine field, such as finance or construction, research participants rated them as being just as competent as their male counterparts, but less likable. When it was left ambiguous whether women were qualified in such a field, participants perceived them as less likable *and* less competent than their male counterparts. As a result, participants believed the women should receive lower salary offers and fewer promotions and resources than men with the same qualifications.

"I don't have a traditionally female way of speaking," former Canadian prime minister Kim Campbell once said. "I'm quite assertive. If I didn't speak the way I do, I wouldn't have been seen as a leader. But my way of speaking may have grated on people who were not used to hearing it from a woman. It was the right way for a leader to speak, but it wasn't the right way for a woman to speak."

THE INITIAL RISE OF WOMEN IN THE WORKPLACE WAS DUE TO EXTERNAL CIRCUM- stances. In the United States, during both World War I and World War II, women were needed to fill factory jobs, replacing men who had been killed or injured in battle. During wartime, many women joined the military, working as nurses, driving trucks, repairing airplanes, or performing clerical work so that men were freed up for combat. Others flocked to civil service jobs, while some worked as engineers and chemists, developing weapons for the war. Though many women had to relinquish their roles to returning veterans after both wars, the wars solidified the notion that women were in the workforce to stay. As professional opportunities expanded, women weren't the only ones who benefited. There were gains for the companies they joined and for the economy more broadly.

Those gains are no less a reality today. A recent report by management consulting firm McKinsey & Company used proprietary data on 366 public companies across a wide range of industries in the United States, Canada, the United Kingdom, and Latin America, and found that firms belonging to the top quartile for gender diversity are 15 percent more likely to experience financial returns above the median of their respective national industry. The organizations where women lead show better financial performance. An increase in female participation in the labor force also accelerates economic growth. In fact, increasing the number of women in the workforce can boost a country's GDP by as much as 21 percent.

But change did not happen without resistance. When women initially entered the workforce, venturing into factories and offices during the Industrial Revolution, men typically viewed them (along with the rise of machinery, for that matter) as a threat to their status, and many women were criticized for taking jobs from men—even if this wasn't the case. For women with husbands and children, the backlash was even stronger. Working mothers took the blame for increases in juvenile delinquency. And, unlike men, women faced the double bind of juggling work outside the home with caring for their families.

We now understand the psychology behind the resistance women have faced. We think of women as communal—other-oriented, modest, affectionate, helpful, gentle, pleasant, sensitive, and nice—while men are considered "agentic," or independent, strong, forceful, self-focused, competent, and competitive. As a result, we expect men to pursue their career goals while women stay at home as caretakers. These expectations shape the way we view men and women in the workplace. An authoritative male worker is "the boss," while an authoritative woman is "bossy." An assertive man is "persuasive," an assertive woman "pushy." And so on.

Entrenched gender views lead to bias in hiring, performance reviews, and promotion decisions. In one field study, two female and two male college students were recruited to apply in person to work at sixty-five restaurants in Philadelphia categorized as low-, medium-, or high-priced. The students' résumés made clear their similar personal histories and experience. The job they applied for was also the same: being a waiter or waitress. Most of the job offers made by high-priced restaurants went to men (eleven out of thirteen), and most of the offers made by low-priced restaurants went to women (eight out of ten). Earnings would be substantially higher at the high-priced restaurants; thus, the apparent hiring discrimination resulted in gender-based differences in earnings. But it also would harm the restaurants by depriving them of the best employees.

When women are hired, it's harder for them to get ahead. A 2014 study using data from 248 performance reviews across 28 companies found that 59 percent of the reviews of men had critical feedback in them as compared with 88 percent of the reviews of women. Both men and women received constructive feedback, but women were more likely to be criticized based on their personalities, often being told to be less loud or abrasive, to take a step back to make room for others, and to be less judgmental.

In August 1982, thirty-eight-year-old Ann Hopkins was proposed as a candidate for partner at the accounting firm Price Waterhouse. Since joining the firm four years earlier, she had brought in an estimated $40 million in revenue, more than any other partnership candidate. She had also billed more hours in 1981 and 1982 than any of the eighty-eight other candidates. In the nominating proposal prepared by her group, Hopkins was praised for her "outstanding performance." Yet various male partners evaluated her as being too "macho" and in need of "charm school." More than half the nominees were promoted to partner, but Hopkins, the only woman, wasn't one of them.

One partner who supported her promotion told her about the feedback from the voting partners: She was, according to them, "overly aggressive," "unduly harsh," "difficult to work with," "impatient with staff," "overcompensated for being a woman," and "universally disliked." Another partner advised her to "walk more femininely, talk more femininely, dress more femininely, wear makeup, have her hair styled, and wear jewelry." The praise she received was grudging: One partner said she had "matured from a tough-talking somewhat masculine hard-nosed manager to an authoritative, formidable, but much more appealing lady partner candidate."

It was true that Hopkins was an unconventional woman for the era: She swore like a sailor, drank beer at lunch, smoked, rode motorcycles, carried a briefcase instead of a purse, and wore little makeup or jewelry. Then again, she was allergic to makeup and, even if she weren't, she thought it'd be difficult to apply, given her inability to see much without her trifocals. She found that putting everything she needed in a briefcase was easier than having to also carry a purse, especially when she was managing a suitcase. In any case, she didn't understand what such trivial matters had to do with her job.

Price Waterhouse had given Hopkins one year to demonstrate "the personal and leadership qualities required of a partner." But just four months later, she was informed that she was unlikely to be promoted. In December 1983, she received some unexpected news: She would not be re-proposed for a partnership even if reviews of her work were, on balance, favorable. Meanwhile, the nineteen men who had been placed on hold along with Hopkins fared much better. Fifteen of them were promoted to partner that year. For Hopkins, it was the last straw: Four days before Christmas, she resigned.

Although Hopkins had these experiences in the eighties, women continue to be underrepresented in top management positions today. In 2017, only thirty-two Fortune 500 firms had female CEOs, in part because both men and women believe that effective leadership requires masculine traits. Research suggests that, in our minds, good managers are typically male. Women are often perceived as less competent and as having less leadership potential than men, and thus are more likely to encounter skepticism and backlash when they behave aggressively in the workplace and go for top positions. And other women are as likely to discriminate as men. When women are in charge, both men and women criticize them for being bossy, cold, bitchy, or aggressive—all attributes at odds with traditionally "feminine" features such as compassion, warmth, and submissiveness.

More often, women are found toiling behind the scenes. When teaching at the MBA level, I often ask students to complete group projects in teams of four or five. Though not a favorite among students, these projects are an effective way to teach both the class materials and teamwork. Still, I usually find myself spending many hours dealing with the same issue: One student ends up doing most or all of the work, while everyone on the team earns the same score.

And often, I find, it's a female student who ends up picking up the slack for the rest of the team.

Research suggests that this pattern is common in groups. Women carry at least as much of the load, if not more, than men, but the men get more credit. When male employees bring ideas forward, their performance evaluations are higher; when women propose the same ideas, managers' perceptions of their performance do not change. Similarly, when executives speak up rather than staying silent, they receive competence ratings that are 10 percent higher when they are male, but when the executives engaging in the exact same behavior are female, their ratings suffer: They are 14 percent lower.

This is bad not just for the women who carry the weight of their groups, but also for their organizations. Think of how much potential is yet to be tapped. If some members are slacking off just because they know someone else will step up to the plate, the team won't live up to its potential, and the organization won't either. It is hard to overstate how much there is to gain when everyone contributes.

IN JULY 2010, LESS THAN A MONTH AFTER BEING PROMOTED TO ASSOCIATE PROFES-sor at Harvard Business School, I had to teach my first executive education class, part of a one-week program designed for leaders from all sorts of businesses across the globe. I was initially a bit nervous about telling a group of almost ninety experienced executives how to be effective negotiators, but by the end of the week, I felt good about how things had gone.

Later, the chair of the executive education program came by to tell me that he was about to send out the student feedback from the course. There was, he warned, one comment that would probably upset me. He was giving me a heads-up in the hope that I would read it and then move on, without dwelling on it. About an hour later, the email came. The ratings were good, overall, but as my colleague had warned, one comment stood out: "Professor Gino should wear less well-fitted clothes. This would allow the students in her classes to pay more attention to what she is saying rather than being distracted by her clothes."

Had I worn a slinky, low-cut dress? No. I had worn a dark, conservative pantsuit. Yes, it was cut for a woman, but it was not tight or revealing.

A few years later I taught another executive class. This time I had more experience under my belt, and I also had a larger belly—I was eight months pregnant. Before the start of the session, a male executive approached me to say that pregnant women are known for tiring easily and that I probably should have asked somebody else to teach my class. I didn't know how to respond. "Good luck, though," he said, breaking the awkward silence. "We'll see how it goes."

Once the class began I looked around at the executives, most of whom were men. I couldn't help but imagine that they were wondering why they did not have a more experienced, thinner professor leading the class—someone not at risk of passing out from exhaustion or suddenly going into labor. They were leaning back in their chairs, as if signaling that they were not interested in what I had to tell them—as if they doubted my teaching skills. Were my perceptions correct, or had the student's comment rattled me?

Moments like this have stuck with me over the years. Sometimes they come to mind when I'm preparing for an executive education class or a consulting meeting, or running a training session in the field. They make me wonder what expectations my audience might have based on my female first name—and then, after I enter the room, what additional assumptions they make. Women in my classes often relay feedback they have received in their own organizations, comments that they doubt male colleagues get: observations about their dress, criticisms of their assertiveness, and other remarks that have nothing to do with their actual work.

The effect of such judgments is truly insidious. Imagine, for example, that you are a woman (likely easier for some of you than others!). You walk into a meeting and see that all the other participants are male. Before anyone speaks, you feel less confident than the men about how you will come across, so you find yourself hesitating before speaking. That's when one of the men jumps in and proposes an agenda. You try to argue a certain point, but your voice betrays your nervousness. Detecting your insecurity, the men dismiss your concerns. Their dismissal leaves you shaken, and you fall silent. Too bad, because the subject under discussion is one you know well. When you speak up again, you have trouble holding the floor to present your view. The final decision suffers the absence of your expertise.

This is common. Especially when outnumbered, women are frequently interrupted, talked over, shut down, and penalized for speaking out. Men, research consistently shows, dominate both conversations and decision-making processes in corporate offices, school boards, town meetings, and government. In fact, the more power men have, the more they talk—which is not the case for women. Similarly, men who show anger at work are rewarded with more respect and authority, but angry women are seen as incompetent and unworthy, and are penalized. These experiences, in turn, affect confidence, expectations, and future behavior. For instance, the sexist comments I received in my executive classes made me nervous about teaching or even interacting with executives in the future.

Psychologist Claude Steele refers to this phenomenon as "stereotype threat," or the tendency to "choke" and underperform due to the fear of bias. Consider the stereotype that female students are naturally inferior in math and science. In a study in which women were reminded of their gender before taking a math test, they scored lower than equally qualified men who took the same test. The women's performance suffered because they were worried about confirming negative stereotypes, the researchers found. However, when reassured of equal ability before the test, the women matched the performances of men. Similar results have been found for African-American and Latino students: Stereotypes predict they will underperform in academic pursuits relative to whites, and they do underperform when primed to think about race. Reminders can also be visual: Studies have shown that women score higher in math when surrounded by other women than when testing in a mixed-gender group.

The consequences of stereotype threat go well beyond poor performance on tests; we can also find ourselves closed off from others, less ambitious, and disengaged from our work, unable to fulfill our potential as leaders, negotiators, entrepreneurs, and competitors. Of course, the consequences hurt not only those who experience the threat, but also their organizations. And a vicious cycle develops: When women experience stereotype threat, their mental energy is taxed as they work to disprove the stereotype, leaving them with less mental energy to perform the task at hand. This creates more stress and lower performance—thus maintaining the underrepresentation of women in the workplace, especially in leadership positions. All of us are part of some group that can be affected by negative perceptions, and we know we may be judged by it. No one is immune to stereotype threat.

But here's the good news: Expectations can influence results. This insight has been demonstrated for years through the use of medical placebos. In one study, patients received intravenous injections of morphine over the course of two days to reduce the pain created by dental work. On the third day, the same patients received an injection of saline that they thought was a powerful painkiller. Patients who received the placebo tolerated the pain much better than what one would normally expect even from people given morphine.

Outside of medicine, the same phenomenon holds. The simple

fact of knowing that I'll soon be in a meeting with a potential client, working on a joint project with new colleagues, or in a class full of executives leads to expectations of how well I think I'll do. The interaction proceeds accordingly: If I expect to do well, I'll feel more comfortable and excited. As a result, I'll not only perform better, but I will also be judged, research shows, as more competent and even wittier.

In a similar way, we can shape our expectations about the behavior of *others*. For instance, when looking over the roster for my executive class, I might tell myself that I expect my students to make particularly clever comments and to do well in even the most challenging exercises. Once my expectations are set, research shows, I'll behave differently toward my students in a way that confirms my positive expectations.

A story from Greek mythology has inspired much research on the topic of how expectations influence behavior: Pygmalion. According to the story, told most vividly in the ancient Roman poet Ovid's *Metamorphoses*, Pygmalion was a talented sculptor from Cyprus who had become disgusted by some local prostitutes and as a result had lost all interest in women. Dedicating himself to his work, he spent long hours crafting a beautiful statue of a woman, Galatea, out of ivory.

When he finally put his chisel down, he was captivated by the woman he had created. She was so perfect that Pygmalion, despite his professed disdain of all women, fell deeply in love. He began to bring the statue gifts, such as beads, seashells, songbirds, and flowers. Pygmalion prayed to the goddess Aphrodite to bring Galatea to life, and she granted his wish. In a sense, though, his expectations were what had brought her to life.

The story of Pygmalion has resonated across the centuries. In George Bernard Shaw's 1912 play *Pygmalion* (which was later turned into a 1956 Broadway musical and then into the popular film *My Fair Lady*), Professor Henry Higgins works hard to transform an uncouth cockney flower girl named Eliza Doolittle into a refined young lady, becoming besotted with her in the process. Psychologists have studied what they call the "Pygmalion effect," in which a person's expectations of another person turn into a self-fulfilling prophecy. Evidence of the effect emerged in 1965, when students in a California school completed a test that was described to them as one that would identify "growth spurters," students who were poised to make strides in their academic journey. Teachers were given the names of elementary school children who allegedly had great intellectual potential. Although these children were cho-sen at random, they showed a larger gain in performance than their peers when they were tested again at the end of the year. The only significant difference between them and their classmates was in the minds of the teachers.

These days, I find that I often benefit from the Pygmalion ef-fect in my own teaching. When my colleagues—usually male and older than me—introduce me to my executive education classes now, they stress that I have won various teaching awards or that I became a full professor at an unusually young age. These accolades, presented by a clear authority figure, seem to improve any low, stereotype-based expectations the students may bring to the class.

We can also choose to rebel against low expectations that oth-ers set for us. Research has found that approaching high-stakes per-formance situations by telling ourselves that we're excited, rather than telling ourselves to simply calm down, lowers our anxiety and improves our performance. If we fear a backlash, we can frame the upcoming task as an opportunity to learn and improve rather than dwelling on our anxiety. Rebels know to expect the most out of everyone, including themselves.

I made the conscious choice to harness this rebel spirit (rather than succumbing to stereotype threat) in the fall of 2010 when I was asked to teach in the same executive education program in which I had previously received the comment about my supposedly too-tight clothes. I agreed, but after seeing the list of who else would be on the teaching team—all incredibly accomplished men, with many years of teaching and consulting experience—I felt nervous. I was the only woman, I had a weird accent, and I was clearly younger than the other instructors (not to mention the executives I would be teaching). But as I walked to campus for the first class in the program, I decided to focus on the fact that it would be a great learning opportunity for me. I told myself to be excited to be part of such an accomplished teaching team rather than stressed. Ultimately, the program went well, and I eventually became a regular member of the team.

When we fight stereotype threats and reframe situations by focusing on opportunities rather than potential problems, we make personal gains by embracing challenging situations that we would otherwise shy away from. But fighting a stereotype threat also has an added benefit: Our behavior, once we are part of the action, can motivate others to follow our lead. Our examples and stories can change how others think, often in powerful ways.

In February 1966, twenty-three-year-old Roberta "Bobbi" Gibb reached into her mailbox in San Diego and eagerly tore open the letter she found from the Boston Athletic Association. She was expecting to see her race number for the upcoming Boston Marathon. Instead, she found that her request to compete had been denied because women were not allowed to race. Women, the letter said, were not "physiologically able" to run the race. Gibb was a lifelong runner who had been training for Boston for two years. On the day of the marathon, she showed up at the starting line, the hood of her sweatshirt pulled over her head to disguise her gender. When her fellow runners figured out that she was a woman, they encouraged her, and she lifted the hood. The press got wind of the news, and soon spectators were seeking her out and cheering her on. Gibb finished ahead of two-thirds of the men in the race and found the governor of Massachusetts waiting to congratulate her at the finish line. In 1972, partly inspired by Gibb, Boston Marathon officials opened the race to women.

Examples are powerful. The daughters of working mothers grow up to benefit from their mothers' choices in their own careers, despite the old attitude that women who stay home to take care of their children are better, more devoted mothers than those who work. Women raised by working mothers are more likely to hold managerial roles than women whose mothers stay home full time, research shows. They also earn more money. In the United States, for example, the earnings of daughters of working mothers were 23 percent higher than those of daughters of stay-at-home moms. As for the sons of working mothers, their mothers' choice of work had no effect on their employment, but, as adults, they were more likely than sons of stay-at-home mothers to share in the chores and child care.

At Harvard Business School, the issue of having a diverse set of role models was discussed a few years ago in relationship to our curriculum, which is heavily based on case studies. In 2014, women comprised about 20 percent of case study protagonists. A case study, in a way, conveys to students who should be in leadership roles. With this realization, the HBS dean of the faculty, Nitin Nohria, encouraged the faculty to seek out more cases with females and minorities as main characters.

People who are brave enough to call out discrimination, despite the fear of how it may affect their career, can have an especially potent effect. In an October 2017 *New Yorker* article, journalist Ronan Farrow reported allegations that Hollywood movie mogul Harvey Weinstein had sexually assaulted multiple women. In the weeks that followed, new accusations of sexual harassment and abuse against other powerful, high-profile men surfaced. When actress Alyssa Milano urged women to share their stories using the #MeToo Twitter hashtag, thousands of women did so; at its peak, the hashtag was used half a million times in tweets in just a day. At first, the tweets were coming from women in Hollywood. But they were soon joined by women in the media, then in the art world, in comedy, in politics—in all walks of life. When a few women had the courage to speak up, others were no longer afraid.

We all have opportunities, big and small, to change attitudes. When I was visibly pregnant with my second daughter, Emma, I could sometimes be seen on campus doing jumping jacks. People who walked by smiled. Others asked me what I was doing. "I am breaking common stereotypes," I told them.

IN 2009, EILEEN TAYLOR, DEUTSCHE BANK'S MANAGING DIRECTOR AND GLOBAL head of diversity, found herself staring at some puzzling internal data: Female managing directors were leaving the firm. The post involves stress and long hours, so it seemed possible that these women were leaving due to work-life balance issues. But when Taylor dug deeper, she found that this was not the case: They were leaving because they were taking better positions elsewhere—and after being passed up for promotions. If Deutsche Bank was neglecting the needs of promising employees and losing them as a result, that was clearly a problem that could not be ignored, Taylor realized.

Companies that can maintain and expand leadership roles for women, as Taylor wanted Deutsche Bank to do, reap large benefits. Using data from 1992 through 2006, Cristian Dezsö of the University of Maryland and David Ross of Columbia University looked at the size and gender composition of executive management teams of most of the companies in Standard & Poor's Composite 1500 list, a group that reflects the U.S. equity market. The researchers found that, on average, female leadership generated an additional $42 million in firm value, all else being equal. The study also found that firms with a particular focus on innovation experienced larger gains when women had positions in the executive ranks.

In a study of 2,360 companies using data from 2005 to 2011,

researchers at the Credit Suisse Research Institute found that businesses with at least one woman on their board had lower net debt to equity, higher average returns on equity, and better average growth. Gender diversity isn't just a laudable goal; it also makes bottom-line business sense.

But the benefits of more women in the workforce go beyond financial performance, surfacing in every level of an organization, including in the quality of ideas and decision-making. My own research shows that gender diversity helps companies attract and retain more talent by providing a more stimulating workplace. When a potential candidate learns that a company has a gender-diverse workforce, he or she puts more effort into getting the job.

Eileen Taylor took action, spearheading an internal sponsorship program called Accomplished Top Leaders Advancement Strategy, or ATLAS, that paired women leaders at Deutsche with women mentors from the bank's executive committee. Research on the careers of both whites and minorities shows a common thread among people of color who advance the furthest: a strong network of sponsors and mentors inside their organization. Developmental relationships are important for everyone climbing the organizational ladder—but especially so for women and minorities. When DuVernay needed to hire directors for OWN's *Queen Sugar*, she sought to hire only female directors. "I always say if *Game of Thrones* can have three seasons of all male directors, why can't we have three seasons of all women directors?" said DuVernay in an interview for *Hollywood Reporter*. All the directors chosen for the first season of the show had directed one film that had been in competition at a film festival but had not been able to find a job that would allow them to direct an episode of television. And, after *Queen Sugar*, all of them ended up getting booked for other pilots or TV shows.

Taylor's initiative at Deutsche Bank raised the visibility of women leaders and connected them with powerful advocates. A third of program participants won larger roles with the firm; another third were deemed ready to move up when positions became available. Since ATLAS launched in 2009, the number of women managing directors at Deutsche Bank has grown by 50 percent.

The effort was worth it. Research shows the benefits of diversity in organizations, nations, communities, and groups. A 2009 analysis of data from 506 firms found that those with greater gender or racial diversity had higher sales revenue, a greater number of customers, and higher profits. Another study of management teams found that those that had more diverse work and educational backgrounds came up with products that were more innovative. And analyses of international data show that nations thrive by many measures, from business to medicine to art, after opening their borders to travel and immigration.

People who live in more diverse geographic areas and interact with people in other regions also reap benefits from diversity. Telephone calling patterns reveal that interaction with different geographic regions—or social network diversity—is associated with greater economic prosperity in a community. Similarly, correlational evidence indicates that U.S. cities with a greater share of foreign-born inhabitants are more financially solid. And in competitive trading markets, ethnic diversity encourages more care, less bias, and greater accuracy in judgments, which in turn prevents price bubbles.

For the most part, this data is correlational—showing that more diversity is related to better outcomes—but it does not allow one to conclude that greater diversity is the *cause* of those better outcomes. Laboratory experiments, though, have shown the causal effect that diversity has on performance. Given the constraints of the lab, these studies focus on smaller groups. But it's clear that homogeneous groups are more vulnerable to narrow-mindedness and groupthink. Diversity, by contrast, has been found to produce more innovation and better decisions in both cooperative and competitive contexts, and to strengthen teamwork.

Despite the compelling evidence behind it, diversity often fails to take hold for the simple reason that homogeneous teams can *feel* more effective. We all tend to seek out comfort and familiarity, and this often translates into choosing to work with those who are like us. The feeling of comfort and ease in homogeneous groups was well captured in a 2008 study of fraternity and sorority members at Northwestern University in Chicago. Membership in these groups conveys a strong sense of identity, much like affiliation with a religious or political group, and can thus intensify a sense of internal similarity among members, while deepening a sense of separateness from outsiders. In this particular experiment, 132 sorority members and 68 fraternity members were asked to solve a fictional murder mystery. Each participant wore a color-coded nametag with the name of their Greek house and had twenty minutes to study the clues and pinpoint the likely suspect out of three possible individuals. Next, each student was assigned to a team of three with two other members of their fraternity or sorority. Each team had a total of twenty minutes to discuss the case and come up with an answer. Five minutes into the discussions, a fourth team member joined each group. This new member was either from the same Greek house (i.e., someone like them) or a different house (i.e., someone who was likely different).

After a team named the suspect they'd agreed on, each member answered questions about various aspects of their team's interactions. More diverse groups—those that included a person from outside their sorority or fraternity—judged the interactions within the team as less effective than did the groups of insiders. The diverse groups also showed less confidence in their final choices. This supports what we knew to be true: That members of homogeneous teams easily and readily understand one another, and collaboration on such teams flows smoothly, creating a feeling of good progress. Dealing with outsiders generates disagreements and friction, which naturally does not feel productive. Yet the subjective experiences of the team members did not match reality: Adding an outsider actually *doubled* a group's chance of solving the mystery correctly, from 29 to 60 percent. Working in a diverse group was uncomfortable, but the outcomes were better.

In fact, contrary to our intuition, greater diversity produces better outcomes exactly because it *is* harder to work among a mix of perspectives. Part of the reason we associate homogeneity with greater performance is our preference for information we can process easily, a bias that psychologists have named the fluency heuristic. Easy-to-digest information seems truer or more beautiful—which explains why we often appreciate songs and artwork more as they become more familiar. And when we face opinions we disagree with, discomfort is only one issue. We may also believe that disagreement will make reaching our goals more difficult and time-consuming. Again, this belief is misplaced. Think of working effectively in a group as being like studying (or exercising, for that matter): No pain, no gain.

Businesses can help to dilute the power of stereotypes, but only if their leaders are thoughtful about it. Even seemingly benign decisions, such as which magazines are kept in a reception area, have been found to shift perceptions of an organization's stance on diversity. Whether women and minorities feel accepted depends on many workplace cues, from physical environment to offer letters. For instance, the language used in recruiting documents directly influences application rates. Masculine language in job advertisements ("dominant," "competitive," etc.) lowers the appeal of these jobs for women, not because women worry that they lack the skills, but because they feel they do not belong. Such cues can set off stereotype threat and shape ideas about a company's views toward a particular group.

In addition to making changes to workplace cues, managers can confront stereotypes by increasing minority representation within the organization. Increasing minority representation not only increases the value placed on diversity in the eyes of potential recruits, it also aids in the development of role models—a strong predictor of success for stereotyped individuals.

It's important to remember that we tend to overestimate the amount of conflict a diverse group will experience. In one study, researchers instructed MBA students to act as if they were co-managing various four-person teams of interns and to imagine that one of these teams had asked for more resources. They were shown photos of the members—four white men, four black men, or an even split. Next, they were given a transcript of a group discussion and asked to rate the team on various factors. Everyone read the same transcript, yet participants viewed teams of four white men and four black men as having the same amount of relationship conflict, and diverse teams as having more. Believing that these teams would experience greater conflict led the participants to be less likely to give additional resources to mixed-race groups.

Such beliefs prompt leaders to make bad decisions when it comes to diversity, whether they are hiring, building teams, or encouraging collaboration. Fearing tension, they balk at adding diversity to a group. Rebels understand that conflict can lead to growth and that disagreement is a feature rather than a flaw.

IN JUNE 2014, THE SAN ANTONIO SPURS WON THEIR FIFTH NATIONAL BASKETBALL Association championship in sixteen seasons. The team was often described as "the United Nations of Hoops." The oldest player, thirty-eight-year-old Tim Duncan, had been with the Spurs for about as long as his youngest teammate had been alive. Other players hailed from the Virgin Islands, France, Argentina, Canada, Italy, Brazil, and Australia. In fact, more than half the squad came from outside the United States, making the Spurs much more geographically diverse than the other teams in the league. They were also the first NBA team to have a female assistant coach, Becky Hammon.

The Spurs' superb head coach, Gregg Popovich, and top-notch players were obviously key to the team's success. But a diverse culture also played a role. Popovich, the son of a Serbian father and a Croatian mother, made it a point to learn about his players' backgrounds and to try to speak to them in their native tongues. Players spoke English most of the time to ensure that no one felt left out, but occasionally the international players would switch things up, boosting both camaraderie and tactical advantage. Two French players, Tony Parker and Boris Diaw, turned to their native language when they needed to communicate quickly on the court. The two Australians on the team, Patty Mills and Aron Baynes, often spoke to each other in their own dialect. In teamwork, diversity encourages members—whether they're in the majority or the minority—to search for new information and novel viewpoints, and to process that information more deeply and accurately, which leads to better decision making and problem solving.

Just being exposed to diversity changes the way we think. In a 2006 study, undergrads at the University of Illinois were assigned to work in three-person same-gender groups on a murder-mystery task in which sharing information was the key to success. Some of the groups had only white members; other groups had two white members and one nonwhite person (Asian, African-American, or Hispanic). Information was shared among all members of a group, but each was also given key clues to the mystery that only he or she had. To correctly identify the murderer, members had to share all the information they collectively had during their discussion. The diverse groups were more successful. Being with others who are similar, the results suggest, leads us to think that we all have the same information, which discourages engagement.

Differences in beliefs and personal preferences also bring benefits. In one study, 186 people who identified as either a Democrat or a Republican worked on the same murder mystery task I just told you about and decided who they thought committed the crime. Next, each person wrote an essay about their suspicion in preparation for a meeting with another group member. Participants were told that their partner disagreed with their opinion; their task was to change his or her mind. Half of the participants were told their partner supported the opposing political party, and half were told the person supported their own party. The results showed that Democrats didn't prepare as well for meetings with Democrats as they did for meetings with Republicans, and the same pattern was true for Republicans. In general, people who anticipate joining ethnically or politically diverse groups are more thorough in their preparation.

Whether we are trying to solve a murder mystery, come up with creative solutions to complex problems, enter new markets, develop new products, or improve workflow, diversity can challenge our thinking in constructive ways. Even before we begin to interact with others in a diverse group, the simple fact of diversity promotes better preparation, more creativity, and deeper thinking by encouraging us to consider a range of viewpoints. We may not enjoy the decision-making process as much because of the greater effort required, but in the end, we'll usually reach a better outcome than a less diverse group would have produced.

When organizations and their leaders commit to diversity, the benefits are deep and wide. But increasing diversity in an organization often requires leaders to fight attitudes and practices that are holding their employees back. Rebels help their organizations reap the benefits of greater diversity by focusing on how to best leverage differences. Rebels recognize that initiatives to increase or effectively manage diversity often fail because they treat the issue as a problem rather than as an opportunity. Rebels know that to effectively leverage differences, their organizations should work beyond race and gender. In the rebel mind, all differences matter. Diversity is not a quota system; it's a long-range vision for growth.

When Ava DuVernay was starting her new career, she spent a lot of her energy trying to figure out how to break into the film-making business. She sought out people who could advise her, give her support, and show her the way to success. Eventually, though, she realized that in doing this she was wearing a "coat of desperation" and would be better off making her own films, with her own ideas, on her own budget. "I think there have been cracks made in the glass ceiling by women who can get close enough to hit it," she told *Time* magazine. "But I'm mostly bolstered by folks who create their own ceilings." By following their dreams, women and minorities can change their organizations and inspire others to do the same. By finding a way to ignore the barriers that others may create for them, intentionally or not, rebels like DuVernay create their own ceiling, one set only by their own potential.

6

COACH CHEEKS SINGS
THE NATIONAL ANTHEM
A TALENT FOR AUTHENTICITY

*No one man can, for any considerable time, wear one face
to himself, and another to the multitude, without finally
getting bewildered as to which is the true one.*
—**NATHANIEL HAWTHORNE,** *THE SCARLET LETTER*

On the night of April 25, 2003, twenty thousand eager basketball fans streamed into the $267 million Rose Garden arena in
Portland, Oregon, for the third game between the Portland Trail
Blazers and the Dallas Mavericks in the first round of the NBA
Western Conference playoffs. The Blazers had won thirteen of fifteen games against the Mavericks in Portland, but the Mavericks
already owned a 2–0 lead in the best-of-seven series. The first two
games had been played in Dallas, and now the Blazers were back
on their home court.

Excitement and tension were high, but the raucous crowd
quieted for the singing of the national anthem. Thirteen-year-old
Natalie Gilbert would do the honors, as winner of the Trail Blazers'

"Get the Feeling of a Star" promotion. She had woken up with the flu that day, but the aspiring Broadway star knew the show had to go on. Gilbert stood before a massive American flag, all dressed up in a black-and-white sparkly prom dress, rhinestones glittering on her neck, her blond hair pulled up in a topknot. Facing the thousands of amped-up fans and millions of TV viewers, she took a last look around the arena, raised the microphone, and began to sing in a mellow alto.

"O say can you see . . ."

At first, Gilbert showed the poise of a pro, but when she hit the second line she stumbled, singing "starlight's" instead of "twilight's." She broke off and nervously chuckled, then tossed her head from side to side, trying to shake off the mistake. But she couldn't. She raised her right hand and covered her face with the mic as embarrassment set in. The music continued, but Gilbert, shaking her head, appeared on the verge of tears. The crowd's encouragement was for naught: She had lost her composure. Out of ideas, she looked to her right, then behind her, searching for her father, Vince, but with no luck. Gilbert was all alone. In just a few excruciating seconds, her dream had turned into a nightmare.

Blazers head coach Maurice Cheeks, standing near the bench in a gray suit and tie, had been focused on the game—one of the biggest of his coaching career. But he quickly strode over to Gilbert. The forty-six-year-old coach gently put his arm around her, helped her raise the mic, and began singing the words at Gilbert's side. She regained her confidence, no longer alone. Cheeks gestured to the crowd, leading the twenty-thousand-strong choir in a patriotic sing-along. By the end, the voices of players, coaches, and fans soared as one behind "the home of the brave."

The Trail Blazers lost that night. They fought hard to win the next three games, tying the series, but fell in the seventh game. Yet Cheeks is remembered less for those nail-biter wins and losses than for his moment as an on-court savior. Ministers praised him as the very definition of a Good Samaritan. Gilbert called him her "guardian angel."

"I never thought about doing it before I did it," Cheeks told the *New York Times*. "I just saw a little girl in trouble and I went to help her. I'm a father. I have two kids myself. I'd have wanted someone to help them if they could."

IN 2005, PATRICIA FILI-KRUSHEL, AN EXECUTIVE VICE PRESIDENT AT AOL TIME Warner, was about to deliver an important speech to her staff. For months, she had been working to bring flextime to the company. More and more people, she thought, valued flexibility in their work, and she worried that AOL Time Warner was in danger of losing the war for talent because they didn't have a flextime policy. But she was having trouble getting colleagues to take the idea seriously—many worried that flextime would be abused. So Fili-Krushel had decided to run a flextime pilot program with her own group of about five thousand employees. In the speech, she was going to explain the pilot to the entire staff. She needed and wanted to make the strongest case possible.

But she was also thinking a lot about her teenage daughter, who had been struggling that year. Fili-Krushel was planning to hire a therapist to work with her daughter, and she had also sought permission to work from home during the coming summer so that they could spend more time together. "Should I mention this to the staff?" she asked herself. It would be risky. Her employees might judge her for her daughter's problems, wondering if perhaps she was to blame for having focused more on her career than on her child.

Fili-Krushel took the stage and outlined the value of flextime for employees. Using flextime, she said, would not keep them from getting ahead. Taking a deep breath, she explained that, although this wasn't the reason she was advocating for the program, she would be the first employee to take advantage of it. She needed to be with her daughter. "We are all human beings," Fili-Krushel said, "and things happen in life we can't always control." Fili-Krushel's flextime pilot turned out to be a success. The program was eventually rolled out to other groups in the company, and it ultimately helped with hiring and retention. Fili-Krushel's worries about being judged gave way to a strong sense that her openness had resonated with her staff.

We all hesitate before making ourselves vulnerable, fearful of being judged by others, but these worries are usually misplaced. Opening up wins us trust, perhaps even more so when it involves showing weaknesses—whether an off-key voice, as in the case of Maurice Cheeks, or a personal problem, as with Fili-Krushel. Revealing our deepest emotions takes courage, which inspires emulation and admiration in the people around us, and allows them to connect with us more quickly and more profoundly. Rebels understand all of this. They are willing to stand "naked" in front of others.

Sharing personal information is key to developing and maintaining strong relationships. When we do, our peers trust and like us more, and also feel closer to us. In addition, self-disclosure makes us feel (and appear) more real. For one study, my colleagues and I invited college students to the lab and paired them up for computer chats. Participants asked to disclose their flaws got a more positive response from their partners. Next, during a game that required trust, the participants who disclosed their weaknesses outperformed their more circumspect peers. Even a star stands to gain from the occasional slip. When Jennifer Lawrence was named Best Actress for her role in *Silver Linings Playbook* at the 2013 Academy Awards, she tripped and fell as she climbed to the stage in her pink ball gown. She looked mortified, but the crowd gave her a standing ovation. "You guys are just standing up because you feel bad that I fell," she joked in her acceptance speech. "That's really embarrassing."

Psychologist Elliot Aronson has identified what he calls the "pratfall effect." In one of his experiments, Aronson trained a paid actor to act as a quiz-show contestant. Students listened to the recording of the actor answering a series of extremely difficult questions and getting almost all of them correct. He then described his highly successful academic career. For some students, the recording ended. For others, it continued, and the students could hear the actor knocking over a cup of coffee on himself. The students who heard the spill judged him to be more likable. We find it hard to relate to people who are highly competent, but we tend to warm to those who are flawed—because we know that we are, too. The psychologist Joanne Silvester has found that job candidates who admitted past mistakes during interviews were actually more appealing to employers than those who covered them up. When we own our blunders, people are impressed.

In May 2015, I saw this happen in person, when Intuit cofounder Scott Cook delivered an unexpected sort of commencement address to the graduating MBAs at Harvard Business School, his alma mater. Cook was following in the footsteps of many other distinguished business leaders, including Facebook COO Sheryl Sandberg. Cook, who now serves as the chairman of the executive committee of Intuit, had earned an MBA from HBS in 1976. He worked as a brand manager at Procter & Gamble and then with the corporate-strategy consulting firm Bain, taking on assignments in banking and technology. A few years later, Cook and his wife, Signe, moved to Silicon Valley when the software explosion was at its peak. He was in his early twenties. One day, the two were sitting at their kitchen table when Cook saw Signe writing out checks, one after the other. Cook started thinking that there had to be a simpler way to pay the bills. Why not create software to handle household finances? That question eventually led to Intuit Inc. and the creation of leading financial software products like TurboTax, Quicken, QuickBooks, and Mint. Starting from nothing in 1983, the company is now a $5 billion giant with over eight thousand employees.

Nine hundred and eight members of the MBA Class of 2015 were awaiting their well-deserved degrees after two long years of classes, group projects, and internships (and yes, a lot of parties at the end). With their families and friends, they were sitting under a warm sun and blue sky on the Baker lawn of the HBS campus, ready to hear an inspiring speech that would assure them that they could do pretty much anything if they applied themselves. But then something unexpected happened. Cook spoke to them about his failures.

"I realized I was holding the company back," he said. "I could feel in my gut that there were a lot of duties I had to do that I didn't enjoy, nor was I good at doing them." Cook recalled that when his limitations as a chief executive first dawned on him, Intuit was flying high: a market leader expanding into the UK after a successful IPO. And yet the man at the top worried that he was in over his head, that he didn't have the skills the company needed at the helm, and that he didn't know how to tackle its most pressing problems. Cook ultimately decided to step down. It was a decision he should have made much earlier, he told the crowd. He had failed to develop as a leader, and he had let the company down.

As the only person in the company who didn't receive a performance review during his time as CEO, Cook had sought out an executive coach and asked for a 360-degree evaluation. The results were poor. But rather than hiding them, he shared the feedback with employees. "I went to colleagues and said, 'This is what I've heard. I'm going to fix it. Please help me,'" he told the HBS students. That a person at his level was willing to admit to his flaws and even ask for help from people below him on the corporate ladder was, needless to say, uncommon. After receiving a long, warm applause, Cook was swarmed by graduates who wanted to hear more. Such is the power of authenticity.

In a recent study, a team of Harvard researchers demonstrated that it is also a good idea to show weaknesses in the context of "pitch" competitions, where entrepreneurs give "fast pitches"—short presentations of a minute or two—before a panel of investors. The investors then judge the entrepreneurs and award capital to the winners. The study focused on one actual pitch competition. In it, after entrepreneurs had made their presentations, but before the results were revealed, they listened to a recording of what they believed to be a fellow competitor's pitch and were told that they would be asked to evaluate this competitor. Some listened to a recording in which the entrepreneur only discussed successes. For example, the entrepreneur stated: "I have already landed some huge clients—companies like Google and GE. I've had amazing success, and in the past year I have single-handedly increased our market share by 200 percent." Other entrepreneurs listened to the same recording but then heard the speaker reveal her failures: "I wasn't always so successful. I had a lot of trouble getting to where I am now. . . . When I started my company, I also failed to demonstrate why potential clients should believe in me and our mission. Many potential clients turned me down." When they heard the entrepreneur describe her successes *and* her failures, rather than only the former, listeners felt less envious and more motivated to work hard to improve their own ventures.

Discussing failure in the classroom can also be inspiring and motivating to students, and research has shown that it usually results in higher grades. For example, the following details are worth mentioning when we study a genius like Einstein: As a boy, Albert Einstein saw his father struggle to provide for his wife and children, moving the family from place to place as he looked for work. Having to change schools was difficult for Albert. Not only did he constantly feel out of place, but he was always playing catch-up in class. It's not just success that inspires others to greatness. Sometimes, in fact, it's just the opposite.

About four hundred freshmen and sophomores at a low-income, mostly nonwhite high school were asked to read stories about Einstein, Marie Curie, or Michael Faraday. The stories, each just eight hundred words, focused on one of three themes. "The Story of a Successful Scientist" was about great accomplishments—winning Nobel Prizes, publishing groundbreaking papers, or pioneering new fields of study. "Trying Over and Over Again Even When You Fail" focused on intellectual and professional struggle, including failed experiments. "Overcoming the Challenges in Your Life" covered personal ordeals, such as dealing with poverty or discrimination. Six weeks after the students read the stories, the researchers asked the teachers how the students were doing in science class. The answer was that students who had read about struggle—whether intellectual or personal—now had higher grades than their peers who had read about achievements. The differences were especially pronounced in students who weren't getting good grades to begin with, suggesting that this exercise may be most beneficial to those most in need of help. Understanding the scientists' struggles helped the students see them as role models.

In another study, researchers found that exposing firefighters to case studies of experienced firefighters who committed errors brought better performance in a post-training task as compared to case studies where there were no errors. And in research I conducted with colleagues, we examined data from seventy-one surgeons who completed more than sixty-five hundred cardiac procedures over the course of ten years and found that surgeons learned more from others' failures than from others' successes, and that this vicarious learning reduced patient mortality.

In early 2016, after posting a revised CV on his professional website, Princeton University professor Johannes Haushofer became a kind of folk hero of failure. In this "CV of failures," he listed the many positions and awards for which he had applied and been rejected. When asked about the revision, Haushofer gave a simple explanation to the *Washington Post*: "Most of what I try fails, but these failures are often invisible, while the successes are visible. I have noticed that this sometimes gives others the impression that most things work out for me. As a result, they are more likely to attribute their own failures to themselves, rather than the fact that the world is stochastic, applications are crapshoots, and selection committees and referees have bad days."

We are always looking for ways to hide—whether by covering up aspects of our personality, keeping our emotions to ourselves, or concealing our fears and flaws. But vulnerability helps us create stronger connections with others. Listening to Maurice Cheeks's voice as he led Gilbert through the anthem, you'd have never mistaken him for a great singer. Nobody cared. The audience joined in because of the connection he had made. We worry that rejection awaits those who reveal their true selves. To connect, we try our best to appear perfect, strong, intelligent, and polished, without realizing that this strategy often has the opposite effect.

WHEN I FIRST ARRIVED IN THE UNITED STATES, BACK IN 2001, I SHARED A BOSTON apartment with two roommates, both Americans, who were just a few years older and who had been living together for two years. The day I moved in, they invited me to join them for dinner. "We were thinking of taking it easy and just ordering Chinese," one of them told me. "That's what we often do on Sundays."

"Sure," I said. "That would be great." Chinese is not my favorite, but I was pleased to be asked to join them and didn't mention it. Chinese takeout became a Sunday tradition in our apartment, and one that I grew to dread. I vividly remember the night my roommates added spicy chicken feet to the usual dishes. "There's not much food on the foot itself, but you can eat the tendons off the bones," my roommate pointed out. I couldn't bring myself to put anything on my plate. Eventually, my roommates served me. I slowly played with the food, taking small bites and swallowing almost without chewing. *This*, I thought, *isn't working*.

It may seem harmless to fake it, especially in a context as relatively unimportant as what to order for dinner. But it's not—our self-esteem, job performance, and relationships all take a hit. Small challenges seem bigger. We hesitate to speak up. Our health suffers. The more inauthentic we feel, the higher our stress, the lower our sense of well-being, and the more prone we are to burnout. Think about a time in your personal or professional life when you behaved in a way that made you feel untrue to yourself. My colleagues and I asked participants in a study to write about such a moment. We asked another group to write about their last visit to the grocery store, an experience we assumed would be somewhat neutral. After writing about inauthentic behavior, participants felt more anxious and less moral than those who wrote about their last visit to the grocery store. They wanted to clean themselves.

There are other, subtler costs of pretending. I often see people in organizations claiming to know things that they don't. In a meeting, for instance, the more seasoned employees may use obscure acronyms, and the new recruits nod to signal that they are following the discussion, when, in fact, they are not. They do so to make a good impression. But, interestingly, when we are praised for behavior that is inauthentic, our self-esteem suffers. In one study, a group of college students first answered a questionnaire that measured their self-esteem and then took one of two tests. One group took a test that could not be completed without the students pretending to understand several fake vocabulary words, such as "besionary." The second group took a test in which no pretending to understand words was necessary. Once they completed the test, students in both groups received praise for their performance and then answered questions about their self-esteem again. Those who had pretended experienced a loss in their self-esteem, while the others experienced gains.

Inauthenticity can also make it tougher to land a job. Research conducted by Celia Moore of Bocconi University and her colleagues found that 92 percent of job candidates actively misrepresented themselves in interviews. That behavior has consequences: Those who are inauthentic, deflecting questions about weaknesses and concealing their personalities, are less likely to be hired. Much better is the path Anne Hathaway's character chose in *The Devil Wears Prada*: She lands a job at an elite fashion magazine despite admitting she is neither skinny nor glamorous and has little interest in fashion.

And if you're trying to raise money to launch a new business, it's best to be real. In a field study, my colleagues and I looked at data from 166 entrepreneurs participating in a fast-pitch competition. The three judges, experienced private investors interested in funding start-up ventures, filled out a brief scorecard after each pitch. At the end of the event, they deliberated before choosing ten semifinalists who would be invited to participate in the competition's final round. After making their pitch, entrepreneurs, at our request, answered two questions designed to reveal how much they were being themselves when presenting: "Reflecting on the pitch you just delivered, to what extent do you feel you were being authentic?" and "Reflecting on the pitch you just delivered, to what extent do you feel you were being genuine?" When their responses were authentic, not just telling judges what they wanted to hear, the entrepreneurs were given higher ratings by the judges and had over three times higher odds of being one of the winners.

Inauthenticity also works as a drag on motivation. I showed this in a study that will send a shiver down the spine of any Boston Red Sox fan. My colleague Maryam Kouchaki of Northwestern University and I recruited a group of Red Sox fans and gave half of them Red Sox wristbands to wear. The other half was stuck with

New York Yankees wristbands. Then we had everyone put their dominant hand in a bucket of ice and measured how long they could last. The longer they endured, the more we'd pay them. Inauthenticity worked against those wearing the Yankees wristbands. Their times were lower.

This is also true for "social pain," the discomfort we experience when we feel excluded or rejected. In another study I ran with Kouchaki, we primed participants by asking them to recall a time when they felt either authentic or inauthentic. Next, we had them play a computer game called Cyberball, which involves tossing a virtual ball with two pre-programmed "players." At first, the pair tossed the ball to each other and to the study participant. Then, suddenly, the pair started tossing the ball only to each other. Participants primed to feel authentic experienced much lower levels of psychological and physiological stress. Authenticity gives us the courage, energy, and confidence we need to rebound from negative experiences.

It's also easier to be around. People can tell when we're being inauthentic. In fact, they register that inauthenticity in their bodies. When someone hides his feelings, those who interact with him experience a rise in blood pressure. This physiological response helps explain our discomfort around people who seem "fake."

This response is so strong that we actually prefer honest boasting to the dreaded "humblebrag," those phony complaints that provide an opportunity to brag about luck or talent. In other words, the friend who can't stop complaining about what a bad job she did applying to grad schools, now that she can't keep up with all the acceptance letters she's received. My research shows that people disapprove of humblebragging even more than outright bragging. Nonetheless, it survives, even thrives. Having received the mixed message that it's impolite to brag *and* not safe to share our *actual* challenges with others, we fear being rejected and judged—and end up being rejected and judged.

When Bottura opened Osteria Francescana in 1995, he met with considerable opposition from tradition-bound Italians. "It was more than resistance," the chef told me. "They were actively fighting against us. They wanted to see us dead because they didn't want me to touch their grandmothers' recipes." Bottura struggled to keep the restaurant alive in the early years. He persisted, though, in part thanks to lessons from his experience in the summer of 2000, when he worked at El Bulli, often described at the time as the best restaurant in the world. El Bulli chef Ferran Adrià taught Bottura that he had to stay true to himself. "Right away, I realized that it wasn't just about technique," Bottura told me. "What changed me was the message of freedom that Ferran gave me, the freedom to feel my own fire, to look inside myself and make my thoughts edible." He added, "Everybody looked at Ferran as the master of technique. To me, the most important focus of what he did is freedom. He gave us freedom to express ourselves in any way."

Part of freedom is expressing oneself honestly. Even pretending to be happy can take a toll. I thought about this recently when I was visiting London's Victoria and Albert Museum, whose collection of decorative arts and design is the largest in the world. Two of the 4.5 million objects really got my attention: statues of Heraclitus and Democritus, Greek thinkers known as the "weeping and laughing philosophers." Fittingly, Heraclitus looked sad and melancholic, while the cheerfulness on the face of Democritus brought a smile to my own. As many studies have found, we prefer people who appear happy. In research on speed dating, for instance, participants who appeared positive provoked uplifting emotions in others and were deemed better candidates for a second date. Yet we're not always going to be in a Democritus-like mood, and to pretend otherwise is folly. Dozens of studies, on populations ranging from students to working adults, show that inauthenticity exacts heavy costs on physical and emotional health. Among the negative consequences: sleep deprivation, headaches, and chest pain. Of course, for some of us, smiling at work isn't a matter of choice. When we board a plane or a bus, for example, we generally expect to be welcomed by flight attendants or bus drivers who are happy to see us. The problem is, sometimes they're really not.

Across two weeks, seventy-eight bus drivers working for a company in the northwestern United States took surveys before work, after their shifts, and just before they went to bed. They were asked about their sleep, their moods during and after work, and whether or not they had put on a "performance" or a "mask" that day. In the results, emotional acting was associated with insomnia, anxiety, and distress, and it also increased the likelihood of conflict at home. Meanwhile, drivers who reported behaving authentically—either by not faking smiles at all or by smiling because they felt genuinely happy—had much better sleep quality.

Doctors and nurses are no strangers to pressure, but one fascinating study shows that having a safe space to express real feelings can make a big difference. Psychologist Alicia Grandey of Penn State and her colleagues collected survey data in different health care units in a large Australian hospital. One of their measures was the extent to which members of a medical team felt free to express real feelings to colleagues when the group was not dealing with patients or otherwise in the public eye. The idea was to capture how much of a climate of authenticity existed in a given group. When such a climate was present, members were better able to cope with tough situations such as mistreatment by patients and their families. A climate of authenticity within a team, in fact, gave members a chance to replenish their emotional resources and recover from the harm of surface acting.

Authenticity is a rule at Osteria Francescana. Once a week, Bottura asks team members to cook a dish from their own culture for the rest of the staff. This tradition allows the cook to tell his or her stories, and it also reveals different ways of using the same ingredients. One morning, as workers polished dishes and cutlery, an intern with a degree in art history showed them pictures of paintings and talked in detail about the ideas behind the brush-strokes. Why did he do this? Because Bottura had kept asking him to be himself and bring more of himself into work. Bottura pushed other interns to do the same, as well as everyone else working at Osteria. And as each member of the staff found their way to be unique, in the kitchen and in the front of the house, the dishes at Osteria became more refined and delicious. In 2001, one of Italy's most prominent food writers got stuck in traffic on his way from Rome to Milan and stopped in at Osteria Francescana for a meal. A rave review followed. Within a year, the first Michelin star arrived. It was only the beginning.

IT'S A CURIOUS REALITY THAT MOST LARGE ORGANIZATIONS MANAGE THEIR EMployees based on weakness. Just think about how performance reviews typically work. Gaps between ideal behaviors and actual ones are identified, and feedback follows. Thanks to feedback, the employee gains a sense of where he's failing and then starts to think about making improvements. It's true that feedback sometimes covers strengths, but none of us escape the negativity bias, or the tendency for negative information, thoughts, emotions, and experiences tend to make a more lasting impression on us. When we give feedback to others, we often focus on the problems that performance reviews identify, rather than on words of praise or encouragement.

Even outside of work, when we think about self-improvement, we tend to focus on weaknesses. Consider the usual suspects in New Year's resolutions: "get healthy," "lose weight," "spend less," "get organized." These goals have the feel of a negative job review: You're just not cutting it. A study conducted by psychologists Andreas Steimer of Universität Heidelberg and André Mata of the

ISPA Instituto Universitário revealed one of the primary reasons that we tend to focus on weaknesses as opposed to strengths. Participants were told to list a personality trait that they really liked (a strength) and another that they really disliked (a weakness). Next, they answered questions aimed at determining how changeable they believed these traits to be. The results showed that people generally believed their weaknesses to be more malleable than their strengths.

In fact, we've got it backward: We improve faster in areas where we are strong than in areas where we are weak. Research on self-efficacy shows that we are more motivated toward self-improvement when we are confident of results and more likely to think that our efforts will produce good outcomes when we focus on our strengths rather than our weaknesses. One of the best reasons to focus on our strengths is that doing so encourages us to be authentic and allows our true selves to shine. Think of how coaches work with professional athletes: They might do some work on "weaknesses," but mostly they build on areas of tremendous skill.

A study conducted decades ago unintentionally proved this idea. In the 1950s, the Nebraska School Study Council commissioned statewide research that included a test of a method for teaching rapid reading to tenth graders. Before the course, the students were reading, on average, about 90 words per minute. After it, they had improved to about 150 words per minute. But there was a group who had made much larger gains: the students who were strongest at the outset. Before any training, these super readers were covering 300 words per minute. After the course, they jumped to about 2,900 words per minute. Some of the greatest gains in human development may come from investing in what people naturally do best.

In 2013, Deloitte decided to get rid of its performance management system. Deloitte is one of the "Big Four" accounting corporations and the world's largest professional services network, with more than $35 billion in revenue and 244,000 employees. Their old process was in many ways typical. Managers set objectives for each employee and then rated the employees on how well those objectives were met. These evaluations formed the basis for annual ratings that were set at "consensus meetings," where counselors represented employees to discuss where each of them stood in comparison to their coworkers. There were preset categories for the ratings, which were required to conform to a forced distribution. This is what determined any changes in compensation.

Company leaders worried that the company was failing in the ultimate goal of developing stronger employees and leaders. In addition, the performance review cycle—which included filling out forms, participating in meetings, and doing the actual ratings—took about 1.8 million hours a year. Most of this time seemed to be consumed by discussions of ratings rather than being used productively to talk to employees about their performance and potential. Deloitte replaced the system with one aimed at investing in employees for the long term. There would still be performance reviews, but they would be streamlined. The new system redistributed time and energy to coaching, more timely feedback, and career guidance. The emphasis across all these activities would be on strengths, not weaknesses. Each employee would be assigned a coach to help him or her discover and apply strengths and make sense of feedback.

In 2014, Deloitte ran a small pilot to test the new system. Six hundred U.S. workers participated. The initiative was such a success that the company soon ran a larger pilot on about seven thousand people. Data from the two pilots indicated that participants performed better, felt greater commitment to the organization, and became more energized in their work. These trends became more pronounced the longer the employees participated in the new system. The data also found that one predictor of job performance stood above all others: playing to strengths. By the end of 2017, about 85,000 Deloitte employees were working under the new process.

In a multiyear study of team performance Gallup conducted involving more than 1.4 million employees working in 50,000 teams across 192 organizations, high-performing teams and lower-performing ones responded to statements related to purpose, pay, and opportunity. A small group of items explained most of the variation between the two types of teams. The most powerful was a measure of applied aptitude: "At work, I have the opportunity to do what I do best every day." Teams whose members chose "strongly agree" as a response to this item were 38 percent more productive, 50 percent more likely to have low turnover, and 44 percent more likely to have high customer satisfaction scores.

But the introspection of a firm like Deloitte is rare. As organizations grow, they often lose sight of what made them successful in the first place: their employees. In a survey I conducted of about 280 students who attended executive education classes at HBS, I found that larger organizations were less likely to treat investing in people as a priority. It can be easy to forget about all the talent in the room, especially as a company grows and demands that its top leaders grow with it. Focus turns to investments in other markets, products, or services, and in new technologies and equipment. All the while, potential investments in employees are neglected—and huge opportunities are squandered.

According to Gallup research, people who use their strengths daily are six times more likely to get satisfaction out of their job and report less stress and anxiety. Research by the Corporate Leadership Council found that when managers focus on an employee's weaknesses, his or her performance *declines* by 27 percent, whereas a focus on strengths boosts performance by 36 percent. Similar data from Gallup suggests that employees develop better relationships with their managers and are more likely to improve and feel energized at work when their bosses focus on their strengths. When strengths are brought to the foreground, the employee's focus shifts from worrying about what others think they should be to becoming the best version of who they truly are.

It can be incredibly empowering to figure out what we're good at. We are stuck in our own heads 24/7, but we don't often *see* ourselves or take the time to examine our strengths. In a study I conducted with Julia Lee of the University of Michigan, Dan Cable of London Business School, and Brad Staats of the University of North Carolina, Chapel Hill, participants provided us with contact information for various people in their professional and personal networks, including family members, friends, and coworkers. We reached out to the people the participants had listed and asked them to write a story about a time when they had witnessed the participant at his or her best and to share it with us. Each participant received five to ten stories that were overwhelmingly and often unexpectedly positive. Consider this narrative about a boss, with names changed for privacy reasons: "Laura has good forethought for business and does anything and everything she can to help keep us employed. In 2012, when Hurricane Sandy hit the East Coast, here in Florida we did not really think much of it. But Laura was obviously worried that it would impact her business, because a lot of our accounts receivables are in the NYC/New Jersey areas. She ended up borrowing from her retirement savings to keep the business going. I even suggested that maybe she could let the couple of part-timers go, but she responded that the people there always gave their best, so she wouldn't want to do anything less for them. It took about six months to get things back on track, but we all managed to keep our jobs thanks to Laura."

We gave half of our participants the narratives about them and asked them to read through them and identify the strengths the stories highlighted. We then divided participants into teams and had them engage in tasks that would allow us to measure their performance. Those who had read about their strengths before the exercise were less concerned about being socially accepted by their team members, and, as a result, their teams exchanged more information and achieved higher performance. This is the power of self-reflection: It instills the confidence we need to accomplish our goals.

Back in 2011, the Indian IT company Wipro was experiencing some tough issues in its business-process-outsourcing division. The company was spending a lot of money training people, only to see them leave within two months. To understand why, my colleagues Dan Cable, Brad Staats, and I talked to the employees. Workers told us that the organization was asking them to strip away their identities and not allowing them to play to their strengths. So we conducted a field experiment designed to encourage self-reflection and measure its effects. We had some of Wipro's incoming employees go through a new onboarding process where we asked them to spend a designated half-hour thinking about what was unique about them, what their strengths were, and how they could bring out more of themselves authentically at work. Seven months later, these employees had found ways to tailor their jobs to their strengths—for example, they used their own judgment and words when answering customer calls instead of strictly following the firm's script. They were more committed to their jobs, performed at higher levels, and were more likely to still be at Wipro—all thanks to a half-hour reflection exercise. In another study at the company, we asked a group of employees who were going through training to spend their last fifteen minutes at the office each day reflecting, in writing, on the lessons they had learned that day. Over the course of a month, reflection increased performance on the final training test by an average of 23 percent.

Self-reflection can have significant effects over time. When Rachael Chong was working as a young investment banker, she participated in a volunteer opportunity with a group of other bankers in which they all helped to build a house in the Bronx. One day, as Chong, who is five foot two, was slowly hauling lumber across the construction yard, she realized that this task was not exactly making the best use of her strengths or of those of the other bankers. Why, she wondered, are bankers building houses when they could be using their unique skills to build financial models for nonprofits that desperately need that type of help? Fired up, she spent several months looking for an alternative way to volunteer her skills, but came up empty. A year later, Chong moved to Bangladesh to help launch the U.S. affiliate of BRAC (Building Resources Across Communities), one of the largest nonprofit organizations in the world. Eleven college students had come along to serve as BRAC volunteers. The students learned about microfinance and worked on projects pro bono. More important, they developed a deep, lasting appreciation for helping others. By watching the students, Chong realized that "a good experience opens a mind to possibilities of how much you can achieve as an individual," she told me when I interviewed her. "When you volunteer, you may think, am I really making a dent in big problems? A good volunteer experience would lead you to feel—yes!" Chong started thinking that volunteering could be an activity that empowered people, inspiring them to do more. For this to happen, they would have to be involved in activities that energized them, work they believed they were good at.

In time, Chong founded Catchafire, a firm that connects professionals who want to donate their skills with nonprofit and social enterprises that need help. She borrowed the name from a Bob Marley album. Songs like "Stir It Up," Chong says, provide a nice parallel to what volunteering should be about. "It's about finding fire in yourself," she says. Volunteering, in her mind, should help people find their spark and make the best use of their passion.

"I SAW THE ANGEL IN THE MARBLE, AND I CARVED UNTIL I SET HIM FREE." THIS IS how Michelangelo Buonarroti, the legendary artist behind the Pietà in Rome and the David in Florence, described the process of sculpting in a 1547 letter to famed Italian humanist Benedetto Varchi. For Michelangelo, sculpture was a process in which the artist allows an ideal figure to be released from the block of stone in which it slumbers. All of us possess such ideal forms within ourselves—our signature strengths. Our task is to find ways to sculpt work and life to bring out our uniqueness.

Every day, we have opportunities to be "naked" in front of our colleagues, to make ourselves vulnerable, and to be more open about discussing our mistakes. We can also make time to reflect on what our signature strengths may be so that we can make use of them more often. There is no need to wait for a nudge from the boss. We can start the process ourselves. But leaders have an important role to play.

Mellody Hobson is the president of Ariel Investments, a Chicago-based money management firm. When she first joined the company right after graduating from college, at twenty-two, she was given license to be herself. As she told me, "I received precious and unforgettable advice on my first day at work from Ariel's founder and CEO John W. Rogers Jr. He said to me, 'You are going to be in rooms with people who make a lot of money and have big titles. But it does not mean your ideas are not as good or even better. I want to hear your ideas. It is incumbent on you to speak up.'" Hobson has told that story many, many times since then because to hear it is a gift, she believes. Last year, in the process of hiring a person who is now part of the company's research team, Hobson told the candidate she expected her "to be a source of spark in the conversation and a source of difference to really push us, and to say the uncomfortable thing." If you want to see this type of attitude in the organization, Hobson believes, you can't be shy about letting people know. When we play to our strengths and find ways to be authentic at work, we feel more committed to the organization we work for and experience more joy in our pursuits.

There's a video I like to show to my students that opens with a little boy strutting through a backyard, toting a ball and bat and wearing his baseball cap.

"I'm the greatest hitter in the world," he announces. Then he tosses the ball into the air. A swing—and a miss.

"Strike one!" he yells.

Undaunted, he picks up the ball and again says, "I'm the greatest hitter in the world!" He tosses the ball in the air, only to whiff again.

"Strike two!" he cries out.

The boy carefully examines the bat and the ball. He spits on his hands and rubs them together. He straightens his cap and says, once again, "I'm the greatest hitter in the world!" He throws the ball in the air. He swings. He misses.

"Strike three!"

He pauses, confused. Then he exclaims, "Wow! I'm the greatest pitcher in the world!" And he smiles. This is the smile of finding your strength.

7

THE SECRET OF STORY
THE TRANSFORMATIVE POWER OF ENGAGEMENT

To win in the marketplace you must first win in the workplace.
—DOUG CONANT

It's 6:36 a.m. I've boarded a plane at Boston's Logan Airport and am waiting anxiously in my seat. The pilot comes on to make an announcement, and I sigh with relief: The heavy snow that was expected has been downgraded to just a few flakes, so our flight is on schedule. I'm headed to Newark for a full day of teaching. As the final few passengers take their seats, a flight attendant begins the boarding announcement: "Ladies and gentlemen, the captain has turned on the fasten seat belt sign. If you haven't already done so, please stow your carry-on luggage underneath the seat in front of you or in an overhead bin."

She continues on, about emergency exits and smoke detectors, but my thoughts turn to the classes I'll be teaching. I am planning a group exercise for forty executives, and I wonder whether the directions are clear enough. The plane door closes and the flight attendant launches into another announcement: "Ladies and gentlemen, my name is Jennifer Capstone, and I'm your chief flight attendant. On behalf of the captain and the entire crew, welcome aboard United Airlines flight 343, nonstop service from Boston to Newark." As she tells us about the flight time, altitude, and speed, my mind again wanders. I scribble a few notes on the day's first teaching session. The flight attendants position themselves for their safety demonstration. I look up for a moment, but my gaze quickly returns to my notes. Soon, we're airborne. A few other announcements drift by during the flight, but none really register. It seems we've barely reached peak altitude when the plane starts to descend for landing.

I make it to my class with plenty of time to spare, and I begin with an exercise where I auction off a $100 bill to my students. I explain to them that both the highest and second-highest bidders will have to pay for their bids, but only the person with the highest bid will win the money. Bids start at $5, and go up $5 at a time. I don't allow them to talk to one another, and I ask them to just shout out their bids. As I start the auction, many students raise their hands when they want in. The price of the bids is fast increasing, and when we get close to $100, just two of the executives keep on bidding: They seem to realize that the lower bidder will be stuck having to pay, so neither is willing to drop out. They end up bidding well over $100 for that $100 bill. The highest bid? $360! (The second highest was $355.) This turns out to be a good way to begin a discussion about common errors that affect our decision-making. The auction, in fact, shows the students that our decisions are often irrational. In the end, I don't pocket the money I made. I give it back to the group so they can buy themselves some drinks after class. I am not cruel.

At 5:00 p.m., I'm sitting on my return flight to Boston. "Ladies and gentlemen, the captain has turned on the fasten seat belt sign . . ."

From the time they are hired, flight attendants learn a variety of procedures that they must follow to the letter. They are trained to deal with everything from medical emergencies to hostile passengers, and they know how to use every piece of emergency equipment on the plane, from the first-aid kit to the life rafts to the fire extinguishers. These measures are vital to the safety of everybody on board. And it is certainly helpful to know how to access and use the oxygen mask in case of an emergency, or to be reminded to turn off electronic devices that could interfere with the flight. But all of this safety information rarely registers with me when I am on a plane, as I'm sure is the case with most passengers. As a customer, then, I'm *less* safe when I tune out during these announcements than I would be if they weren't so scripted and I was actually listening.

And imagine what these announcements are like for the flight attendants. Repeating the same exact words on every flight, using the same exact hand movements, they show a group of strangers how to fasten their seat belts and the right way to put on a life jacket. Almost mindlessly, they point to each of the exits and remind passengers not to smoke in the lavatories. And they can probably tell from the faces of those onboard that their words and gestures are not capturing anyone's attention. With so much of their job scripted, it's bound to get both boring and frustrating.

The quandary of the flight attendant is a familiar one, faced by workers in every kind of job. Most people don't show up for their first day at a new job feeling unmotivated, frustrated, and uninspired. Rather, they are excited to get started, ready to meet new colleagues, hopeful they'll make a good impression. Yet the honeymoon period typically soon comes to an end. Data that my colleagues and I have collected from a wide range of industries reveals that people feel high levels of energy, commitment, and excitement in the first few days of their new jobs, followed by a noticeable drop within the first year. It doesn't matter whether it's a first job or how many alternatives they had to choose from; the decline seems inevitable. Excitement turns into boredom. The desire to bring one's best self to work slackens into a tendency to just go with the flow. After announcing that the captain has turned on the "fasten seat belt" sign for the hundredth time, the thrill is gone.

Since 1998, the Gallup Organization has been studying engagement at work by surveying millions of employees across industries and nations. According to data collected by Gallup in 2016, only 32 percent of U.S. employees feel involved in, enthusiastic about, and committed to their jobs. Almost 20 percent are actively *dis*engaged, the label Gallup uses to refer to employees who are not just unhappy at work, but are busy *acting out* their unhappiness. These are people who, every day, slowly undermine their organizations and the attitudes of their coworkers. The results of a study led by consulting firm Towers-Watson portrayed an even bleaker situation. Only about 15 percent of employees, according to the findings of their research, are fully engaged; 65 to 70 percent of employees are moderately engaged; and 15 percent are totally disengaged. The global average is even worse, according to Gallup's 2016 survey: Across 142 countries, only 13 percent of workers feel engaged with their work.

Disengagement is expensive. It hinders commitment, retention, productivity, and innovation. Engaged employees, Gallup finds, perform 20 percent better than their disengaged counterparts, and they are three times more creative. Gallup estimates that disengagement costs the American economy up to $550 billion per year in lost productivity. Companies with a highly engaged workforce—Google, say, or Recreational Equipment, Inc. (REI)— are 22 percent more profitable and 21 percent more productive. They also have 37 percent lower absenteeism, 41 percent fewer defects, 48 percent fewer safety incidents, and lower turnover (25 percent lower in high-turnover organizations and 65 percent lower in low-turnover companies). Particularly alarming is that the problem increases with growth. According to Gallup, employees in large companies are less engaged than those in smaller ones.

Disengagement isn't just rampant at work. In a survey of nearly one million American K–12 students, Gallup found that only half considered themselves "engaged," while 29 percent answered "not engaged" and 21 percent "actively disengaged." The same problem plagues our personal lives. I recently conducted a survey of more than a thousand people in the United States who reported being in a romantic or close relationship and found that *over 80 percent* felt the relationship was, more often than not, a cause for worry and frustration rather than energy and joy. We are facing a crisis of engagement in our lives.

"Can I pretend to have your attention for just a few moments?" That's Marty Cobb, a Texas-based Southwest Airlines flight attendant, launching into the safety announcement during a 2014 flight to Salt Lake City. "My ex-husband, my new boyfriend, and their divorce attorney are going to show you the safety features of the Boeing 737 800 series," Cobb continues.

"It's been a long day for me. To properly fasten your seat belts, slide the flap into the buckle; to release, lift up the buckle. Position your seat belt tight and low across your hips, just like my grandmother wears her support bra."

"If you're traveling with small children, we're sorry," Cobb continues. "If you're traveling with more than one child, pick out the one you think might have the most earning potential down the road."

Passengers on the flight are giggling, which means they are paying attention. Cobb ends the announcement with a spin on the customary invitation: "If there's anything at all we can do to make your flight more enjoyable, please tell us . . . just as soon as we land in Salt Lake City. And if there's anything you can do to make our flight more enjoyable, we'll tell you immediately. We're not shy at Southwest."

Cobb is not the only Southwest flight attendant who diverges from the standard announcements. David Holmes, a former computer programmer and personal trainer, became known as the "rapping flight attendant" after his performance on a 2009 Southwest flight to Las Vegas went viral. (Sample rhyme: "We won't take your cash. You gotta pay with plastic. If you have a coupon then that's fantastic.") And Southwest flight attendant Jack Sullivan is known for impersonating Elvis, complete with sunglasses and scarves.

When Colleen Barrett served as Southwest's executive vice president from 1990 to 2001, one of her priorities was to encourage workers to be themselves on the job. Unlike other airline executives, she didn't require employees to carefully follow scripts, as long as they covered all the legally required information. To this day, Southwest encourages employees to welcome and entertain passengers in their own authentic ways. The company's recruiting and hiring practices were created based on the belief that authenticity and humor help people thrive during times of change, stay creative even when under pressure, work with greater energy, and remain healthy in the process. This philosophy has helped the company achieve high passenger volume, profitability, and customer satisfaction. Southwest has low turnover and a near-perfect safety record. "We have always thought that your avocation can be your vocation, so that you don't have to do any acting in your life when you leave home to go to work," Barrett has said.

What Southwest has created is a workplace where engagement is high. In a context in which routine can trap employees in mindless repetition, Southwest leadership respects human nature and allows employees to decide how to best do their work, so long as what they do is aligned with the company's main objective: safety for everyone. With this approach, it's not just the employees who stay engaged—the passengers do, too. Engagement can do great things for employees, leaders, and organizations. When we are committed to the organization and energized by our work, productivity is supercharged, ideas are more creative, relationships are stronger, the organization is more successful, and customers are more likely to be satisfied with the company's products and services. I still smile when I think about a comment I once heard from a Southwest flight attendant after a landing: "As you exit the plane, please make sure to gather all of your belongings. Anything left behind will be distributed evenly among the flight attendants. Please do not leave children or spouses."

WE ALL DELIGHT IN BEING ENGAGED. IT'S SO MUCH BETTER TO START A FLIGHT WITH a rap than it is to hear the same tedious announcement we've been subjected to many times before. One of the funny things about human nature, though, is that we tend to succumb to habits, like conformity, that aren't good for us. We are social animals, with a strong desire to be accepted by others, and conformity gives us comfort. But it also reduces our level of engagement, whether in our jobs or in our relationships. Except for the most rebellious among us, we have a strong preference for the status quo. In an organization, this preference can lead to various standard practices that may play an important role in day-to-day operations but that can also leave us feeling stuck, and make everyone around us feel stuck.

The annals of business are full of tales of companies that struggled to keep their workforce motivated in the long term and ended up with employees who were either frustrated or checked out. When Doug Conant became president and CEO of Campbell's Soup Company in 2001, he arrived at corporate headquarters in Camden to find that the parking lots were surrounded by barbed wire, the walls needed a paint job, and the floors needed new carpets. Campbell's had been struggling financially, and the problems had taken a toll on everyone. Employees described headquarters to Conant as a "prison." It had been clear that the company was in serious trouble since the end of the 1990s, when senior management had raised prices, and sales began falling as a result. By 2001,

Campbell's share price had sunk to half of the high it had reached in November 1998. To correct the error made by raising prices, Campbell's management cut costs, slashing advertising spending and laying off about four hundred employees. As Conant noted, "They had to cut costs to the point where they were literally taking the chicken out of chicken noodle soup, and the product was no longer competitive." The downward spiral continued.

The pride that employees had once taken in working for Campbell's also suffered. The company started in 1869 and grew steadily over the years. By the early 1970s, it had gone international and become one of the largest food companies in the world. In the United States, the Campbell's brand turned iconic, as Andy Warhol signaled with his pop-art soup cans. Many Americans could hum the "Mm, Mm, Good!" advertising jingle. A bowl of Campbell's Tomato Soup (one of the firm's best-selling products) and a grilled cheese sandwich had become quintessential comfort food, almost as American as baseball and apple pie.

Soon after arriving, Conant announced that his top priority was to increase employee engagement. Many company executives scoffed, believing that Campbell's faced more pressing issues. Rather than investing in its people, some doubters said, the company would be better off continuing to cut costs. Other critics believed the company had to invest in its product portfolio and marketing efforts. But, in Conant's words, the firm had "a very toxic culture." The management system had gone off the rails, and employee morale was abysmal. To turn around the company's prospects, Conant believed he needed to start with its twenty thousand employees.

The problems Conant saw in the company's workforce were confirmed by the results of a survey he asked Gallup to conduct in 2002. The goal was to assess the level of personal commitment employees felt toward the company and its goals. The survey results were dismal, among the worst Gallup had ever seen in Fortune 500 companies. More than 60 percent of Campbell's employees reported they were not engaged in their work, and over 10 percent reported that they were actively disengaged—that is, they were so unhappy at work that they were actively undermining the efforts of the few people who were actually performing. As for those in top management positions, over 40 percent operated in a state of being "tuned out," with little interest in contributing to the company's work and goals.

To take action, Conant first got moving—literally. He wore a pedometer on his belt and put on a pair of walking shoes, whether at the company's New Jersey headquarters or at production plants in Europe and Asia. He set the goal of logging ten thousand steps each day and having meaningful interactions with as many employees as possible. Conant also introduced a series of meetings he called "One-Over-Ones," so named to convey a sense that everyone was in it together. These meetings began with a regular review between an employee and his or her manager. Then the employee and manager would be invited in to meet with Conant and the head of human resources. The conversation was purposely kept informal and candid. Both the manager and their direct report could ask questions, discuss whatever issues were on their minds, and propose ideas—in fact, they were encouraged to do so. The meetings gave managers and employees the opportunity to approach the CEO with any question or idea. By including four people rather than the usual two that are present in a performance review, One-Over-Ones extended the reach of the discussion. Conant and the head of HR got access to more information than they would have by only talking to their direct reports. And, at the same time, the CEO's vision made its way down throughout the company.

These two initiatives—Conant's walks and the One-Over-Ones conversations—showed employees that they were truly valued. Conant also started sending out personalized notes, up to twenty per day, thanking employees for their successes and specific contributions. He spent about an hour each day writing these notes by hand. A staffer helped him find success stories he could thank employees for at all levels of Campbell's. Why handwritten notes? Because more than half of the workforce didn't use a computer. In his ten years with the company, Conant sent more than thirty thousand handwritten thank-yous, which recipients hung in their offices or above their desks.

Conant had the razor wire surrounding the building removed and the weeds and overgrowth cleared. He had estate-fencing installed, and the curbs painted. Then he started to fix the inside of the building: updates to the carpet, décor, and paint. Conant wanted to give employees visible signs of a turnaround, a better future for themselves and for the organization. To reinvigorate employees, Conant believed, the company needed to eliminate barriers, whether razor wire or departmental silos, that held back ideas and conversation. As a result of Conant's changes, employees were happier. Performance and retention started to improve. Engagement started to rise. And now that employees were more fired up for the workday, they offered ideas that improved product quality and led to innovations, like easy-to-open pop-top cans and new shelving systems for supermarkets that would help customers find the soup they wanted.

At the management level, Conant was ruthless. According to Gallup's research over the years, managers are key to building and maintaining employee engagement. When people quit, in fact, they're not quitting their jobs, they're quitting their bosses: Managers account for at least 70 percent of the variance in employee engagement. In Conant's first three years, he pushed out over 300 of the company's top 350 leaders. To replace those who had been fired, he promoted about 150 people from within, and for the rest, he brought in high-performance leaders from other companies. By 2009, Campbell's was doing much better than the S&P Food Group and the S&P 500. Between 2001 and 2011, the company's total sales and revenue grew about 24 percent. The revenues of Standard & Poor's 500 firms declined nearly 10 percent, on average, in the same period.

Both analysts on Wall Street and investors gave Conant full credit for Campbell's turnaround. From a psychological perspective, Conant became a model of how to inspire employees and release their talents by bringing to the company three ingredients of employee engagement: dedication, absorption, and vigor. In his walkabouts and in the One-Over-Ones, the CEO made employees feel that their work and contributions to the organization were valued. It was clear that he cared about their development and their satisfaction.

When we feel that the work we do matters, our dedication deepens. The changes Conant made to the physical environment removed distractions so that employees could focus on their jobs. When our attention is focused, we reach a state of absorption and time passes quickly. The handwritten notes also likely made a difference. When we receive expressions of gratitude, my research shows, we are more likely to persist when the road gets tough. As energy and mental resilience increase, we experience vigor. Bring together dedication, absorption, and vigor, and employees are highly engaged. When Gallup surveyed Campbell's employees in 2009, the results were quite different than they had been in 2002: 68 percent said they were actively engaged by their work, and only 3 percent reported being actively disengaged. Conant proved that employee engagement had been the main problem at Campbell's and the key to a turnaround.

Think about the times when you've most felt engaged. Maybe you were attending a concert and found your mind bouncing with creative ideas, captivated by the music. Perhaps you sat down at your desk and started writing after attending an inspiring lecture. Maybe you struck up a conversation with a stranger on the subway and felt like you could have talked for days. When we are engaged, our happiness, our outside-the-box thinking, and our productivity all increase, and the organizations we work for benefit as well. In one field study my colleagues and I conducted at Morning Star, the tomato-processing company in California, we asked harvesters to watch a short video in which a colleague told them about the positive impact their work had in the factory. Then we surveyed Morning Star employees, and those who had seen the video indicated feeling more engaged at work than those who hadn't seen it. Their productivity was also higher: They achieved a 7 percent increase per hour in tons of tomatoes harvested in the weeks after watching the video. In a follow-up study, a similar message increased not only participants' engagement and performance, but also their creativity.

For organizations, lack of employee engagement negatively affects quality, productivity, customer satisfaction, and financial outcomes. According to a study by Dale Carnegie Training, for instance, billions of dollars are lost each year to employee turnover, and companies with engaged employees outperform those with employees who report lack of engagement by over 200 percent. Lack of employee engagement is linked to higher healthcare costs and lost productivity, according to Gallup.

The positive effects of being engaged extend beyond the workplace. College students who report feeling engaged have been shown to be more likely to pass their exams. When students are energized by what they are learning, they perform better academically. In close relationships, engagement and passion lead to longer commitments, greater happiness and satisfaction, and a stronger willingness to work together in the face of adversity. In parenting, engagement leads to greater trust between parents and children, greater commitment to the family, and more joy in family dynamics.

In this book, I've introduced you to the talents that we see, again and again, in rebels: novelty, curiosity, perspective, diversity, and authenticity. What is fascinating, though, is what binds all these "talents" together: They are all paths to engagement. The talent for novelty allows us to fight the boredom that comes with routines and traditions. The talent for curiosity allows us to combat the tendency to stick with the status quo. The talent for perspective allows us to rebel against our narrow focus when we approach problems or decisions, which usually includes only one view—our own. The talent for diversity allows us to defy the stereotypes that are so ingrained in human nature. The talent for authenticity allows us to be honest about our preferences, emotions, and beliefs.

At their core, rebels are *engaged*. They have abundant energy and mental resilience, they invest in their work and in their personal relationships, and they persist even when the road gets tough. They feel inspired by and passionate about what they do and who they know—and they inspire those around them. Thanks to their engagement, rebels are successful. And yet, as individuals and members of organizations, we struggle to understand how to boost engagement. Doug Conant arrived at a failing soup company and successfully turned it around by walking the floors, repainting the walls, having honest conversations with his staff, and saying thank you again and again. Yet this is not the only way of achieving engagement and reaping its many benefits.

A GREEN-SKINNED ALIEN WITH THREE EYES, THREE-FINGERED HANDS, AND AN OB-long head with pointy ears and a single, club-tipped antenna stared up at me from the ID badge I'd been given to wear for the day. My name appeared on the badge alongside a warning: "A stranger from the outside!" It was a sunny spring day in 2017 in Emeryville, California, north of the Bay Area, and I was at Pixar Animation Studios, a large complex with baseball and soccer fields, lush gardens, a 600-seat amphitheater, tennis courts, and a swimming pool. At the heart of the campus is the two-story Steve Jobs Building:

218,000 square feet of space for hundreds of people to work, eat, and play. After being ousted from Apple in 1985, Jobs bought Pixar (which was called Graphics Group at the time) from Lucasfilm and remained the firm's largest shareholder and CEO until Disney acquired the company in 2006. In front of the Jobs building stands a statue of the company's mascot, Luxo Jr., a desk lamp with human emotions from Pixar's first short film, created in 1986.

Jobs oversaw the construction of the building from the smallest details to the big picture. It was Jobs who came up with the idea of having a very large atrium that every Pixar employee would have to pass through each day, enabling random encounters and conversations. The atrium, built with a mixture of steel and brick for an industrial feel, has lots of natural light, life-sized versions of Pixar characters, and a display case for the company's multiple Oscars, Golden Globes, and Annie Awards. The building's décor changes regularly to feature whatever Pixar film is coming out that year and to showcase off-screen employee artwork. The Jobs building also houses Pixar's main restaurant, Café Luxo, which offers wood-fire pizza, a burrito bar, daily specials, and free fountain drinks. The building also has a mailroom, a free cereal bar, a gift shop, and plenty of lounging areas. The only bathrooms on the first floor of the building are in the atrium—a compromise from Jobs, who reportedly suggested at one point that the atrium's floor have the only bathrooms for the whole main building. Having only one set of restrooms creates more opportunities for people to run into one another, ask questions, and exchange ideas.

In 2016, I had become interested in visiting Pixar after meeting Ed Catmull, a cofounder and the company's president. Pixar has had an unprecedented run of highly acclaimed, successful movies. Yet, as Catmull explained to me when we first met, Pixar probably has about the same failure rate as other studios. The difference, in his mind, is that the failed Pixar films were not released. He listed other Pixar films that had drastically changed over time. In *Rata-*

touille, for instance, only a single line from the initial script made it into the final version of the film. In its first version, *Up* was about a floating castle in the sky. Catmull described the revisions that took place on the subsequent incarnations of the film: "The only thing left was the bird and the word 'up.' In the next version, there was a house that floated up and landed on a lost Russian dirigible. In the next version, the bird laid eggs that conferred long life." No Pixar movie ever starts out as well written, funny, and heartfelt as what we see in theaters. Each one goes through all sorts of changes along the way. Rather than calling these digressions "failures," Catmull describes them as "just things that we tried."

Along with animated filmmaking, Pixar has mastered the art of engagement. The company's movies appeal to audiences of all ages, from children to adults. A child may laugh at the unexpected roles that characters take on, like toys that talk, while an adult may be impressed by the ability of the writers to cover complex topics with humor or by the sheer ingenuity of it all. Pixar movies touch a wide audience, captivating viewers from beginning to end. What is it about Pixar's storytelling that keeps everyone so engaged? And what might the rest of us learn?

The studio is one of the most successful in the world, with fifteen Academy Awards and an average international gross of over $600 million per film. Moreover, unconventional plots and ideas are in the company's DNA. The Pixar universe includes a world of talking cars (*Cars*), an elderly man whose house floats to South America thanks to thousands of balloons (*Up*), a rat who wants to be a chef (*Ratatouille*), and the emotions residing in a young girl's brain (*Inside Out*). I watched every single Pixar movie again before visiting the campus and was glued to my seat, at times laughing out loud. I was struck by how fully *transporting* the stories are.

But even the best storytellers may not get engagement right on the first try. Meet Pete Docter, the director of *Monsters, Inc.*, *Up*, and *Inside Out*. Docter, who started working at Pixar in 1989 when he was twenty-one, the day after he graduated from college, comes across as a cartoon character himself. He's impossibly tall, with a reed-thin torso, bendy arms, and eyes full of wonder. His colleagues once compared his narrow head to a pencil eraser. After starting at Pixar with limited responsibilities, Docter soon began to take on larger roles in writing, animation, sound recording, and music. As one of the three key screenwriters behind the concept of *Toy Story*, he created Buzz Lightyear partially in his own image, pausing to check the mirror while he drew the character.

Next he was charged with directing *Monsters, Inc.* Not only would this be his directorial debut, but he would be only the second person to direct a Pixar film after Pixar cofounder and chief creative officer John Lasseter had helmed the first three. *Monsters, Inc.* is set in a factory run by two monsters, James P. (Sulley) Sullivan and Mike Wazowski, whose work involves generating the screams of frightened children, which are needed to power the monster universe. With his blue fur, large frame, and leonine roar, Sulley (voiced by John Goodman) comes from a generation of kidscarers. His best friend and coach, Mike (voiced by Billy Crystal), is a lime-green, potato-shaped monster with one all-seeing eye. Monsters who scare kids for a living, Docter thought, was a promising hook for engaging an audience. But at an early test screening, viewers began checking their watches about fifteen minutes into the movie. Disaster.

This was a difficult time for Docter, personally. For years, he had been single-mindedly devoted to Pixar. But he had recently become a father and found himself focusing on something other than work. He felt a great emotional connection to his son, Nick, the little creature who had entered his life, and wanted to make sure he took good care of him. As he struggled to figure out how to fix his movie, Docter had a key insight: Sulley, too, needed someone to care for. Sulley was solely focused on his career, and the audience was having trouble empathizing with him.

Revising the story, Docter introduced Boo, a pig-tailed two-year-old girl with big brown eyes and dark brown hair, whom Sulley saves from the clutches of his and Mike's biggest rival, Randall. Over the course of the (revised) movie, Sulley and Boo grow ever closer as Sulley and Mike help her out of one tight spot after another, all while trying to evade Randall. At one point in the movie, Boo runs away and is captured by Randall, who tries to use her in an experiment to forcibly extract screams for the growing energy crisis. But Sulley comes to the rescue. As he transforms from being "all work and no play" to caring for Boo, Sulley becomes a character audiences can relate to.

The most engaging stories have this type of deep emotional core. As a main character faces challenges, he reacts to them in authentic ways and exposes his vulnerabilities. The character might not be totally sympathetic, but if his reactions and emotions seem real, the audience will begin to care deeply about what happens to him, almost as if his story is their own. "The main character is like a surrogate for you, the audience member," Docter told me. "They're learning and discovering information at the same time you are, so that by the time the film ends, you feel like you've gone on the same emotional journey the character has." As Docter sees it, Sulley's emotional connection to Boo saved the movie, both at the box office and in the eyes of critics.

This same idea—emotional connection—can be used to spark engagement at work. At Campbell's, Conant created an emotional connection with his employees by getting to know them and celebrating their contributions. Or consider the analytics software giant SAS, whose founder and CEO, Jim Goodnight, promotes emotional engagement by giving workers plenty of freedom. When people are free to make choices at work, they feel more authentic and in control, my research finds. Employees often welcome this sense of freedom as a true gift, as it makes them look at their relationship with the organization as emotional rather than just transactional. At SAS, it's not uncommon to see employees at the company gym long after the traditional lunch hour—or to see Goodnight himself getting a haircut on campus in the middle of the afternoon.

Stories, as Pixar understands them, become memorable in a way that resonates with people when they appeal to some fundamental truth about human nature—even if monsters, clownfish, robots, or cars are standing in for humans. Think back to a recent movie or novel that moved you. What triggered your emotions? The magic typically happens when we see a character's vulnerabilities or imperfections. When a story feels authentic, we connect. Similarly, in organizations, we feel engaged when we are encouraged to be authentic by leaders who exhibit the same freedom. Organizations can encourage employees to bring more of themselves to work in small and big ways. At Pixar, for example, animators can decorate their office space however they like. The result? One animator's space is decorated like a tiki cabin. Another has a second floor built on top of the first. And several cubicle-like spaces have been converted into tiny duplex houses. The whimsical decorating is actually beside the point. It's what it says about the people who work there, the freedom they feel, and the relationships—real, emotional relationships—they build.

PIXAR PRESIDENT AND COFOUNDER ED CATMULL HAS A LARGE, BRIGHT WORKSPACE on the second floor of the Steve Jobs building. Windows overlook green lawns, and toy versions of characters from my favorite Pixar movies fill the shelves of his office. When we met, Catmull sat on a couch in his office across from me, dressed in a colorful short-sleeved shirt and jeans. He told me that, despite all the signs of comfort and whimsy I saw around me, Pixar had experienced real trouble. In 2013, seven years after being acquired by Disney, the studio had gone through some tough times. Film budgets were rising, the DVD market was shrinking, and production costs were soaring. Pixar management was also increasingly feeling that a key aspect of the company culture—employees' willingness to speak their minds freely—was not what it used to be.

"A hallmark of a healthy creative culture is that its people feel free to share ideas, opinions, and criticisms," Catmull said. He went on to note that when a creative group draws on unvarnished perspectives of all its members and the collective knowledge, decision-making stands to benefit. Candor is key to effective collaboration, says Catmull. "Lack of candor leads to dysfunctional environments," he told me. This belief has been at the core of Pixar's culture since the company was founded. At its inception, Pixar formed a group called the "Braintrust," which consisted of four or five Pixar creative leaders who oversee development on all movies, meeting every few months to assess progress and challenges. Catmull described the Braintrust in simple terms: "Put smart, passionate people in a room together, charge them with identifying and solving problems, and encourage them to be candid." The whole idea behind the Braintrust is that members should speak freely, arguing without fear of conflict, with the interests of the company in mind. The group has no authority, so when members evaluate a movie in production, the director can decide whether or not to follow any of their specific suggestions.

In the 2010s, Pixar was expanding and growing, so it hired more and more people. The new recruits were excited, sure, but the talent in the room was usually pretty intimidating and left them nervous about sharing their own ideas. Executives decided to try something bold to improve the situation. In early 2013, Catmull and a few other managers began planning a special day, Notes Day, during which Pixar would shut down to elicit honest feedback from its employees. Notes Day was an expansion of the spirit of the Braintrust. Catmull and other executives at Pixar wanted to bring the same style of safe sharing to the entire organization. For Notes Day, employees were invited to brainstorm ways to improve the company, drawing on topics and problems they themselves had identified. So that employees would feel comfortable offering candid feedback, managers were excluded from Notes Day.

Notes Day was inspired by a widespread practice among studios of screening in-progress films for executives, who offer written suggestions and criticisms, or "notes." At most studios, directors are generally encouraged, if not required, to follow the direction of these notes. But Pixar decided to handle notes differently. All employees are invited to screenings at the very early stages of a film, long before a story line is finalized, and everyone is welcome to give notes. Moreover, directors do not have to use the notes they receive; the notes are merely suggestions. Pixar's version of the practice is more like crowdsourcing.

Notes Day applied the same principles to the overall practices of the company, as opposed to a specific film. One initial goal of Notes Day was to solicit ideas from employees on how to lower costs by 10 percent. Pixar executives asked employees to prepare themselves for Notes Day by imagining they'd been transported four years into the future and to answer the following questions: "The year is 2017. Both of this year's films were completed well under budget. What innovations helped these productions meet their budget goals? What are some of the specific things we did differently?" Questions were sent out to all employees, generating over four thousand responses on more than one thousand unique topics, such as reducing implicit gender bias in Pixar films, shortening production time, and improving the workplace.

Out of the thousands of responses, executives chose 106 issues for employees to discuss in separate sessions. The sessions were spread across three buildings on Pixar's main campus, and employees could choose for themselves which sessions to attend. Trained internal facilitators led each session, which culminated with specific proposals, brainstorms, or best practices. The group also assigned certain members to be their "idea advocates"—those who would help advance their suggestions. After identifying their recommendation, employees were treated to hot dogs and beer. Out of the 106 topics, the company immediately started working on 21. Some were small changes, like implementing a faster, more secure way of delivering film cuts to directors. But even the smallest changes added up to something bigger. "They were changing Pixar—meaningfully and for the better," Catmull said. And improving efficiency may not have been the most notable benefit. "I believe the biggest payoff of Notes Day was that we made it safer for people to say what they thought," Catmull writes in his book *Creativity, Inc.* "Notes Day made it OK to disagree."

In the years that followed, Pixar saw the benefits of its Notes Day candor. It released two successful films in 2015, *Inside Out* and *The Good Dinosaur*, then *Finding Dory* in 2016, followed by *Cars 3* and *Coco* in 2017. *Inside Out* was one of Pixar's most successful movies, with an adjusted net profit of about $689 million and the best opening weekend of all time for a film using an original idea rather than existing characters.

The company, Catmull told me, has always recognized that conflict is a key aspect of creativity. With a smile, Catmull told me a story about the late Steve Jobs, Pixar's chairman—a story that Catmull also recounts in detail in his book, *Creativity, Inc.* Catmull once asked Jobs what happened when people working with him disagreed with his point of view. Jobs's answer was simple: "I just explain it to them until they understand." Though their relationship was no different in nature, Catmull developed a clever solution to voice his opinions. In the twenty-six years they worked together, Catmull told me that he and Jobs never had an angry argument, but they did disagree quite often. "I would say something," he told me, and Jobs would "immediately shoot it down because he could think faster than I could." Catmull would then wait about a week or so and reach out to Jobs. "I'd call and give my counterargument, and he'd shoot it down again." Catmull would wait another week and call again. "Sometimes this would go on for months," he told me. "In the end, [Jobs] would say, 'Oh I get it, you're right,' or I would realize he was right. And the rest of the time, we didn't reach consensus; he'd just let me do it my way and wouldn't say anything more about it."

Jobs had a reputation for being difficult and demanding, and no one would say he was an expert in conflict resolution. Catmull clearly had to work hard to make sure his boss heard his voice. But it's notable that neither Jobs nor Catmull took the disagreements personally or allowed them to create barriers to collaboration.

In the creative process, tension and conflict need to be embraced for good ideas to emerge. A sense of conflict triggers exploration of novel ideas. For instance, the sense of disorientation and conflict people experience when reading a short story that seems absurd has been shown to enhance their desire to learn novel information. People experiencing conflict have been found to generate more original solutions to difficult situations than individuals who are in a more cooperative mood. Similarly, when members of a team experience conflict, they tend to scrutinize and deeply explore alternatives, which leads them to novel insights. In my own research, I find that when people are asked to meet goals that appear to be at odds—for example, "create an original product cheaply"—their ideas are more innovative than when they have to meet only one of those goals.

When people disagree constructively, their ideas improve. At Ariel Investments, the Chicago money-management firm, constructive dissent is actively encouraged by assigning devil's advocates to meetings and other dialogues. The devil's advocate is charged with poking holes in the decision-making process. During the financial crisis of 2008 and 2009, the devil's advocate became a key feature of Ariel's research process. One person would follow a stock; another was instructed to argue the opposite. Each person tried to represent their opinion constructively while being open to debate. Mellody Hobson, the company's president, regularly opens team meetings with a reminder to those attending it: They don't have to be right; rather, they simply need to voice concerns and be willing to disagree to help the team make the right decisions.

Most of us fear conflict, and understandably so. Conflict stirs up negative emotions and makes us feel vulnerable. But when expressed constructively, conflict allows us to explore new possibilities, arrive at surprising solutions, and gain important insights into ourselves and others. Without conflict, there would be no Pixar movies. How could there be a *Finding Nemo* without Nemo getting lost? *Up* would lose its power if seventy-eight-year-old balloon salesman Carl Fredricksen, the main character, hadn't lost his wife and grown bitter. Insights and innovations seldom arise when we're feeling satisfied with the status quo. Rather, they come from the energy that's created when we crave change. In storytelling and organizations, as well as in our personal lives, conflict leads to engagement. Different perspectives work to heighten our attention.

Rebels embrace tension and conflict. "Ideas only become great," Catmull told me, "when they are challenged and tested." The right amount of conflict makes for a good story and a more rewarding life.

IN 1996, PIXAR STARTED WORKING ON THE SEQUEL TO *TOY STORY*, THE STUDIO'S first full-length picture. At the time, Pixar's second feature, *A Bug's Life*, was still in production. As Catmull recounts in a *Harvard Business Review* article on how Pixar encourages creativity, the company had enough technicians to mount a second project, but its proven creative leaders—those who succeeded with *Toy Story*—

were busy finishing their work on *A Bug's Life*. So a new creative team was put in charge, made up of people who had never run a film production.

The original concept for the sequel seemed solid. Woody, a cowboy doll, is excitedly anticipating a trip to Cowboy Camp. Finally, he'll have quality time alone with Andy, the boy who owns him. Woody is one of Andy's favorite toys. At the same time, Woody is worried about what will happen to the considerably less responsible toys in Andy's room while he's gone. But these worries are forgotten when Woody faces a major crisis: His arm is ripped, and the injury keeps him from going to Cowboy Camp. Another crisis soon follows: A toy collector kidnaps Woody and takes him to his apartment, where a new group of toys is introduced. Among them is a Cowgirl named Jessie, a horse named Bullseye, and a mint-quality doll named Stinky Pete. They explain to Woody that they are all toys based on *Woody's Roundup*, a TV show from the 1940s and 1950s. Now that Woody has joined them, the *Woody's Roundup* toys can all be sold to a museum in Japan, doomed to spend the rest of their lives separated from children by thick glass.

As part of the process of making an animated movie, storyboards are drawn early on, and these initial storyboards are then edited together with dialogue and music that is only temporary. These make up the "story reels," as they are called in the business, which are typically rough, but help illuminate problems that need to be solved in the film. Next come new versions of the reels, each typically improving on the previous one. But that was not the case for *Toy Story 2*. The initial idea was creative enough, but the reels were not getting better. By the time Pixar began animation, the reels were not where they needed to be. "Making matters worse," Catmull writes, "the directors and producers were not pulling together to rise to the challenge."

The problem was that the story was too predictable: It did not allow the audience to imagine what might happen next. At a key moment in the story, Woody faces an important decision: whether to leave his home to travel to Japan or attempt an escape from the collector's apartment and go back to Andy. As *Toy Story* fans well know, Woody and Andy have a deep connection—after all, Woody is Andy's favorite toy. This makes Woody's choice too predictable: Clearly, he'll want to go back home to be with Andy. When viewers can predict how the story will unfold, there's no drama, and they will disengage.

Pixar faced the challenge of introducing unpredictability—that is, making the audience come to the realization that Woody had a tough decision to make and it was unclear which option he would choose. But the team working on the movie was unable to come up with a solution to the challenge. Luckily, the team working on *A Bug's Life* finished up in time to take over the leadership driving the creative efforts for *Toy Story 2*. They were now on a very tight deadline, as the release date for the sequel could not be moved. Having eighteen months to work on the film would have been an aggressive schedule. At that point, only eight months were left for the job.

They created a scene called "Jessie's story" in which Jessie, a cowgirl doll, sings an emotional song to Woody to explain why she does not want to escape, but rather is willing to go to Japan. In the song called "When She Loved Me," Jessie reveals that she had been the favorite doll of a young girl, but once the girl grew up, she got rid of her. Jessie is convinced that losing someone you love is far worse than never having known that person in the first place. By going to Japan, she believes, Woody can avoid the heartache of being discarded by Andy when he grows up. And then there's the sad story of Stinky Pete. Left behind on a shelf with no chance to ever play with a child, he would also prefer to be in a museum. After all, at least he'd have a long life. Plus, as Jessie and Stinky Pete make clear, if Woody returns to Andy and his friends, he dooms the *Woody's Roundup* toys to life inside the collector's dark boxes, as he wouldn't ship them to Japan except as a set.

All of us can relate to the fears that grip Woody and his new friends. Suddenly, Woody's choice is no longer predictable, and the audience is engaged. When a Pixar movie starts, it's difficult to predict where it's going or how it will end. This is true of the most engaging stories in general—they are full of surprises. Docter gave me an example of creating surprises and unpredictability from *Toy Story*. At some point in the film, the creative team wanted to make use of the rocket strapped to Buzz Lightyear's back. But they wanted to do so in a way that was unexpected and surprising to the audience. Sid, a boy living next door to Andy's house, is rather sadistic, as he enjoys torturing toys. For instance, in one scene of the film, Sid puts a mask on as if he were a surgeon, and starts "operating" on his sister's doll. He ends up removing the doll's head and replacing it with that of another toy, and then he returns the mutilated doll to his sister, saying, "All better now." Once the surgery is over, Buzz observes, "I don't believe the man's ever been to medical school."

Buzz and Woody are trapped at Sid's, though, and have to devise an escape plan. By that point, Sid had taped Buzz to a fat firecracker, as he was planning to blow him up as he'd done with other toys. Earlier, Sid had tried to burn Woody on the grill, so Woody, being close to fire, had put a match in his holster. The storytellers thought the match could be used to light the firecracker on Buzz's back and bring Woody and Buzz "flying" back home. But they realized that the audience would see that coming. So instead, Woody lights the match, only to have it blown out by a passing car. All seems lost until Woody remembers the power of the sun. He uses the reflection of Buzz's helmet to light the fuse, and off they go.

Organizations can use unpredictability to improve engagement. The thank-you notes at Campbell's both surprised and motivated employees. As another example, an HBS study of the freelancer contracting site oDesk (now renamed Upwork) found that surprise incentives resulted in greater employee effort than higher pay. Harvard Business School researchers posted a data-entry job on oDesk that would take four hours. One of the postings offered $3 per hour for the job; the other offered $4 per hour. People with past data-entry experience were hired at either the $3 or $4 rate. But some of those who were initially told they'd be paid $3 were later told that the hiring company had a bigger budget than what they expected: "Therefore, we will pay you $4 per hour instead of $3 per hour." The group initially hired at $4 an hour worked no harder than those hired at $3. But those who received the surprise raise worked substantially harder than the other two groups, and among those with experience, their effort more than made up for the cost of the extra pay.

Surprises quench our thirst for the new and feed our curiosity, making us wonder what could happen next.

AT THE END OF MY DAY AT PIXAR, I WALKED PAST THE DESK WHERE I HAD PICKED up my badge and smiled at the Buzz Lightyear statue. The people who created him, and characters like him, had held my attention all day. I didn't want to leave. When we are engaged, time flies, and life and work take on a different, deeper meaning. The passion and engagement of the Pixar employees I'd observed that day reminded me of a story I once read about President Kennedy visiting NASA back in 1962. This was not long after his famous speech about going to the moon, at the height of the Cold War. He saw a janitor who he noticed was fully immersed in his work, sweeping the room the president was touring. "Hi. I am Jack Kennedy," the president said to him. "What are you doing here?"

Without any hesitation, the janitor gave him an answer: "I'm helping put a man on the moon, Mr. President."

8

BECOMING A REBEL LEADER
BLACKBEARD, "FLATNESS," AND THE
8 PRINCIPLES OF REBEL LEADERSHIP

Every man shall have an equal vote in affairs of the moment.
**—FIRST ARTICLE IN THE CONSTITUTION GOVERNING
THE PIRATE SHIP OF THE LEGENDARY BLACK BART**

In the deep heat of an early eighteenth-century summer, a crew of pirates was sailing off the Virginia coast when a lookout spotted a merchant ship to the south. The pirates launched their attack, rocking the merchant ship with a cascade of musket balls and grenades. When a wounded helmsman abandoned the merchant ship's wheel, the vessel swung around, drifting out of control. The pirates boarded, swinging axes and cutlasses. Behind them came the captain, his face clouded by smoke. Sashes holding daggers and pistols crisscrossed his large chest. Black ribbons flapped in his braided beard. The most feared pirate of his era had taken another ship.

Blackbeard was a notorious English raider who terrorized sailors around the West Indies and North America in the early 1700s. Sometimes he plotted sneak attacks; sometimes he relied on trickery, such as flying the home flag of the targeted ship before hoisting his own at the very last moment. After first targeting the man at the wheel, the pirates would snare their quarry with grappling hooks, pull it closer, and leap aboard. When the attack was over, they made hostages of the passengers and crew, and went through the cabins looking for gold, silver, and jewelry.

We usually associate pirates with violence, theft, and mayhem. That's all true, but their ships were also forward-looking in a number of surprising—and instructive—ways.

On the open sea, a merchant ship was a floating dictatorship. With the blessing of the vessel's owner, the captain treated crewmen as he saw fit, often harshly. Sailors were beaten, overworked, underpaid, and sometimes starved. Morale was low. Dissent was punished as mutiny. Pirates, by contrast, practiced a revolutionary form of democracy. To keep the ship running smoothly for months on end and to discourage revolt, pirates elected their captain democratically, limited his power, and guaranteed crew members a say in the ship's affairs. They also elected a quartermaster, who in addition to his primary duties—settling minor disputes and distributing supplies and money—served as a check against the captain's authority. Except in the heat of battle, when the captain took full command, no one man ruled the others. Captain and crew took a vote on everything: where to go, from whom to steal, how to steal it, where to go next, the fate of prisoners. With enough votes, the crew could demote or even dismiss the captain. They could maroon him on an island or dump him into the sea. And when the rules were disputed, it was a jury of crewmen who decided the matter, not the captain. As Bob Dylan sings in "Absolutely Sweet Marie": "To live outside the law, you must be honest."

Any pirate could lodge complaints or concerns without fear of reprisal, as crew members were protected by "articles"—essentially, a constitution drafted for each ship. The articles were democratically formed and required unanimous agreement before an expedition launched. They set the rights and duties of the crew, rules for the handling of disputes, and incentives and insurance payments to ensure bravery in battle. Pirate ships developed highly detailed schemes to compensate injured crewmen. That the crew elected and could depose their leaders stood in dramatic contrast to the tyrannical rule common on most merchant vessels. After capturing a ship, raiders would ask their prisoners if they might want to switch sides. Given the relative freedom and power that pirates enjoyed, and the spirit of antiauthoritarianism and self-governance characterizing their endeavors, it was not uncommon for merchant sailors to seize the opportunity. As they sailed the high seas, pirates picked up mariners from different races, religions, and ethnicities, which made for a cosmopolitan lot. The democratic nature of the ships and the pirates' defiance of custom meant blacks were welcomed as equals. Slavery was easy to find on the mainland, but at sea, black pirates had the right to vote, were entitled to an equal share of the booty, could bear arms, and were even elected captains of crews that were predominantly white. The goal was competent, hardworking deck hands: Skin color didn't matter. Pirates even raided slave plantations and ships for better crews. Blackbeard's ship was arguably more democratic than America was at the time. "[P]irates constructed [a] world in defiant contradistinction to the ways of the world they left behind," writes historian Marcus Rediker.

There's another surprising detail about Blackbeard, whose real name was Edward Teach. Yes, he braided his beard and tied the braids with black ribbons. Yes, he stuffed slow-burning rope under his hat to make himself look more menacing. Yes, he had a reputation as a ruthless cutthroat. But Blackbeard did not kill a single man during his career at sea. He captured other sailors but did not take their lives. The image he cultivated for himself and his crew was a brilliant bit of eighteenth-century marketing that won him glory and riches—and did not require the loss of lives.

BACK IN THE 1950S, THE SOCIAL PSYCHOLOGIST ROBERT FREED BALES RAN AN experiment in which he divided a cohort of college students into groups of three to seven members. He was interested in studying group interactions. The groups, which had no appointed leader, met for several hours to make decisions and solve assigned problems. The students didn't know one another, but they had something in common: They were all men in their sophomore year at Harvard. Despite the initial lack of group structure and the fact that the members were very much alike, Bales repeatedly found that a hierarchy developed smoothly and quickly in each group, often within minutes. It would arise from simple behaviors, such as how much people talked, which signaled status, influence, and good ideas. Bales's results suggest that even when members seem to be of equal footing, hierarchies based on status—the respect, influence, and prominence that members enjoy in the eyes of others—take shape.

Across the globe, groups and organizations rely on some form of social hierarchy to instill order and efficiency. In groups, leaders naturally emerge from interactions, and a few central people gather most of the status. Organizations take the shape of a pyramid, with fewer people at the top than at the bottom. Both human and primate societies rely on this stratified structure. Watch children as young as four years old play together, and you'll see hierarchies develop. When organizations attempt to dodge or suppress hierarchy, they usually fail.

Hierarchies have certain benefits: They satisfy a common psychological need for order; make it easier for people to learn about one another; and can work well when coordination is needed to produce a product or service. But hierarchies have powerful consequences, and not all of them are good. Resources and power tend to be distributed unequally across members of the organization and outsiders based on role. An idea from a talkative group member is judged more valuable than a less talkative colleague's same suggestion. Groups overestimate the performance of high-status members and underestimate that of low-status members, giving the skills and competence of the former an unfair sheen.

Hierarchies, then, can be costly and ineffective. Part of the problem is that groups often fail to grant status based on merit, and the wrong people end up at the top—a situation that leads to poor decisions and performance. Steep hierarchies have been linked to lower job satisfaction, morale, and motivation; reduced employee loyalty; and more stress and anxiety among workers. Because people often do not feel at ease bringing concerns to their bosses, hierarchy can also suppress dissent. One study of over fifty-one hundred Himalayan mountain expeditions found that groups with participants from more hierarchical countries—in Africa, Asia, and the Middle East, for example, as compared with Western Europe and the United States—were less likely to survive the trek. Organizations that lack steep hierarchies are sometimes called "flat organizations." I prefer "rebel organizations." A rebel organization—be it a pirate ship or a restaurant like Osteria Francescana—exemplifies the rebel talents we've discussed in this book. It avoids the traps of routine and complacency.

If you are ever in Berkeley, California, and feeling hungry, stop in at Cheese Board Pizza, which is part of a worker-owned collective that has no explicit status hierarchy. The shop serves just one type of pizza daily. If today's toppings are red pepper, onion, feta, tapenade, and parsley, expect something entirely different tomorrow. It may sound quirky, but it works: In 2016, Yelp users rated Cheese Board the best pizza place in America. (It sure tasted that way when I visited.) The shop's democratic spirit may be part of its success. Since 1971, the collective, which includes a cheese shop (the original business) and bakery, relies upon "a shared work ethic, high standards, and the strong emotional connections among the group," according to its website. Employees run the business and share in the profits.

A flatter structure may work for pizza joints, where roles and tasks are fairly predictable, but what about at larger, more complex ventures? Just a few months after I visited Cheese Board, I wrote a Harvard Business School case study about Valve Software, which, in addition to genre-busting games such as Half-Life and Counter-Strike, counts among its successes the dominant platform for distributing PC games, Steam. Valve is a private, self-funded firm whose per-employee profitability is higher than that of Google, Amazon, or Microsoft. Valve employees arrive at decisions through argument and persuasion. When you want to make a case for a new project, you just need to find enough people to build a team to start working on it. Sure, some employees are better at persuading their colleagues than others. (If they have a good track record, this works in their favor.) But no one has the formal power to tell anyone else what to do. The firm has been boss-free since it launched in 1996.

Before founding Valve, Gabe Newell and Mike Harrington worked at Microsoft. The experience set them on a different course, like merchant sailors who take a chance with the pirate ship. Newell and Harrington made the conscious choice to create a flat organization that would give employees maximum flexibility. "This company is yours to steer—toward opportunities and away from risks," Valve's employee handbook explains. "You have the power to green-light projects. You have the power to ship products." Employees choose for themselves what project to work on, which is why desks at Valve are on wheels and why you only have to unplug to join a different team.

When you give freedom to employees, Newell believes, you liberate their talents and creativity. Self-management builds pride in the work and commitment to the company. And yet, most CEOs don't see (never mind act on) these benefits. Newell told me that people who join Valve from other firms or industries often suffer culture shock. A section in the employee handbook advises new hires on "how not to freak out." Valve's ideas have been tried in other companies, albeit in less radical ways. In the late 1940s, Toyota gave its employees total control over the assembly line so that even someone at the very bottom of the pyramid could halt the production line if he spotted a problem. The company soon reaped the benefits, in terms of product quality, productivity, and market share. Competitors adopted the method on their own assembly lines, with similar success, ultimately giving Japanese cars a reputation as among the most reliable and well built in the world. Under this new system, each employee had a clear way to contribute to the organization's goals. Realizing they had to overcome their fears of losing some control in order to meaningfully engage their employees, managers gave them a voice and their trust. As a result of gaining responsibility and taking ownership of their performance—Toyota employees solved problems faster.

According to a study of over 800 employees, those with a strong sense of ownership in their organizations are more committed, satisfied, and productive. In one study, my colleagues and I asked over 750 employees from various organizations to think about their current job. Some were asked to write about an idea, project, or workspace that they felt they personally owned. The rest were asked to write about how they spend their days at work. After everyone answered a few other unrelated questions, we presented them with an opportunity to help the research team by participating in a five-minute survey without extra pay. The people primed to feel a sense of ownership were more likely to say yes. By flattening the power structure, ownership of problems and ideas becomes shared, rather than concentrated in the hands of a few, and workers thrive.

You may or may not be interested in starting a business, but we all face a choice in life: how to best structure our relationships with others. We can let our job title, our accomplishments, or a booming voice take the lead. Or we can choose to organize our lives so that every person in it "shall have an equal vote in affairs of the moment"—the first article that governed the pirate ship of Welsh pirate Black Bart, known as the most successful pirate of the Golden Age of Piracy, based on ships captured.

REBEL LEADERSHIP IS NOT JUST FOR PEOPLE WHO THINK OF THEMSELVES AS LEADERS. And you don't need a staff of people working under you to be a rebel leader. Rebel leadership means that you prefer working in a rebel organization and that you support your organization in that mission. Rebel leadership means fighting our natural human urges for the comfortable and the familiar. We have an innate desire to be accepted by others and thus regularly conform to their views, preferences, and behavior. We rarely question the status quo. We easily accept existing social roles and fall prey to unconscious biases like stereotypes. It's human nature to stay narrowly focused on our own perspective and on information that proves us right. By contrast, rebels know themselves and are aware of these limitations, but they don't believe there are limits on what they can accomplish.

Like the pirates, rebels follow their own "articles." I call these the Eight Principles of Rebel Leadership:

1. SEEK OUT THE NEW

In a large room, men and women sit at individual desks, positioned in a row and equipped with screws, pliers, a hammer, and a few other tools. Conveyor belts deliver parts. Workers look down, intent on the job of piecing together the components that will become a completed typewriter. This is what the assembly lines at Olivetti looked like in the 1950s.

As we discussed, when he took over his father's business, Adriano Olivetti extended lunch breaks so that workers could eat lunch for an hour and then "eat culture" for another hour. Guest speakers included philosophers, writers, intellectuals, and poets from across Italy and the rest of Europe. If workers preferred to read, they could visit the factory library, which was stocked with tens of thousands of books and magazines. Meanwhile, the company prospered.

Chef Bottura has his own home library. He keeps an extensive collection of records, art books, installations, and paintings, all sources of inspiration. His kitchen creations, in fact, often find their roots in art and music. The dish *Almost Better than Beluga*, in which pearls of black lentil are placed in a caviar tin layered over dill-flavored sour cream, references the René Magritte painting *This Is Not a Pipe*. For *Beautiful Psychedelic Veal, Not Flame-Grilled*, Bottura found inspiration in the work of Damien Hirst. While he was listening to Thelonious Monk one night, Bottura came up with *Tribute to Thelonious Monk*: black cod served with daikon white radish and green onion, in squid ink, after the jazz great's keyboard.

At Bottura's restaurant, contemporary art surrounds you—from works by Maurizio Catellan to Carlo Benvenuto to the world-famous *Capri Battery* of Beuys. Even the staff bathroom doubles as a small gallery. Music plays in the kitchen and in the front of the house at every hour of the day, other than during service (there is no music playing while customers are dining). Inspiration is everywhere.

This embrace of the arts by people in two very different lines of work demonstrates the first principle of rebel leadership: Always look for the new. The rebel is voracious, with interests that are wide-ranging. A new interest does not need a justification in the moment, for it might lead to a larger insight down the road.

I've always been interested in motorcycles, particularly in their engines and in motorcycle racing. Growing up, I'd go to local races, and every Sunday afternoon I'd sit down with my dad and brother on the couch for our weekend ritual: watching motorcycle races on TV. I still remember the first time I visited a racetrack. Nestled in the Tuscan hills about nineteen miles northeast of Florence, l'Autodromo del Mugello is the jewel of Italian motorsports. The three-mile-plus track has fifteen turns. Fans hoisted the colors of their favorite teams. Sitting on a hillside, I watched motorcycles tempting the edge of calamity on dangerous turns. Fans cheered loud and long, but the sound that stuck with me was that of the engines.

Today, I smile whenever I hear that familiar roar. There is nothing practical behind my interest in motorcycles. But it's something that inspires me. My interest in motorcycles once led me to interview riders in MotoGP, the premier motorcycle-racing World Championship, which consists of eighteen different races across fourteen countries and four continents. It was fascinating to hear them talk about how they keep their focus, even when it's raining. The same interest led me to the desert at the outskirts of Dubai to interview people working at stores renting quads. I'm always looking to know more about motorcycles, from learning about models I've not tried in the past or reading about how different companies design them. Who knows where else this slightly odd interest may take me. I'm not worried.

Speaking of racing, there is a famous story about Juan Manuel Fangio, the legendary Argentine driver who dominated the early years of Formula One racing. Well into the 1950 Monaco Grand Prix, he was blazing into a blind corner when, for no apparent reason, he slammed on the brakes. It turns out that he had caught a glimpse of the crowd as he came into the curve and realized that he was seeing the backs of everyone's heads, not their faces. Just the day before, Fangio had seen a similar photograph from 1936. They were looking away because, around the corner, there was a crash. The pieces fell into place: Fangio stopped, saving himself from joining the pileup. Even situations that we've experienced many times in the past or routes that look familiar can come across as novel if we approach them by focusing on what seems new.

2. ENCOURAGE CONSTRUCTIVE DISSENT

October 18, 1962, was a chilly night as Attorney General Robert Kennedy took a seat in the front of his car. A driver was behind the steering wheel, and the chairman of the Joint Chiefs of Staff, the director of the CIA, and six other officials, all high-level, were crammed in the room left in the front and the back. They had decided to take Robert Kennedy's car rather than a limousine or two to avoid raising any suspicion. The car left the State Department for the White House, where Robert's older brother, President John F. Kennedy, was waiting. A few days before, President Kennedy and his team had learned that the Soviet Union was installing nuclear-armed missiles in Cuba—missiles with the potential to kill 80 million Americans within minutes. The United States and the Soviets were on the brink of war, and the time for a decision had come.

One of the most remarkable details about President Kennedy's management of the Cuban Missile Crisis was what he sought from his advisors: disagreement. A year and a half before, he had supported an ill-conceived secret operation to unseat Cuban leader Fidel Castro, a fiasco remembered as the Bay of Pigs. In its wake, the president ordered a review of the decision-making process, which produced a series of changes. First, each member would take the role of a "skeptical generalist," approaching a given problem in its entirety, rather than focusing only on one department's perspective (usually their own). Second, to encourage freewheeling conversations, the members would use settings free of any formality, with no specified procedures or formal agenda to follow. Third, the team would be divided into subgroups that would work on different options and then come back together to discuss them. Finally, Kennedy sometimes would have his aides meet without him to keep them from simply agreeing with his views. These changes, Kennedy believed, would stimulate debate, challenge assumptions, and clear a path for the best plan to emerge on its merits. All of the measures were aimed at defeating what psychologists call "groupthink"—the tendency for members of a group to agree with one another, which quiets dissent and suppresses alternatives.

The men in Robert Kennedy's car had divided into subgroups, with one working on a position paper that argued for a military strike and the other for a blockade of the island nation. They then swapped papers, applying merciless scrutiny in search of the superior strategy. "There was no rank, and in fact we did not even have a chairman . . . the conversations were completely uninhibited and unrestricted," Robert Kennedy would comment. In the end, the blockade in combination with deft diplomacy led to the removal of the missiles and prevented a nuclear conflict with the Soviet Union. The rebel understands that a certain amount of tension is healthy, that discomfort leads to striving. Rebels seek out diverse perspectives and experiences. Knowing when to listen is just as important as knowing when to speak up.

At Ariel Investments, the practice of assigning someone to play devil's advocate during meetings to challenge the consensus and raise different perspectives produces better decisions. At Pal's Sudden Service, when a new idea is proposed—adding an item to the menu, for example, or a change in workflow—the idea is tested in three stores at the same time: one that supports the idea, one that is against it, and one that is neutral. At Catchafire, when Rachael Chong interviews new hires, she looks for people who disagree with her. She describes decisions the company has made or ones it is grappling with and looks for people who think differently from her and the rest of her team. A study of seven Fortune 500 companies revealed that the most successful top management teams were those that encouraged disagreement in private meetings.

Alfred Sloan, chairman of General Motors from 1937 to 1956, once concluded a meeting with executives discussing a critical, high-stakes decision by saying, "I take it we are all in complete agreement on the decision here . . . Then I propose we postpone further discussion until our next meeting to give ourselves some time to develop disagreements and perhaps gain some understanding of what the decision is all about." This is rebel talent.

3. OPEN CONVERSATIONS, DON'T CLOSE THEM

At Pixar, when writers and directors are working on a story, there is a premium on developing creative solutions. Group leaders encourage a technique they call "plussing." The point of plussing is to improve ideas without using judgmental language. You add to, or "plus," what has been said. Instead of criticizing a sketch, the director might build on a starting point by saying, "I like Woody's eyes, and what if we . . ." Someone else might then jump in and add her own plus. The idea resembles the "yes, and" principle of improv. People listen, respect the ideas of others, and contribute their own. This type of collaborative atmosphere requires great effort to maintain. We all seem to feel an urge to judge others and their ideas. Sometimes our disapproval takes the form of silence—"the death pause," as Pixar's Ed Catmull describes it.

The rebel keeps an open mind, understanding that communication drives insight, and that closed conversations generally fail. Dissent is welcome, but only when there is shared respect and everyone feels they are on the same team. So many things can close a conversation—laziness, distraction, someone who talks too much or not enough, a cutting comment or slavish politeness—and the rebel resists them all. Rebels solicit honest feedback and new knowledge by sparking new conversations—even difficult ones—and sticking with them even when the going gets tough.

When James E. Rogers was the CEO and chairman of Cinergy (which then merged with Duke Energy), he conducted anything-goes listening sessions with groups of managers, which alerted him to issues that might have otherwise not reached his desk, such as complaints about unequal compensation. He also invited feedback on his own performance, even asking employees for an anonymous letter grade. His communication skills needed work, he found out, and so he worked on them. Crew members on pirate ships could bring concerns to their captains without fear of reprisal. When conversations are open, a ship runs fast and nimble.

4. REVEAL YOURSELF—AND REFLECT

Soon after becoming CEO of the Campbell Soup Company, Doug Conant got to know his senior executives in one-on-one meetings. As Conant put it, he talked about "what's important to me both in and out of work, what I look for in an organization, how I operate, why I do what I do, and much more." His goal? To convey a full picture of who he was, what he was all about, and what he wanted to accomplish as CEO. "If I do what I say I'm going to do," he told the executives, "I guess you can trust me. If I don't, I guess you can't." Conant considered this approach to be key to an effective and healthy working relationship. "I explain[ed] that my goal is to take the mystery out of our relationship in a personal way as quickly as possible so that we can get on with the business of working together and doing something special," he told me. Rebels understand the power of showing themselves—and knowing themselves. They don't hide who they are or pretend to be someone they are not. They encourage others to find and express their strengths.

Coach Maurice Cheeks had prepared to lead his team to victory, not to sing the national anthem in front of over twenty thousand fans. But when he saw a young woman struggling, he stepped in and sang with her. Nobody cared that he couldn't carry a tune. Before her time at AOL Time Warner, Patricia Fili-Krushel was hired by WebMD Health to work as chief executive. As the leader of WebMD, Fili-Krushel met with a group of engineers in Silicon Valley, all men. When they asked her right off the bat what she knew about engineering, she made a zero with her fingers. "This is how much I know about engineering," she told them. "However, I do know how to run businesses, and I'm hoping you can teach me what I need to know about your world."

We are all quick to judge ourselves and our colleagues, but it is so much better to learn to focus on strengths, not weaknesses. We are quick to judge our coworker for blowing a deadline rather than praising him for his meticulous attention to detail. We comment on the sloppy way our partner loaded the dishwasher rather than thanking her for cooking dinner. Too often, our focus is on where others are falling behind rather than on their successes.

Most organizations fall into the same trap, but some get it right. Mellody Hobson took to heart the advice she got from Ariel Investments CEO and founder John W. Rogers Jr. when she joined the firm to speak up and be herself. Hobson credits her success in part to her ability to stay authentic as she climbed the corporate ladder.

Once we're in touch with our talents, the thrill of potential takes hold. When Greg and I attended improv comedy classes, we each at our own pace became more comfortable in our skin. Chef Bottura followed his passion for cooking when he decided to leave law school, though he knew he would disappoint his father—at least at first. He reached fame by cooking Italian food in a way that inspired him and that was entirely unique to him. He faced years of resistance. But he could not stop himself from doing what he loves and being who he is.

5. LEARN EVERYTHING—THEN FORGET EVERYTHING

The legendary UCLA basketball coach John Wooden would open the first practice of every season by having his players practice putting on their socks and lacing their shoes. If the players got blisters from improperly laced shoes, they wouldn't move as well. If they couldn't run or jump to their potential, they would lose rebounds and miss shots. And if they missed rebounds and shots, the team would lose. Master the fundamentals, Wooden figured, and the team would prosper.

Rebels know the limits of their knowledge, and that mastering the basics is a lifelong project. But a rebel is not a slave to the rules either. Sometimes you return to the fundamentals only to discover a strategy that is very different—and better. In most fast-food chains, a new employee receives about two hours of training per process before starting on the line. At Pal's Sudden Service, training for new workers averages 135 hours and can span six months. With a strong foundation, employees perform at a higher level and are well positioned to think of improvements. Leila Janah, CEO and founder of Samasource, spent years learning everything she could about providing aid to the developing world and working for organizations, such as the World Bank, that operate with this goal in mind. In time, she started to wonder whether giving people aid (such as money, clothes, and food) was the most effective way to reduce poverty. It wasn't, she decided, and created a company that helps poor people by giving them jobs, not aid.

Consider another of Bottura's signature dishes, whose name is a mouthful in itself—*Le cinque stagionature del Parmigiano Reggiano in diverse consistenze e temperature*, or "the five different ages of Parmigiano Reggiano in five different textures and temperatures." The dish was first imagined twenty years ago, starting as an experiment with textures and temperatures. The twenty-four-month-aged cheese is made into a hot soufflé, the thirty-month-aged cheese is made into a warm sauce, the thirty-six-month-aged cheese is made into a chilled foam, the forty-month-aged cheese is made into a crisp, and the fifty-month-aged cheese is transformed in an "air." It is a celebration of what *stagionatura*, or aging, does to a wheel of Parmigiano. By exploring fundamental questions of how the cheese behaves, Bottura ended with a dish that had never been experienced before. "If you want to innovate," he often reminds his team, "you need to know everything, then forget everything."

6. FIND FREEDOM IN CONSTRAINTS

In April 1970, an explosion rocked the moon mission of Apollo 13. The service module in the spacecraft supplied the command module, where crew members would spend most of their time during the voyage, with electrical power and oxygen. Five and a half million pounds of explosives and two tanks of liquid oxygen were in the service module. Tank No. 2, ten feet below the astronauts' couches, had a crack in its wiring—something neither NASA nor the crew realized before launch. Nineteen hours into the flight—Apollo 13 had completed four-fifths of her outward voyage and was 200,000 miles from Earth—the cracked wires became exposed. When the crew turned on the fans in the oxygen tanks before going to bed, a spark between the cracked wires ignited a fire. The explosion severely damaged the spacecraft, leaving the three astronauts with a dwindling oxygen supply. On the ground, a team of engineers had to come up with a way to clean the air using only the equipment on board in a very short amount of time. The remarkable constraints and pressure drove them to a completely novel solution: They figured out a clever way to use the square air cleaners located in the command module in the round receivers of the lunar module. Who says that a square peg can't fit in a round hole?

Rebels work through constraints to the freedom on the other side. Human nature introduces some of the most formidable challenges: bias; a preference for the status quo; blinding self-regard. Rebels are aware of these constraints and fight against them. Research tells us that when we're faced with constraints, we dedicate our mental energy to acting more resourcefully and doggedly, and surpass expectations—or better. In 1960, Dr. Seuss made a bet with Bennett Cerf, the cofounder of Random House, that he could write a whole book relying on only fifty different words. Though challenging, the bet resulted in *Green Eggs and Ham*, a classic that's beloved in my house (and maybe yours) and Dr. Seuss's bestselling book.

Constraints, then, can open our minds and drive creativity rather than hinder it. Poetic masterworks spring from the boundaries of verse and rhyme. Masterpieces of Renaissance art started as commissions in which the painter was bound to adhere to narrow specifications on subject matter, materials, color, and size. In our own work, constraints take many different forms, from tight budgets to standardization. If you ask a team to design and build a product, you might get a handful of good ideas. But if you ask that same team to design and build the same product within a tight budget, you'll likely see even more creative results. Research examining how people design new products, cook meals, and even fix broken toys finds that budget constraints increase resourcefulness and lead to better solutions. While we all need resources to perform our jobs, scarcity can sometimes spur innovation.

7. LEAD FROM THE TRENCHES

The sixteenth-century French pirate François Le Clerc was incredibly successful—so successful that, recently, he nabbed the #13 spot on Forbes's list of highest-earning pirates. (Yes, Forbes made a list of top-earning pirates.) Legend has it that Le Clerc was a "lead from the front" pirate, often the first to board an enemy ship. This trait cost him a leg, and henceforth he was known as "Jambe de Bois" ("Peg Leg"). He went on to lead a fleet of ten vessels and over three hundred men. Why were so many other pirates willing to follow Le Clerc into battle, even after he lost his leg? Because he fought beside them.

In the TV show *Undercover Boss*, executives go undercover as entry-level employees in the companies they lead. There are almost always some unpleasant surprises. In one episode, Frontier Airlines CEO Bryan Bedford discovered major flaws in company operations when he joined the front lines, from employees having only seven minutes to clean a plane between flights to agents shifting between checking in patrons to loading luggage, by hand, in 104-degree heat. By being in the trenches with their own employees, the executives see the problems in their businesses and how they are experienced, and they also better understand what working in the organization entails for their employees.

Rebels know where the action is, and that's where they want to be—not up in a tower or secluded in a corner office. The rebel knows that the best way to lead is from the trenches. Rebel leaders are comrades, friends, and fellow enthusiasts. Napoleon would not have spent all his time in the executive suite. Chef Bottura is often found sweeping the streets outside his restaurant, unloading deliveries, and cleaning the kitchen. In Navy SEAL teams, as I've learned from naval officers who have attended my classes at Harvard Kennedy School, this hands-on philosophy is ingrained in candidates from the first day of training. Indeed, naval officers are taught to lead by example in everything they do. You'll find them at the head of the pack during runs and swims.

In a survey I conducted of over seven hundred employees, I found that the most respected leaders are those most willing to get their hands dirty. When I asked the employees to think about leaders they don't respect, they zeroed in on managers removed from the nitty-gritty. When an organization is flat, it's not just good for the leader, of course. One study of group assignments found that the more control a single member had, the worse the team did as a whole. When talking about Osteria Francescana, Bottura uses "we" rather than "I." He also shares meals with the staff, plays soccer with them in the afternoon, and constantly checks in when he's traveling. When he is not in Modena, they miss him, but the team does not falter just because one member is away.

8. FOSTER HAPPY ACCIDENTS

After World War II, a flood of veterans enrolled in the Massachusetts Institute of Technology. To accommodate this new population and their families, MIT built Westgate West, a maze of one hundred low-rise housing units for families on the far western edge of campus. A pair of psychologists were interested in knowing more about the social network in the housing complex, so they asked residents to list their three closest friends. The people listed most often as best friends tended to live in a first-floor apartment, right at the bottom of the staircase. Forty-two percent said one of their best friends was a direct neighbor. Friends are the people you bump into.

When Steve Jobs needed a new home for Pixar back in the 1980s, he bought a dilapidated Del Monte canning factory. The initial plan was to create separate spaces for each department (animators, computer scientists, etc.), but instead he decided to configure the old factory as one large space, centered on an atrium. He put employee mailboxes in the atrium, as well as the café, gift shop, and screening rooms. (He even considered putting the only restrooms there, but changed his mind.) Jobs believed that separating the groups, each of which had its own unique culture and approach to problem solving, would discourage idea sharing.

These fruitful connections happen not only by designing workspaces differently, but by designing teams differently. Bottura's two sous chefs are Davide di Fabio and Kondo Takahiko. The two not only differ in their origins (Italy and Japan), but also in their strengths: one is more comfortable with improvisation, and the other is obsessed with precision. Bottura believes that such "collisions" make his kitchen more innovative. Too often, leaders believe that success depends on hierarchical command and control. Rebels, on the other hand, know the value of happy accidents. They believe in workspaces and teams that cross-pollinate. The rebel realizes that a mistake may unlock a breakthrough.

One day at Osteria Francescana, Takahiko dropped a lemon tart . . . and Bottura transformed it into the now famous dessert "Oops! I Dropped the Lemon Tart." The story of how the dish was created found its way into his book, which I happened to pick up one day at a bookstore in Massachusetts. Which, eventually, brought me to Modena to watch as Bottura's dishes, and the stories behind them, were ferried from the kitchen out to the hungry customers, all waiting in anticipation, ready to be astonished.

CONCLUSION
RISOTTO CACIO E PEPE

You should always keep the door open to the unexpected.
—MASSIMO BOTTURA, OWNER AND CHEF, OSTERIA FRANCESCANA

Shortly after four a.m. on May 20, 2012, the ground began to buckle. Bricks fell to the ground, and the sounds of shattering glass filled the air. The windows of parked cars caved in. The walls of churches, schools, and residential homes started to give out. The power failed, leaving entire towns in darkness. Mobile phones didn't function.

A magnitude 6.0 earthquake had hit the Emilia Romagna region in Northern Italy, affecting the historic cities of Bologna, Ferrara, and Modena. As dawn broke, the aftershocks were still not over, but the extent of the damage was already clear. Large cracks ran from the top to the bottom of many apartment buildings. The streets were filled with architectural remains. In one of the towns shaken by the earthquake, a centuries-old clock tower was sheared in two, with one half collapsing into rubble and the other half standing precariously. In another town, the battlements and towers of an imposing fourteenth-century castle had crumbled into dust. Many households were left with no water. In yet another, the town hall was severely damaged, and the public-school buildings had collapsed. Nearby, the roof of a beloved chapel had caved in, leaving statues of angels and saints exposed to the sky.

Emilia Romagna sits at the top of the Italian boot, stretching from the Adriatic Sea on the east coast all the way to the Liguria region on the west coast. In the south of the region, castle-capped hills, green fields, and breathtaking views of the forested Apennine peaks are dotted with remote, sparsely populated villages. In stark contrast, the north of the region is pool-table flat: The landscape mainly consists of the fertile farmlands all across the Po River valley. Emilia Romagna is considered Italy's gastronomic heartland. Modena's balsamic vinegar, Parma ham and Parmesan cheese, and Bologna's meat ragù, lasagne, and mortadella are all Italian icons.

The region also boasts an unusually rich architectural and artistic heritage. There are medieval castles, Romanesque churches, Christian mosaics, and striking Renaissance palaces dating back hundreds of years, when the region was a patchwork of city-states, each independently governed by local dynasties with a lot of power. The damage to this heritage from the quakes was extensive. More aftershocks occurred throughout the day. Fearful of staying in weakened buildings and damaged homes, hundreds of people spent the night in their cars, while others took shelter in tents. Nine days later, with the worst seemingly over, people found themselves searching through debris for the second time, after a 5.8-magnitude earthquake shook the same region, bringing down buildings damaged by the previous quake. Many lives were lost. Countless homes had been leveled. The earthquake damage was estimated at more than $15 billion.

The earthquakes also threatened an entire industry: that of Parmigiano-Reggiano cheese. Parmigiano-Reggiano was first produced in the Po Valley by Cistercian monks as large wheels of cheese that could be easily stored and sustain pilgrims on their long journeys. Today, official Parmigiano-Reggiano can only be made in a few provinces in Emilia Romagna. The cheese must be produced in a very specific way that includes what is fed to the cows that produce the milk. Experts check the quality of wheels of Parmigiano-Reggiano by tapping the rind with a little hammer created just for the job. At a retail price of some $15 a pound in Italy, and even more abroad, Parmigiano-Reggiano is one of the most expensive Italian cheeses. Wheels of Parmigiano-Reggiano are key to the region's economy. Every year, the area produces over three million wheels of Parmigiano-Reggiano, generating about $2.3 billion in consumer sales. Many Italian banks still accept interest payments in Parmigiano.

The cheese is aged in humidity-controlled warehouses, which were hit hard by the earthquake. Hundreds of large wheels of cheese—each as big as truck tires—fell from twenty-three-foot-high shelves, tumbling to the floor like books in a bombed-out library. All in all, about 400,000 wheels of Parmigiano-Reggiano from thirty-seven factories were damaged. These damaged wheels could not be sold as usual, threatening losses in the hundreds of millions. Cheese producers started to worry they'd have to close the doors on businesses their families had tended for generations. In the span of nine days, the tremor had placed an entire industry in danger.

MASSIMO BOTTURA HAD ALWAYS FELT A SPECIAL CONNECTION TO PARMIGIANO-Reggiano. For most big dinners in the house where he grew up, his father brought home some of the cheese to be used as an ingredient in pasta sauces and ravioli or tortellini, eaten in big chunks as appetizer, or grated on pasta. Bottura would steal pieces of it while his mother and grandmother were cooking. The taste was intense and complex. Even today, Bottura considers a piece of Parmigiano and some fruit to be the perfect snack.

When Bottura learned about the damage the earthquake had done to his beloved wheels of Parmigiano-Reggiano, he wondered

if there was something he could do to help. He couldn't stop thinking about it and decided to focus on what he does best: developing
new recipes.

What if he came up with a new dish that had this almost magical cheese as the star? He wanted to devise a recipe for a dish that
would be delicious, but simple enough for almost anyone to make.
If Parmigiano-Reggiano was the star of the dish, he reasoned, those
who were interested in cooking it would buy cheese from the damaged wheels.

Then he started experimenting. Bottura thought about traditional dishes that are made with just a few ingredients unique to
a specific region. One of Rome's traditional dishes seemed to fit
the bill: a classic pasta dish called *cacio e pepe* (pasta with cheese
and pepper). It can be made in minutes with four of the most basic ingredients: salt, pasta, black pepper, and a type of cheese often used in Italian cooking called Pecorino Romano. Pecorino is
a sheep's-milk cheese with a sharp flavor that has been made in
Campania, a region in southern Italy, since ancient times. *Cacio*
is the local Roman dialect word for Pecorino Romano. Bottura
saw a parallel in what Pecorino meant for Campania and what
Parmigiano-Reggiano meant for Emilia Romagna. So he decided
to give this traditional recipe his own creative spin. Instead of the
usual Pecorino, he would use Parmigiano. And instead of pasta,
he would use rice—another product greatly affected by the earthquake. He called the dish *Risotto Cacio e Pepe*.

Though the traditional *cacio e pepe* recipe calls for only a few
ingredients, the way the dish is prepared elevates it to an elegant
creamy twirl of noodles that makes your palate sing. For Bottura's
new dish, he opted to prepare the risotto with a Parmesan water,
instead of the usual stock. He grated some Parmigiano-Reggiano
and soaked the shredded cheese in a pot full of water. He brought
it up to a boil, turned the heat off, and then stirred until it became
creamy. He then stored the creamy mixture in the refrigerator over-

night. By the next morning, the liquid had separated into three different layers. There was a milk protein at the bottom; a thick, viscous broth in the middle; and a cream of Parmigiano at the top. He toasted some rice, and then he started adding the Parmigiano broth until the rice was ready. The dish was finished with the cream of Parmigiano from the top layer. The recipe, as Bottura described it, "borrowed an iconic Roman spaghetti dish . . . and transformed it into an Emilian symbol of hope and recovery."

But that, alone, would not solve the problem. There were so many wheels of damaged cheese, and they could be saved only if they were sold soon. Bottura and the consortium of Parmigiano-Reggiano producers decided to sponsor a one-day event when people across the globe could make *Risotto Cacio e Pepe* at the same time. So, they organized an online fund-raiser: On October 27, 2012, people were encouraged to make the new recipe or a dish of their own featuring Parmigiano-Reggiano.

This special night kicked off at eight o'clock on a major Italian food show, broadcast live via the Internet from the Salone del Gusto, a biannual gastronomy exhibition held in Turin. Over a quarter of a million people had dinner "together" that night. Some of them got together with friends and family and ate Bottura's dish at home. Others ate it at restaurants. Still others devised their own Parmigiano-Reggiano concoctions. The event gathered a lot of attention, not only from people living in Italy, but also from people abroad—from New York City to Tokyo—who wanted to help save one of Italy's culinary treasures. In the end, all 400,000 wheels of damaged Parmigiano-Reggiano were sold. No one lost a job. No cheese makers closed their doors. An industry was rescued by a recipe.

WHEN BOTTURA IS IN MODENA, HE WORKS AT THE RESTAURANT, VISITS THE LOCAL markets, and goes to farms to check on his suppliers. Dressed in his chef's whites, he preps dishes, carefully plates them, tastes pretty much everything that leaves the kitchen, expedites between the front and back of the house, chats with the staff, and works with his team on new recipes. The same month might find him in Tokyo, Melbourne, New York, Rio de Janeiro, and London, returning between each trip to cook at Osteria Francescana. The year the earthquakes struck was also the year that Bottura's restaurant won its third Michelin star, so it was an especially busy time, with a surge in customers, requests for speeches from conference organizers, and constant inquiries from the media.

And yet, when so many wheels of his dear cheese were damaged, he made time to help. Indeed, this is part of a pattern in his life, which continued in 2015, when he started an initiative called Refettorio, which uses leftovers to feed people who do not have access to good food. His first Refettorio was in Milan. The ones that followed occurred in Brazil, Spain, New York, and in other parts of the world where Bottura found the time to travel. Each time he organized a Refettorio, he created menus using leftover ingredients from big ongoing culinary conferences or other cooking events and served his creations to children and homeless shelters in the area.

Somehow, with Bottura, there always seems to be time for more, for sucking the marrow out of life and making the most of every moment. On the evening I worked the front of the house at his restaurant, the doorbell rang about forty-five minutes into the dinner service. The restaurant was full, and Beppe, surprised, went to see who it was. As he opened the door, the bass rumble of a Ducati motorcycle filled the room. The rider, who had a boy of about ten years old perched behind him, asked, "Table for two?" He revved the engine again. And then there was laughter: It was Bottura, who was spending part of the day with a kid who had asked to meet him through the Make-A-Wish Foundation.

We tend to think that the more we have to do, the less time and mental space we will have for other tasks. This is a matter of basic logic, and it is hard to imagine life being any other way, right? But it turns out this is wrong. When we are fully engaged in our work and in our lives, we actually have the energy to accomplish more. Bottura, who often plays a game of soccer out on the street with the staff before dinner starts, has discovered this. This is another secret of the rebel: What seem like tangents, or doing extra—or helping someone when it seems that there is no time—become paths to a more vibrant life. Doing more gives us more.

Psychologists are catching up with this rebel insight. Cassie Mogilner of the University of California in Los Angeles and her colleagues have shown that when we give our time to others, we actually feel less time-constrained. Of course, giving time to others gives us a "connected" feeling and brings us meaningful experiences. But people who give time, Mogilner's research shows, also feel more capable, confident, and useful. They feel they've accomplished something and, as a result, that they can accomplish more in the future. I've seen a similar effect in my own research. I recruited participants to work on a data-entry task, and I deliberately made some of them busier than others by giving them more work to complete in the same amount of time, telling them that they would be helping a researcher's project by doing so. The participants who got more work done within the same allotted time, and thus were objectively busier, felt less time constrained, and were more willing to take on more.

Perhaps this explains the almost magical quality I sensed when I was with Bottura and the other remarkable people I met during my research for this book. In their joy of doing—in their total engagement with life—their recipe for success turned out to be rebelling against time itself.

EPILOGUE
REBEL ACTION

The way to get started is to quit talking and begin doing.
—WALT DISNEY

On a chilly day in the late 1970s, a teenage Massimo Bottura was sitting in the passenger seat of his father's blue Alfa Romeo. His older brother was outside, standing next to a gas pump, filling up the tank. As he was waiting, Bottura decided to have a look at a little red book his father kept in the car: a beat-up edition of the *Michelin Guide*. A decade and a half later, in 1986, Bottura went to speak with his father, who was not happy that his son had decided to leave law school to try his hand at being a chef. He reminded his father of the book he'd discovered in the car that day. "You'll see, Dad, someday I'll have a Michelin star, too!"

Taking the first step wasn't easy for Bottura. He had long looked up to his father, who didn't want him to become a chef. He didn't have the experience or skills that many told him he would need. He didn't have connections. But he had an idea—breaking with the traditions of Italian cuisine—and a lot of passion for it. And so, even in the early years, when tradition-bound Italians criticized his cooking, he refused to give up.

In your own journey toward embracing your rebel talent, you

may also find that the hardest part is getting started. For help, visit www.rebeltalents.org, where you will find a variety of resources and tips to set you on the right path.

WHAT TYPE OF REBEL ARE YOU?

In the years I've been studying rebels, I've realized that they come in many varieties. They behave in different ways, and need different approaches to develop their talent. Understanding what I refer to as your Rebel Quotient is an important first step. On www .rebeltalents.org, you'll find a free assessment to determine which rebel ingredients come most naturally to you and where you have the most room to grow. Are you the kind of rebel who speaks your mind to a charismatic boss who's on the wrong track? Or are you the kind who is more apt to recognize what's new in a project you've completed a dozen times before? Being rebellious is uncomfortable. But becoming more aware of your own rebel profile will help you become more comfortable with the uncomfortable.

It's hard to bring out the rebel inside of you on a regular basis. After all, being a rebel means fighting against elements of human nature. But it can also be incredibly exciting and satisfying: Even small changes in your approach to work and life can produce powerful results. You'll find concrete tips based on the habits and strategies rebels rely on regularly—and some stories about how those techniques can pay off.

REBEL WAYS TO KEEP LEARNING

Rebels value learning and stay humble. As Bottura told me when I first met him, "When you think you know everything, you've stopped growing. . . . Keep your eyes open and ask questions." To help you in your continuous learning, www.rebeltalents.org also includes stories and case studies of other rebels who I hope will inspire and teach you. You'll also find links to research on rebel talents, which—like a Bottura menu—keeps evolving over time.

THE WAY FORWARD

Fortunately, Bottura's father lived long enough to see him receive that first Michelin star, in 2001. It was just the beginning of an amazing journey. In December 2001, about a month after receiving the honor, Bottura gave a commemorative T-shirt to each Osteria Francescana team member as a Christmas gift. Printed on the T-shirt was the date when the first Michelin star arrived, a Michelin star symbol, and the sentence: *Ma dove vuole arrivare questa pasta e fagioli?* (Where do these pasta and beans want to go?) They had traveled far. In fact, Bottura went well beyond his initial promise to his father. He had reached for the stars and eventually got three of them from Michelin.

Like Bottura and the other characters you met in this book, rebels go about their work and life a bit differently: They break rules and bring about positive change in the process. They smile at life and feel fulfilled. There is no better time for rebel action than now.

ACKNOWLEDGMENTS

Great things are done by a series of small things brought together.
—VINCENT VAN GOGH

In February of 2016, *Harvard Business Review* approached me to see if I was interested in being part of an experiment to test ideas about what a digital "article of the future" might look like. "Experiment?" I thought: "I am in." In the end, the feature included videos, case studies, and even a live event in San Francisco, all focused on the idea that acts of rebellion could be positive and productive. The enthusiastic response we received kindled my desire to write the book you hold in your hands today.

At HBR, I worked closely with Senior Editor Steve Prokesch, who held my hand through the process, asking insightful questions, giving candid feedback, and making everything I wrote more compelling with his thoughtful edits and clever suggestions. I am so grateful for all of his outstanding help. Thank you also to HBR's Scott Berinato, Amy Meeker, Sarah Cliffe, Amy Bernstein, Gretchen Gavett, Tina Silberman, Karen Player, Kate Adams, Amy Poftak, and Editor-in-Chief Adi Ignatus. Their creative ideas, encouragement, and willingness to try new things were thoroughly invigorating. I want to express my gratitude to the entire HBR organization.

When I first wrote *Rebel Talent*, the ideas were clear in my head. Or so I thought. I was getting ready to submit the manuscript and shared it with a journalist, Gareth Cook, for a look. I ended up rewriting every chapter thanks to his incredibly helpful feedback and ingenious guidance. I wrestled through each idea in the book with him, and I am grateful for his patience, high standards, and rare ability to shape ideas into much better ones. I thought I had met a book doctor, but I ended up working with an astoundingly curious and sharp "idea coach" who cared about the project as much as I did. Thank you, Gareth, for seeing the potential in my ideas, for pushing me (so, so) hard to make them better, and for keeping me on track despite all the uncertainty about where this adventure would take me.

A big thanks also to my agent, Max Brockman, who saw promise in this project when the book was just a notion. Max provided insightful advice as I chose the right publisher, and he was a pleasure to work with even when my decisions gave him a headache.

I was joined in this journey by my brilliant editor, Jessica Sindler, at Dey Street, who read through many drafts of this book and always found ways to strengthen it with her thoughtful feedback and careful edits. Jessica's excitement for the book kept me motivated throughout the process, and I feel fortunate to have found her.

I owe an enormous debt to my friend, the writer and editor Katie Shonk, who read every chapter many times and suggested edits that made the writing much clearer and more compelling. Her wise advice along the way was invaluable, and her willingness to provide so much help speaks to the kind attitude I have benefited from over the many years I've known her.

The research and stories reported in this book are based on many hours spent reading papers and books, hundreds of interviews, countless plane rides, dozens of visits to organizations around the globe, and thousands of conversations with colleagues, executives and friends. I am fortunate I've had the opportunity to collaborate on the research mentioned in this book with such exceptional scholars: Linda Argote, Dan Ariely, Emma Aveling, Silvia Bellezza, Ethan Bernstein, Alison Wood Brooks, Daniel Cable, Tiziana Casciaro, Tiffany Chang, Giada Di Stefano, Molly Frean, Adam Galinsky, Evelyn Gosnell, Adam Grant, Paul Green, Brian Hall, Karen Huang, Laura Huang, Diwas KC, Anat Keinan, Tami Kim, Ata Jami, Li Jiang, Maryam Kouchaki, Rick Larrick, Julia Lee, Joshua Margolis, Julia Minson, Ella Miron-Spektor, Bill McEvily, Mike Norton, Gary Pisano, Jane Risen, Ovul Sezer, Juliana Schroeder, Maurice Schweitzer, Morgan Shields, Sara Singer, Brad Staats, Juliana Stone, Thor Sundt, Leigh Tost, Mike Yeomans, Kathleen Vohs, Cameron Wright, Evelyn Zhang, and Ting Zhang. The research that brings so much joy to my life is thanks to all of you—to the dedication you have for science, your unsparingly honest feedback, your seemingly bottomless well of creative ideas.

For raising questions about rebels I had not thought about, and for providing a delightful environment in which to work, I am extremely thankful to my colleagues in the Negotiation, Organizations and Markets Unit at HBS: Max Bazerman, John Beshears, Alison Wood Brooks, Katherine Coffman, Ben Edelman, Christine Exley, Jerry Green, Brian Hall, Leslie John, Jenn Logg, Mike Luca, Deepak Malhotra, Kathleen McGinn, Kevin Mohan, Matthew Rabin, Joshua Schwartzstein, Jim Sebenius, Guhan Subramanian, Andy Wasynczuk, and Ashley Whillans. I am so lucky to have an office on the same floor as you, and to have the opportunity to keep on learning from you.

The inspiration for this book came from the many rebels I've met throughout the years. I am especially grateful to Chef Massimo Bottura, his wife, Laura Gilmore, as well as Giuseppe Palmieri, Alessandro Laganà, Enrico Vignoli, and the rest of the remarkably talented and joyful crew at Osteria Francescana. I am thankful to Ed Catmull at Pixar for spending a big chunk of his birthday to speak with me; his keen intellect, thirst for learning, and contagious humility are the perfect combination for a truly engaging conversation. I am also grateful to Captain Sully, Scott Cook, Greg Dyke, Doug Conant, Rachael Chong, Pete Docter, Andrew Gordon, Dan Scanlon, Jonas Rivera, Jamie Woolf, Patricia Fili-Krushel, Leila Janah, Mellody Hobson, Andrew Roberts, Peter Leeson, Riccardo Delleani, and all of the other remarkable people who generously made themselves available for interviews and on-site conversations. Their wealth of knowledge, innovative insights, and approach to life left an indelible impact on my thinking.

For help connecting to rebels, I thank Gianni Lorenzoni, Sally Ashworth, Gareth Jones, Bruno Lamborghini, Avi Swerdlow, Anthony Accardo, Mike Wheeler, Taylor Luczak, Sarah Green Carmichael, and Kathleen McGinn.

I also want to acknowledge the precious help I received from research associates and fact checkers, who worked under time pressure with much good cheer, including Susan Chamberlain, Rijad Custovic, Ivan Dzintars, Annisha Simpson, Cam Haigh, and Leoul Tekle. Jeff Strabone's careful work on the Notes likely drove him crazy, but I am grateful to him for being so attentive and precise. Alex Caracuzzo, Jeffrey Cronin, Barbara Esty, and Rhys Sevier, who are all part of Baker Library Services at HBS, worked their magic in finding information on anything I asked about, whether it was a history of the New York's Hippodrome Theater, or details on the techniques used across the centuries to cut diamonds. Thank you for being so responsive to my dozens of requests, even when many of them had "last request" in the subject line. Along the way, I was aided enormously by my faculty support specialist, Meg King, who not only patiently read various drafts of this book but also dealt with all sorts of last-minute requests with such graciousness. Without Meg's support, my life at work would be complete chaos.

I refined many of this book's ideas in classrooms, with hundreds of executives. I am thankful for their insightful feedback and comments, which shaped my thinking as I learned more about rebel talent. For the many opportunities I had to be in front of executives in Executive Education Programs at HBS, I owe a large debt to David Ager, Cathy Cotins, Jim Dowd, Pam Hallagan, Deborah Hooper, Ani Kharajian, Beth Neustadt, Carla Tishler, and many HBS colleagues who gave me the privilege to share my ideas in the classroom.

When I was ready for feedback, Judith Schaab, Carmen Reynold, and Gary Pisano were generous with their time and attentively read every page. I know how precious your time is, and I appreciate that you spent some of it offering ways to improve the manuscript. Thanks also to Elizabeth Sweeny, who read so many versions of the Introduction that I lost count, and yet still always had ideas on how to sharpen it.

At HarperCollins, I want to thank Lynn Grady, Ben Steinberg, Kendra Newton, and Heidi Richter for their innovative plan for bringing the secrets of rebel talent to a wide audience.

I am also indebted to my HBS Research Director, Teresa Amabile, as well as HBS Director of Research Jan Rivkin and HBS Dean Nitin Nohria for being such stalwart supporters of my work. This book would not exist without their devotion to my research over the years, and their insistence that I always aim higher. Special thanks also to Steve O'Donnell, who graciously keeps an eye on my spending: Steve, this year I promise not to blow my budget.

Writing a book with three children under the age of five was not always easy and it would not have been possible were it not for the peace of mind that comes from knowing they were in great hands when I could not be with them. I want to give a special thanks to the people who took good care of my little ones. I am grateful to Glenda and Mena Chavez, for the love you have for our family, and for the sweetness you brought into our home. Thanks also to Jayla Chavez, who often spent her days off school with us, making the little ones laugh, and being a wonderful role model for them.

My mother deserves my deepest gratitude. I can't believe I am still asking you favors as an adult, after all you've done—and that you are willing to fly across the ocean many times a year to pitch in. I couldn't have written this book without your generous help. Thanks to my brother, Davide, my sister, Elisa, and my father, not only for allowing me to "borrow" Mom for long periods of time, but also for being so understanding and supportive of the work that I do.

Last but not least . . . I am forever grateful to my wonderful other half, Greg Burd. I broke many rules while working on this book, from staying up late to filling many of our conversations with research ideas: You are more than a good sport. Greg, thank you for your grace, your steady encouragement for any project I take on, and your generous partnership at home. You are the biggest reason why I keep smiling even when the pages are blank. I feel so lucky to have met you, and am reminded of this whenever I look at the three wonderful little rebels we brought into the world together.

January 3, 2018
Cambridge, Massachusetts

NOTES

INTRODUCTION: *MARCIA!*

ix **Introduction epigraph:** Jane Kramer. (2013, November 4). "Post-Modena," *The New Yorker* 89, no. 35 (November 4, 2014). Retrieved from www.newyorker.com.

ix **Story of Osteria Francescana:** Personal interviews with Bottura, June 7 and 11, 2016; Personal interviews with staff at Osteria Francescana during May and June of 2016. Two-day visit at the restaurant, July 26–27, 2016.

1. NAPOLEON AND THE HOODIE

1 **Chapter 1 epigraph:** Retrieved from AZ Quotes, http://www .azquotes.com/quote/1428582 (accessed November 29, 2017).

1 **"40 centuries look down upon you":** David Chandler, *The Campaigns of Napoleon* (New York: Simon & Schuster, 2009), p. 224.

1 **Story of Bonaparte:** Ibid.; Andrew Roberts, *Napoleon the Great* (New York: Penguin, 2015); Andrew Roberts, *Napoleon: A Life* (New York: Penguin, 2015); Alan Forrest, *Napoleon's Men: The Soldiers of the Revolution and Empire* (London: Hambledon and London, 2002); Stephanie Jones and Jonathan Gosling, *Napoleonic Leadership: A Study in Power* (Thousand Oaks, CA: SAGE Publications, 2015). Personal interviews with Andrew Roberts, summer 2017.

5 **Bonaparte also fought in the trenches:** Ralph Jean-Paul, "Napoleon Bonaparte's Guide to Leadership," *Potential2Sucess,* http://potential2success.com/napoleonbonaparteleadership.html (accessed November 17, 2017).

5 **a job usually performed by a corporal:** Will Durant and Ariel Durant, *The Age of Napoleon,* vol. 11 *The Story of Civilization* (Ashland, OR: Blackstone Audio, 2015).

6 **the subject of a case study:** Francesca Gino, Bradley R. Staats, Brian J. Hall, and Tiffany Y. Chang, "The Morning Star Company: Self-Management at Work," Harvard Business School Case 914-013, September 2013 (revised June 2016).

8 **rules governing many social interactions:** Marco F. H. Schmidt, Lucas P. Butler, Julia Heinz, and Michael Tomasello, "Young Children See a Single Action and Infer a Social Norm: Promiscuous Normativity in 3-Year-Olds," *Psychological Science* 27, no. 10 (2016): 1360–1370.

8 **the stocks or pillory in the center of town:** Gary Ferraro and Susan Andreatta, *Cultural Anthropology: An Applied Perspective* (Belmont, CA: Wadsworth Publishing, 2011).

10 **fourteen-karat gold:** Walter Lord, *The Good Years: From 1900 to the First World War* (New York: Harper and Brothers, 1960).

10 **cheaper, functional equivalents:** Thorstein Veblen, *The Theory of the Leisure Class* (London: Macmillan, 1965 [1899]).

11 **common in the animal world, too:** Gibert Roberts, "Competitive Altruism: From Reciprocity to the Handicap Principle," *Proceedings of the Royal Society B: Biological Sciences* 265, no. 1394 (1998): 427–431.

11 **attract mates and raise their status:** Amotz Zahavi and Avishag Zahavi, *The Handicap Principle: A Missing Piece of Darwin's Puzzle* (New York: Oxford University Press, 1997); Alan Grafen, "Biological Signals as Handicaps," *Journal of Theoretical Biology* 144 (1990): 517–546.

12 **told Bloomberg TV:** Doug Gross, "Zuckerberg's Hoodie Rankles Wall Street," *CNN,* May 9, 2012, http://www.cnn.com/2012

/05/09/tech/social-media/zuckerberg-hoodie-wall-street/index.html (accessed November 27, 2017).

13 **my research shows:** Silvia Bellezza, Francesca Gino, and Anat Keinan, "The Red Sneakers Effect: Inferring Status and Competence from Signals of Nonconformity," *Journal of Consumer Research* 41, no. 1 (2014): 35–54.

17 **in front of an audience of peers:** Francesca Gino, "When Breaking Rules Pays Off: How Nonconforming Behaviors Increase Confidence and Engagement," Working paper, 2016 (available from author).

18 **their personal lives outside of work for a few weeks:** Ibid.

18 **an experiment:** Ibid.

19 **powerful, research says:** Gerben A. Van Kleef, Astrid C. Homan, Catrin Finkenauer, Seval Gündemir, and Eftychia Stamkou, "Breaking the Rules to Rise to Power: How Norm Violators Gain Power in the Eyes of Others," *Social Psychology and Personality Science* 2, no. 5 (2011) 500–507.

20 **what the experimenter might think:** Adam D. Galinsky, Deborah H. Gruenfeld, and Joe C. Magee, "From Power to Action," *Journal of Personality and Social Psychology* 85, no. 3 (2003): 453–466.

20 **ignore situational pressure:** Jacob B. Hirsh, Adam D. Galinsky, and Chen-Bo Zhong, "Drunk, Powerful, and in the Dark: How General Processes of Disinhibition Produce Both Prosocial and Antisocial Behavior," *Perspectives on Psychological Science* 6, no. 5 (2011): 415–427.

20 **a more socially acceptable emotion:** Sally D. Farley, "Attaining Status at the Expense of Likeability: Pilfering Power Through Conversational Interruption," *Journal of Nonverbal Behavior* 32, no. 4 (2008): 241–260.

2. THE DOG NAMED "HOT"

23 **Chapter 2 epigraph:** Raymond Chandler, *The Long Good-Bye* (Boston: Houghton Mifflin, 1954).

26 **seven married women greet them:** These examples are also mentioned in Ovul Sezer, Michael I. Norton, Francesca Gino, and Kathleen D. Vohs, "Family Rituals Improve the Holidays," *Journal of the Association for Consumer Research* 1, no. 4 (2016): 509–526.

27 **improve group performance:** Tami Kim, Ovul Sezer, Juliana Schroeder, Jane Risen, Francesca Gino, and Mike Norton, "Group Rituals Increase Liking, Meaning, and Group Effort," Working paper, *Open Science Framework* (2017), https://osf.io/xcun3/ (accessed November 17, 2017).

28 **they even copy their mistakes:** Derek E. Lyons, Andrew G. Young, and Frank C. Keil, "The Hidden Structure of Overimitation," *PNAS* 104, no. 50 (2007): 19751–19756.

29 **higher levels of fidelity than preschoolers:** Nicola McGuigan, Jenny Makinson, and Andrew Whiten, "From Over-Imitation to Super-Copying: Adults Imitate Causally Irrelevant Aspects of Tool Use with Higher Fidelity Than Young Children," *British Journal of Psychology* 102, no. 1 (2011): 1–18.

29 **folding T-shirts:** Francesca Gino, "Taking Organizational Processes for Granted: Why Inefficiencies Stick around in Organizations," Working paper, 2016 (available from author).

30 **sticking with a status quo position:** William Samuelson and Richard Zeckhauser, "Status Quo Bias in Decision Making," *Journal of Risk and Uncertainty* 1 (1988): 7–59.

30 **the idea of potential gains:** Daniel Kahneman and Amos Tversky, "Prospect Theory: An Analysis of Decision under Risk," *Econometrica* 47, no. 2 (1979): 263–291.

31 **Italian Commedia dell'Arte:** Sources used for the history of improv: Keith Johnstone, *Impro: Improvisation and the Theatre* (London: Routledge, 1987); Steve Kaplan, *The Hidden Tools of Comedy: The Serious Business of Being Funny* (Studio City, CA: Michael Wiese Productions, 2013); Jeffrey Sweet, *Something Wonderful Right Away: An Oral History of The Second City and The Compass Players* (New York: Limelight Editions, 2004); and Kelly Leonard and Tom Yorton, *Yes, And: How Improvisation Reverses*

"No, But" Thinking and Improves Creativity and Collaboration— Lessons from The Second City (New York: HarperBusiness, 2015).

33 **a second look at the snakes:** Alfred Edmund Brehm, *Brehm's Life of Animals: A Complete Natural History for Popular Home Instruction and for the Use of Schools,* trans. R. Schmidtlein (London: Forgotten Books, 2015 [1864]).

33 **friends and threats in our environment:** Wojciech Pisula, *Curiosity and Information Seeking in Animal and Human Behavior* (Boca Raton, FL: Brown Walker Press, 2009).

33 **unfamiliar things:** Adele Diamond, "Evidence of Robust Recognition Memory Early in Life Even When Assessed by Reaching Behavior," *Journal of Experimental Child Psychology* 59, no. 3 (1995): 419–456; Jennifer S. Lipton and Elizabeth S. Spelke, "Origins of Number Sense: Large-Number Discrimination in Human Infants," *Psychological Science* 14, no. 5 (2003): 396–401.

34 **genes linked to novelty seeking:** Specifically, the genes are DRD4 exon 3 gene alleles 2R and 7R. Joel Lehman and Kenneth O. Stanley, "Abandoning Objectives: Evolution through the Search for Novelty Alone," *Evolutionary Computation* 19, no. 2 (2011): 189–223. See also Wojciech Pisula, Kris Turlejski, and Eric Phillip Charles, "Comparative Psychology as Unified Psychology: The Case of Curiosity and Other Novelty-Related Behavior," *Review of General Psychology* 17, no. 2 (2013): 224–229.

34 **northeast Tennessee and southwestern Virginia:** Gary P. Pisano, Francesca Gino, and Bradley R. Staats, "Pal's Sudden Service— Scaling an Organizational Model to Drive Growth," Harvard Business School Case 916-052, May 2016 (revised March 2017).

36 **a Japanese bank:** Bradley R. Staats and Francesca Gino, "Specialization and Variety in Repetitive Tasks: Evidence from a Japanese Bank," *Management Science* 58, no. 6, (2012): 1141–1159.

36 **a list of facts:** Brent A. Mattingly and Gary W. Lewandowski Jr., "The Power of One: Benefits of Individual Self-Expansion," *Journal of Positive Psychology* 8, no. 1 (2013): 12–22.

36 **accomplish new things in the future:** Brent A. Mattingly and Gary W. Lewandowski Jr., "An Expanded Self Is a More Capable

Self: The Association Between Self-Concept Size and Self-Efficacy," *Self and Identity* 12, no. 6 (2013): 621–634.

36 **the act was anonymous:** Timothy D. Wilson, David B. Centerbar, Deborah A. Kermer, and Daniel T. Gilbert, "The Pleasures of Uncertainty: Prolonging Positive Moods in Ways People Do Not Anticipate," *Journal of Personality and Social Psychology* 88, no. 1 (2005): 5–21.

37 **after seeing the film:** Ibid.

37 **skiing, hiking, or dancing:** Charlotte Reissman, Arthur Aron, and Merlynn R. Bergen, "Shared Activities and Marital Satisfaction: Causal Direction and Self-Expansion versus Boredom," *Journal of Social and Personal Relationships* 10 (1993): 243–254.

38 **relationship satisfaction:** Kimberley Coulter and John M. Malouff, "Effects of an Intervention Designed to Enhance Romantic Relationship Excitement: A Randomized-Control Trial," *Couple and Family Psychology: Research and Practice* 2, no. 1 (2013): 34–44.

38 **nine years later:** Irene Tsapelas, Arthur Aron, and Terri Orbuch, "Marital Boredom Now Predicts Less Satisfaction 9 Years Later," *Psychological Science* 20 (2009): 543–545.

38 **they shared novel activities:** K. Daniel O'Leary, Bianca P. Acevedo, Arthur Aron, Leonie Huddy, and Debra Mashek, "Is Long-Term Love More Than a Rare Phenomenon? If So, What Are Its Correlates?," *Social Psychology and Personality Science* 3, no. 2 (2012): 241–249.

38 **the relationship as exciting:** Arthur Aron, Christina Norman, Elaine Aron, Colin McKenna, and Richard Heyman, "Couples' Shared Participation in Novel and Arousing Activities and Experienced Relationship Quality," *Journal of Personality and Social Psychology* 78 (2000): 273–284.

41 **describe who we are:** Brent A. Mattingly and Gary W. Lewandowski Jr., "Broadening Horizons: Self-Expansion in Relational and Nonrelational Contexts," *Social and Personality Psychology Compass* 8 (2014): 30–40. See also Brent A. Mattingly

and Gary W. Lewandowski Jr., "Expanding the Self Brick by Brick: Non-Relational Self-Expansion and Self-Concept Size," *Social Psychological and Personality Science* 5 (2014): 483–489; and Kevin P. McIntyre, Brent A. Mattingly, Gary W. Lewandowski Jr., and Annie Simpson, "Workplace Self-Expansion: Implications for Job Satisfaction, Commitment, Self-Concept Clarity and Self-Esteem Among the Employed and Unemployed," *Basic and Applied Social Psychology* 36 (2014): 59–69.

41 **no matter how tough the road:** Mattingly and Lewandowski, "The Power of One: Benefits of Individual Self-Expansion."

3. THE VANISHING ELEPHANT

43 **Chapter 3 epigraph:** Leo Hardy, *Paranormal Investigators 8: Harry Houdini and Sir Arthur Conan Doyle* (New York: Pronoun, 2017).

43 **"supreme in size and extravagance":** July 1917 issue of *The Green Book Magazine* (p. 788).

44 **Houdini story:** William Kalush and Larry Sloman, *The Secret Life of Houdini: The Making of America's First Superhero* (New York: Atria Books, 2007); James Randi and Bert Randolph Sugar, *Houdini: His Life and Art* (New York: Grosset & Dunlap, 1976); Kenneth Silverman, *Houdini!!! The Career of Erich Weiss* (New York: HarperCollins, 1996); and Daniel E. Harmon, "Houdini— The Greatest Showman of All?," *New York Times*, November 1, 1981, p. D4.

45 **"this strange appearance":** Adam Smith, *Selected Philosophical Writings*, ed. James R. Otteson (Exeter, Eng.: Imprint Academic, 2004).

47 **Houdini remembered:** Kalush and Sloman, *The Secret Life of Houdini*.

47 **a car for the masses:** Willy Shih, "Ford vs. GM: The Evolution of Mass Production (A)," Harvard Business School Case 614-010, August 2013 (revised November 2013); and interviews with Ford employees, May 4, 2016.

48 **"has failed to master change":** National Research Council, *The Competitive Status of the U.S. Auto Industry: A Study of the Influences of Technology in Determining International Industrial Competitive Advantage* (Washington, D.C.: National Academies Press, 1982), p. 27.

49 **curiosity, research suggests:** Alison Gopnika, Shaun O'Grady, Christopher G. Lucas, et al., "Changes in Cognitive Flexibility and Hypothesis Search Across Human Life History from Childhood to Adolescence to Adulthood," *PNAS* 114, no. 30 (2017): 7892–7899; Laura E. Schulz and Elizabeth Baraff Bonawitz, "Serious Fun: Preschoolers Engage in More Exploratory Play When Evidence Is Confounded," *Developmental Psychology* 43, no. 4 (2007): 1045–1050; Maureen A. Callanan and Lisa M. Oakes, "Preschoolers' Questions and Parents' Explanations: Causal Thinking in Everyday Activity," *Cognitive Development* 7, no. 2 (1992): 213–233; Alison Gopnik, "Scientific Thinking in Young Children: Theoretical Advances, Empirical Research, and Policy Implications," *Science* 337, no. 6102 (2012): 1623–1627; and Cristine H. Legare, "The Contributions of Explanation and exploration to Children's Scientific Reasoning," *Child Development Perspectives* 8, no. 2 (2014): 101–106.

50 **Story of Greg Dyke at the BBC:** Greg Dyke, *Inside Story*; Georgina Born, Uncertain Vision: *Birt, Dyke and the Reinvention of the BBC*; Rosabeth M. Kanter and Douglas A. Raymond, "British Broadcasting Corporation (A): One BBC," Harvard Business School Case 303-075, February 2003 (revised July 2005); Rosabeth M. Kanter and Douglas A. Raymond, "British Broadcasting Corporation (B): Making it Happen," Harvard Business School Case 303-076, February 2003 (revised July 2005); and Peter Killing and Tracey Keys, "Greg Dyke Taking the Helm at the BBC (A)," IMD Case, IMD-3-1353, January 2006.

53 **were also put in place:** Rosabeth M. Kanter, *Confidence: How Winning Streaks and Losing Streaks Begin and End* (New York: Three Rivers Press, 2006).

53 **a group of 170 students:** Alison Wood Brooks, Francesca Gino, and Maurice E. Schweitzer, "Smart People Ask for (My) Advice: Seeking Advice Boosts Perceptions of Competence," *Management Science* 61, no. 6 (2015): 1421–1435.

54 **many questions or just a few:** Karen Huang, Michael Yeomans, Alison Wood Brooks, et al., "It Doesn't Hurt to Ask: Question-Asking Increases Liking," *Journal of Personality and Social Psychology* 113, no. 3, (2017): 430–452.

54 **information about themselves:** Ibid.

55 **engaged in small talk:** Todd B. Kashdan, Patrick E. McKnight, Frank D. Fincham, and Paul Rose, "When Curiosity Breeds Intimacy: Taking Advantage of Intimacy Opportunities and Transforming Boring Conversations," *Journal of Personality* 79 (2011): 1067–1099.

55 **in existing relationships:** Todd B. Kashdan and John E. Roberts, "Trait and State Curiosity in the Genesis of Intimacy: Differentiation from Related Constructs," *Journal of Social and Clinical Psychology* 23 (2004): 792–816. See also Todd B. Kashdan and John E. Roberts, "Affective Outcomes and Cognitive Processes in Superficial and Intimate Interactions: Roles of Social Anxiety and Curiosity," *Journal of Research in Personality* 40 (2006): 140–167.

55 **when we respond to a provocation:** Todd B. Kashdan, C. Nathan DeWall, Richard S. Pond Jr., et al.,"Curiosity Protects Against Interpersonal Aggression: Cross-Sectional, Daily Process, and Behavioral Evidence," *Journal of Personality* 81, no. 1 (2013): 87–102.

56 **excuse transgressions:** Diane S. Berry, Julie K. Willingham, and Christine A. Thayer, "Affect and Personality as Predictors of Conflict and Closeness in Young Adults' Friendships," *Journal of Research in Personality* 34, no. 1 (2000): 84–107.

56 **behavior and learning that it inspires:** Todd B. Kashdan, and Michael F. Steger, "Curiosity and Stable and Dynamic Pathways to Wellness: Traits, States, and Everyday Behaviors," *Motivation*

and Emotion 31, no. 3 (2007): 159–173. See also Jaak Panksepp, "The Primary Process Affects in Human Development, Happiness, and Thriving," in *Designing Positive Psychology: Taking Stock and Moving Forward*, ed. Kennon M. Sheldon, Todd B. Kashdan, and Michael F. Steger (New York: Oxford University Press, 2011), 51–85.

56 the top of the glass: Susan Engel, "Children's Need to Know: Curiosity in Schools," *Harvard Education Review* 81, no. 4 (2011): 625–645. Susan Engel, *The Hungry Mind: The Origins of Curiosity in Childhood* (Cambridge: Harvard University Press, 2015).

56 Scott Cook Innovation Award: Personal conversation, May 2015.

58 living in Turkey: FTN News, "General Manager of The Ritz Carlton Istanbul," https://www.youtube.com/watch?v=jmcQdy4 DgdE (accessed November 17, 2017).

60 between efficiency and innovation in 1991: James G. March, "Exploration and Exploitation in Organizational Learning," *Organization Science* 2, no. 1 (1991): 71–87.

60 Olivetti story: Adriano Olivetti, *La biografia di Valerio Ochetto* (Rome: Edizioni di Comunità, 2013); Adriano Olivetti, *Le Fabbriche di Bene* (Rome: Edizioni di Comunità, 2014); Pier Giorgio Perotto, *P101: Quando l'Italia inventò il personal computer* (Rome: Edizioni di Comunità, 2015); interview with Riccardo Delleani, CEO of Olivetti, May 15, 2017; and interview with Bruno Lamborghini, May 17, 2017.

63 "T-shaped" employees: Sources for the story: Morten T. Hansen, "IDEO CEO Tim Brown: T-Shaped Stars: The Backbone of IDEO's Collaborative Culture," *Chief Executive*, January 21, 2010, https://chiefexecutive.net/ideo-ceo-tim-brown-t-shaped-stars-the -backbone-of-ideoaes-collaborative-culture__trashed/ (accessed November 28, 2017); and Haluk Demirkan and Jim Spohrer, "T-Shaped Innovators: Identifying the Right Talent to Support Service Innovation," *Research-Technology Management* 58, no. 5 (2015): 12–15.

63 curiosity and innovation abounds: Spencer Harrison, "Organizing the Cat? Generative Aspects of Curiosity in

Organizational Life," in *The Oxford Handbook of Positive Organizational Scholarship*, edited by Gretchen M. Spreitzer and Kim S. Cameron (Oxford: Oxford University Press, 2011).

64 **people sell handmade goods:** Lydia Paine Hagtvedt, Karyn Dossinger, and Spencer Harrison, "Curiosity Enabled the Cat: Curiosity as a Driver of Creativity," *Academy of Management Proceedings* (2016): 13231 (and working paper).

64 **their company's call center:** Spencer Harrison, David M. Sluss, and Blake E. Ashforth, "Curiosity Adapted the Cat: The Role of Trait Curiosity in Newcomer Adaptation," *Journal of Applied Psychology* 96, no. 1 (2011): 211–220.

65 **Google story:** Interviews with members of the People Innovation Lab at Google (Jennifer Kurkoski and Jessica Wisdom), May and August 2015; and Saman Musacchio, "What Google's Genius Billboard from 2004 Can Teach Us About Solving Problems," *Business Insider*, July 22, 2011, http://www.businessinsider.com /what-google-can-teach-us-about-solving-problems-2011-7 (accessed November 17, 2017).

66 **the most curious candidates:** Scott Simon, "Solve the Equation, Get an Interview," *National Public Radio*, October 9, 2004, https:// www.npr.org/2004/10/09/4078172/solve-the-equation-get-an -interview (accessed November 28, 2017).

66 **exact times of the day that this occurs?:** Here is the solution, in case you are curious. After 12 o'clock, the minute hand races ahead of the hour hand. By the time the minute hand has gone all the way round the clock and is back at 12, one hour later (i.e., at 1 o'clock), the hour hand has moved to indicate 1. Five minutes later, the minute hand reaches 1 and is almost on top of the hour hand, but not quite, since by then the hour hand has moved ahead a tiny amount more. So the next time after 12 that the minute hand is directly over the hour hand is a bit after 1:05. Similarly, the next time it happens is a bit after 2:10. Then a bit after 3:15, and so on. The eleventh time this happens, a bit after 11:55, has to be 12 o'clock again, since we know what the clock looks like at that time. So the two hands are superimposed exactly twelve

times in each twelve-hour period. To answer the second part of the puzzle, you have to figure out those little bits of time you have to keep adding on each hour. Well, after 12 o'clock, there are eleven occasions when the two hands match up, and since the clock hands move at constant speeds, those eleven events are spread equally apart around the clock face, so they are 1/11th of an hour apart. That's 5.454545 minutes apart, so the little bit you keep adding is in fact 0.454545 minutes. The precise times of the super-positions are, in hours, 1 + 1/11, 2 + 2/11, 3+ 3/11, all the way up to 11 + 11/11, which is 12 o'clock again.

67 **"questions, not answers":** Jeremy Caplan, "Google's Chief Looks Ahead," *Time*, October 2, 2006.

68 **"have them stay":** "Cognition Switch: What Employers Can Do to Encourage Their Workers to Retrain," *The Economist*, January 14, 2017, https://www.economist.com/news/special -report/21714171-companies-are-embracing-learning-core-skill -what-employers-can-do-encourage-their (accessed November 28, 2017).

69 **expression turns negative:** Robin Hornik, Nancy Risenhoover, and Megan Gunnar, "The Effects of Maternal Positive, Neutral, and Negative Affective Communications on Infant Responses to New Toys," *Child Development* 58, no. 4 (1987): 937–944. Susan C. Crockenberg and Esther M. Leerkes, "Infant and Maternal Behaviors Regulate Infant Reactivity to Novelty at 6 Months," *Developmental Psychology* 40, no. 6 (2004): 1123–1132. See also: Robert Siegler, Nancy Eisenberg, Judy DeLoache, and Jenny Saffran, *How Children Develop*, 4th ed. (New York: Worth Publishers, 2014).

69 **openly with their colleagues:** Amy Edmondson, "Psychological Safety and Learning Behavior in Work Teams," *Administrative Science Quarterly* 44, no. 2 (1999): 350–383.

70 **apply their new knowledge:** Satya Nadella and Jill Tracie Nichols, *Hit Refresh: The Quest to Rediscover Microsoft's Soul and Imagine a Better Future for Everyone* (New York: HarperBusiness, 2017).

70 **challenge existing practices:** Ed Catmull, "How Pixar Fosters

Collective Creativity," *Harvard Business Review*, September 2008, https://hbr.org/2008/09/how-pixar-fosters-collective-creativity (accessed November 28, 2017).

70 **an online training program for the firm:** Personal conversation with Spencer Harrison, March 17, 2017.

71 **the Vanishing Elephant trick:** Lydia Paine Hagtvedt, Karyn Dossinger, and Spencer Harrison, "Curiosity Enabled the Cat: Curiosity as a Driver of Creativity," *Academy of Management Proceedings* (2016): 13231 (and working paper).

74 **not actually invented by Houdini:** Victoria Moore, "The Yorkshire Man Who Taught Houdini to Make an Elephant Disappear," *Daily Mail*, July 31, 2007, http://www.dailymail.co.uk /news/article-471954/The-Yorkshire-man-taught-Houdini-make -elephant-disappear.html (accessed November 17, 2017).

4. THE HUDSON RIVER IS A RUNWAY

77 **Chapter 4 epigraph:** Chesley B. Sullenberger III, with Jeffrey Zaslow, *Highest Duty: My Search for What Really Matters* (New York: William Morrow, 2009).

77 **Sully story:** Interview with Sullenberger, April 25, 2017; Sullenberger and Zaslow, *Highest Duty: My Search for What Really Matters*; Chesley B. Sullenberger III with Douglas Century, *Making a Difference: Stories of Vision and Courage from America's Leaders* (New York: William Morrow, 2012); and National Transportation Safety Board, Aircraft Accident Report, adopted May 4, 2010, https://www.ntsb.gov/investigations/AccidentReports/Reports /AAR1003.pdf (accessed November 28, 2017).

78 **Sully said:** Sullenberger and Zaslow, *Highest Duty: My Search for What Really Matters*, p. 209.

78 **Air Traffic Control:** "Cactus" is the radio call sign for US Airways flights. The airline chose it after it merged with the former America West Airlines.

83 **Flight 1549 was no different:** Interview with Sullenberger, April 25, 2017.

84 the modern world: Giora Keinan, Nehemia Friedland, and Yossef Ben-Porath, "Decision-Making Under Stress: Scanning of Alternatives Under Physical Threat," *Acta Psychologica* 64, no. 3 (1987): 219–228.

85 we broaden our perspective: Ting Zhang, Francesca Gino, and Joshua Margolis, "Does 'Could' Lead to Good? On the Road to Moral Insight," *Academy of Management Journal* (2018, in press).

86 a group of study participants: Ibid.

87 a vascular stent: Interviews with three surgeons at a major hospital in Boston, April–May 2015.

88 blood clotting and even death: Susan Mayor, "Drug Eluting Stents Are Safe for Licensed Indications, FDA Panel Says," *BMJ* 333, no. 7581 (2006): 1235.

88 what role expertise might play: Bradley R. Staats, Diwas S. KC, and Francesca Gino, "Maintaining Beliefs in the Face of Negative News: The Moderating Role of Experience," *Management Science* (2017, in press).

89 "tactical military aviation," he's said: Carl Von Wodtke, "The 'Miracle on the Hudson' Was No Miracle; It Was the Culmination of a 35-Year Military and Airline Flying Career," *History Net*, September 7, 2016, http://www.historynet.com/sully-speaks-out .htm (accessed November 28, 2017).

89 must be kept alive: Interview with Sullenberger, April 25, 2017.

90 landing planes: Ruth Kanfer and Phillip L. Ackerman, "Motivation and Cognitive Abilities: An Integrative/Aptitude-Treatment Interaction Approach to Skill Acquisition" *Journal of Applied Psychology* 74, no. 4 (1989) 657–690.

90 had learning goals: Don VandeWalle, Steven P. Brown, William L. Cron, and John W. Slocum, Jr., "The Influence of Goal Orientation and Self-Regulation Tactics on Sales Performance: A Longitudinal Field Test," *Journal of Applied Psychology* 84, no. 2 (1999): 249–259.

90 "control over relevant outcomes": Joachim I. Krueger, "Return of the Ego—Self-Referent Information as a Filter for Social Prediction: Comment on Karniol (2003)," *Psychological Review* 110, no. 3 (2003): 585–590. See page 585.

90 **two hypothetical investment options:** Staats, KC, and Gino, "Maintaining Beliefs in the Face of Negative News: The Moderating Role of Experience."

91 **power aggravates the problem:** Adam D. Galinsky, Joe C. Magee, M. Ena Inesi, and Deborah H Gruenfeld, "Power and Perspectives Not Taken," *Psychological Science* 17, no. 12 (2006): 1068–1074.

92 **power over other people:** Leigh Plunkett Tost, Francesca Gino, and Richard P. Larrick, "Power, Competitiveness, and Advice Taking: Why the Powerful Don't Listen," *Organizational Behavior and Human Decision Processes* 117, no. 1 (2012): 53–65.

92 **taking most of the airtime:** Leigh Plunkett Tost, Francesca Gino, and Richard P. Larrick, "When Power Makes Others Speechless: The Negative Impact of Leader Power on Team Performance," *Academy of Management Journal* 56, no. 5 (2013): 1465–1486.

92 **a lot of room to others' perspective:** Deborah Britt Roebuck, *Communication Strategies for Today's Managerial Leader* (Cambridge, MA: Business Expert Press, 2012).

92 **contribute whenever appropriate:** Juliana L. Stone, Emma-Louise Aveling, Molly Frean, et al., "Effective Leadership of Surgical Teams: A Mixed Methods Study of Surgeon Behaviors and Functions," *The Annals of Thoracic Surgery* 104, no. 2 (2017): 530–537.

93 **the detriment of patients:** Amy C. Edmondson, "Speaking Up in the Operating Room: How Team Leaders Promote Learning in Interdisciplinary Action Teams," *Journal of Management Studies* 40 (2003): 1419–1452.

93 **a snowy flight out of Minneapolis:** Interview with Sullenberger, April 25, 2017.

94 **both Friday and Saturday night:** Interview with Giuseppe Palmieri, July 7, 2016.

95 **when we weigh ourselves:** Daniel Gilbert, "I'm O.K., You're Biased," *New York Times*, April 16, 2006, http://www.nytimes.com/2006/04/16/opinion/im-ok-youre-biased.html (accessed November 28, 2017).

95 **a dangerous enzyme deficiency:** Peter H. Ditto and David

F. Lopez, "Motivated Skepticism: Use of Differential Decision Criteria for Preferred and Nonpreferred Conclusions," *Journal of Personality and Social Psychology* 63, no. 4 (1992): 568–584.

95 college admission decisions: Ibid.

97 had certain events not occurred: Hal Ersner-Hershfield, Adam D. Galinsky, Laura J. Kray, and Brayden G. King, "Company, Country, Connections: Counterfactual Origins Increase Organizational Commitment, Patriotism, and Social Investment," *Psychological Science* 21, no. 10 (2010): 1479–1486.

97 do better in the future: Rachel Smallman and Neal J. Roese, "Counterfactual Thinking Facilitates Behavioral Intentions," *Journal of Experimental Social Psychology* 45, no. 4 (2009): 845–852.

97 the unpredictability of life: Laura J. Kray, and Adam D. Galinsky, "The Debiasing Effect of Counterfactual Mind-Sets: Increasing the Search for Disconfirmatory Information in Group Decisions," *Organizational Behavior and Human Decision Processes* 91, no. 1 (2003): 69–81.

97 that was pivotal in their lives: Laura J. Kray, Linda G. George, Katie A. Liljenquist, et al., "From What Might Have Been to What Must Have Been: Counterfactual Thinking Creates Meaning," *Journal of Personality and Social Psychology* 98 (2010): 106–118.

98 people who became their best friends: Ibid.

98 the experience of being *in*experienced: Ting Zhang, Tami Kim, Alison Wood Brooks, et al., "A 'Present' for the Future: The Unexpected Value of Rediscover," *Psychological Science* 25, no. 10 (2014): 1851–1860.

98 recruited expert guitarists: Ting Zhang, "Back to the beginning: How rediscovering inexperience helps experts advise novices." Working paper, 2017 (available from author).

99 relatively cheap lasers: Thomas W. Overton and James E. Shigley, "A History of Diamond Treatments," in *The Global Diamond Industry: Economics and Development*, vol. 2, ed. Roman Grynberg and Letsema Mbayi (Basingstoke, UK: Palgrave Macmillan, 2015).

100 Story of InnoCentive: Karim R. Lakhani, "InnoCentive.com

(A)," Harvard Business School Case 608-170, June 2008 (revised October 2009).

101 **over 300,000 registered solvers:** Ben Shneiderman, *The New ABCs of Research: Achieving Breakthrough Collaborations* (Oxford: Oxford University Press, 2016), p. 134.

101 **an astrophysicist:** Thomas M. Koulopoulos, *The Innovation Zone: How Great Companies Re-Innovate for Amazing Success* (Mountain View, CA: Nicholas Breale, 2011), p. 97.

101 **closer to the problem:** Karim R. Lakhani, Lars Bo Jeppesen, Peter A. Lohse, and Jill A. Panetta, "The Value of Openness in Scientific Problem Solving," *Harvard Business School Working Paper* No. 07-050, p. 11, http://www.hbs.edu/faculty/Publication%20 Files/07-050.pdf (accessed November 17, 2017).

101 **another project:** Oguz Ali Acar and Jan van den Ende, "Knowledge Distance, Cognitive-Search Processes, and Creativity: The Making of Winning Solutions in Science Contests," *Psychological Science* 27, no. 5 (2016): 692–699.

102 **evidence that confirms our views:** Teresa Garcia-Marques and Diane M. Mackie, "The Feeling of Familiarity as a Regulator of Persuasive Processing," *Social Cognition* 19, no. 1 (2001): 9–34; Arie W. Kruglanski, "Lay Epistemo-Logic—Process and Contents: Another Look at Attribution Theory," *Psychological Review* 87, no. 1 (1980): 70–87; Charlan Jeanne Nemeth, "Differential Contributions of Majority and Minority Influence," *Psychological Review* 93, no. 1 (1986): 23–32; Claudia Toma and Fabrizio Butera, "Hidden Profiles and Concealed Information: Strategic Information Sharing and Use in Group Decision Making," *Personality and Social Psychology Bulletin* 35, no. 6 (2009): 793–806.

102 **the nearby neighborhood of Karaköy:** Aslı Çekmiş and Işıl Hacıhasanoğlu, "Water Crossing Utopias of Istanbul: Past and Future," *ITU Journal of the Faculty of Architecture* 9, no. 2 (2012): 67–88; Walter Isaacson, *Leonardo da Vinci* (New York: Simon & Schuster, 2017).

103 **a bridge based on Da Vinci's design:** Doug Mellgren, "Da Vinci

Comes to Life 500 Years On," *The Guardian*, November 1, 2001, https://www.theguardian.com/world/2001/nov/01/engineering .internationaleducationnews (accessed November 17, 2017).

103 **Story of Jessica Rosval:** Interviews with staff at Osteria Francescana, July 26–27, 2016.

104 **what we know is sharply limited:** Tenelle Porter and Karina Schumann, "Intellectual Humility and Openness to the Opposing View," *Self and Identity* (2017): 1–24.

104 **Story of dish *Camouflage*:** Interviews with staff at Osteria Francescana, July 26–27, 2016.

104 **different from the present:** Ethan Kross and Igor Grossmann, "Boosting Wisdom: Distance from the Self Enhances Wise Reasoning, Attitudes, and Behavior," *Journal of Experimental Psychology* 141, no. 1 (2012): 43–48.

5. UNCOMFORTABLE TRUTHS

107 **Chapter 5 epigraph:** George Bernard Shaw, *Pygmalion: A Romance in Five Acts* (New York: Penguin Books, 1957).

107 **Story of Ava Duvernay:** Interview with Tendo Nagenda, November 8, 2017; Interview with Avi Swerdlow, November 3, 2017; Katherine Schaffstall, "Ava DuVernay Unsure How 'Wrinkle in Time' Will Be Received," *Hollywood Reporter*, October 9, 2017, https://www.hollywoodreporter.com/news/ava -duvernay-unsure-how-wrinkle-time-will-be-received-new-yorker -festival-2017-1046858 (accessed November 28, 2017); Kristal Brent Zook, "Queen Ava," *Essence*, March 1, 2017, https://www .questia.com/magazine/1P3-4318030261/queen-ava (accessed November 28, 2017); Dale Roe, " 'Selma' Director Talks Motivations, Revelations," *Austin American-Statesman*, March 15, 2015; Loren King, "Ava DuVernay's March; 'Selma' Director Could Make History, Becoming the First African- American Woman to Get an Oscar Nod for Directing," *Boston Globe*, January 4, 2015; Manohla Dargis, "She Had a Dream: How This Woman Brought Martin Luther King's Epic Story to the Big Screen," *Observer*,

December 14, 2014; Joelle Monique, "Ava DuVernay on Walking into a Room 'Like a White Man'," *Vice*, July 6, 2017, Brittany Jones-Cooper, "Ava DuVernay Shares the Perks of Being a Red-Hot Director in Hollywood," *Yahoo Finance*, October 4, 2017, Ashley Lee, "Ava DuVernay's Advice on Hollywood: 'Follow the White Guys, They've Got This Thing Wired,'" *Hollywood Reporter*, July 18, 2015; Arianna Davis, "How Oprah & Ava Duvernay's Queen Sugar Has Transformed TV," *Refinery29*, June 19, 2017.

114 **I give my students a little test:** The test is known in the psychology literature as "Implicit Association Test." To learn more, you can read the paper that first introduced the test: Anthony G. Greenwald, Debbie E. McGhee, Jordan L. K. Schwartz, "Measuring Individual Differences in Implicit Cognition: The Implicit Association Test," *Journal of Personality and Social Psychology* 74, no. 6 (1998): 1464–1480.

115 **form primitive stereotypes:** Gary D. Levy and Robert A. Haaf, "Detection of Gender-Related Categories by 10-Month-Old Infants," *Infant Behavior and Development* 17, no. 4 (1994): 457–459.

115 **softness as female:** Mary Driver Leinbach, Barbara E. Hort, and Beverly I. Fagot, "Bears Are for Boys: Metaphorical Associations in Young Children's Gender Stereotypes," *Cognitive Development* 12, no. 1 (1997): 107–130; Marsha Weinraub, Lynda P. Clemens, Alan Sockloff, et al., "The Development of Sex Role Stereotypes in the Third Year: Relationships to Gender Labeling, Gender Identity, Sex-Typed Toy Preference, and Family Characteristics," *Child Development* 55, no. 4 (1984): 1493–1503.

115 **boys as being rough:** Cindy Faith Miller, Leah E. Lurye, Kristina M. Zosuls, and Diane N. Ruble, "Accessibility of Gender Stereotype Domains: Developmental and Gender Differences in Children," *Sex Roles* 60, nos. 11–12 (2009): 870–881.

116 **gravitate to people just like us:** William G. Graziano and Jennifer Weisho Bruce, "Attraction and the Initiation of Relationships: A Review of the Empirical Literature," in *Handbook of Relationship Initiation*, ed. Susan Sprecher, Amy Wenzel, and John H. Harvey (New York: Psychology Press, 2008); Miller McPherson, Lynn

Smith-Lovin, and James M. Cook, "Birds of a Feather: Homophily in Social Networks," *Annual Review of Sociology* 27 (2001), 415–444.

116 **people similar to us:** Angela J. Bahns, Christian S. Crandall, Omri Gillath, and Kristopher J. Preacher, "Similarity in Relationships as Niche Construction: Choice, Stability, and Influence Within Dyads in a Free Choice Environment," *Journal of Personality and Social Psychology* 112, no. 2 (2017): 329–355; Silke Anders, Roos de Jong, Christian Beck, John-Dylan Haynes, and Thomas Ethofer, "A Neural Link Between Affective Understanding and Interpersonal Attraction," *PNAS* 113, no. 16 (2016): E2248–E2257.

116 **backlash, researchers have found:** Laurie A. Rudman and Peter Glick, "Prescriptive Gender Stereotypes and Backlash Toward Agentic Women," *Journal of Social Issues* 57, no. 4 (2001): 743–762; Rudman and Glick, "Feminized Management and Backlash Toward Agentic Women: The Hidden Costs to Women of a Kinder, Gentler Image of Middle-Managers," *Journal of Personality and Social Psychology* 77, no. 5 (1999): 1004–1010.

116 **the backlash can be especially strong:** Madeline E. Heilman, Aaron S. Wallen, Daniella Fuchs, and Melinda M. Tamkins, "Penalties for Success: Reactions to Women who Succeed at Male Gender-Typed Tasks," *Journal of Applied Psychology* 89, no. 3 (2004), 416–427.

116 **"the right way for a woman to speak":** Alice Hendrickson Eagly and Linda Lorene Carli, *Through the Labyrinth: The Truth about how Women Become Leaders* (Cambridge, MA: Harvard Business Review Press, 2007), p. 102.

117 **respective national industry:** China Gorman, "Why Diverse Organizations Perform Better: Do We Still Need Evidence?," *Great Place to Work*, February 18, 2015, https://www.greatplacetowork.com/blog/238-why-diverse-organizations-perform-better-do-we-still-need-evidence (accessed November 17, 2017); Vivian Hunt, Dennis Layton, and Sara Prince, "Why Diversity Matters," McKinsey & Company, January 2015, http://www.mckinsey

.com/business-functions/organization/our-insights/why-diversity
-matters#0 (accessed November 17, 2017).

117 **better financial performance:** Lois Joy, Nancy M. Carter,
Harvey M. Wagner, and Sriram Narayanan, "The Bottom Line:
Corporate Performance and Women's Representation on Boards,"
Catalyst, October 15, 2007, http://www.catalyst.org/knowledge
/bottom-line-corporate-performance-and-womens-representation
-boards (accessed November 17, 2017).

117 **accelerates economic growth:** Organization for Economic
Cooperation and Development (OECD), *Gender Equality in
Education, Employment and Entrepreneurship: Final Report to the
MCM 2012*, p. 17, http://www.oecd.org/employment/50423364
.pdf (accessed November 17, 2017). See also Stephan Klasen
and Francesca Lamanna, "The Impact of Gender Inequality in
Education and Employment on Economic Growth: New Evidence
for a Panel of Countries," *Feminist Economics* 15, no. 3 (2009):
91–132.

117 **as much as 21 percent:** Anu Madgavkar, Kweilin Ellingrud, and
Mekala Krishnan, "The Economic Benefits of Gender Parity,"
Stanford Social Innovation Review, March 8, 2016, https://ssir.org
/articles/entry/the_economic_benefits_of_gender_parity (accessed
November 17, 2017).

117 **even if this wasn't the case:** Susan Ware, *Holding Their Own:
American Women in the 1930s* (Boston: Twayne, 1982).

118 **low-, medium-, and high-priced:** David Neumark, Roy J. Bank,
and Kyle D. Van Nort, "Sex Discrimination in Restaurant Hiring:
An Audit Study," *Quarterly Journal of Economics* 111, no. 3 (1996):
915–941.

118 **the reviews of women:** Kieran Snyder, "The Abrasiveness Trap:
High-Achieving Men and Women Are Described Differently in
Reviews," *Fortune*, August 26, 2014, http://fortune.com/2014
/08/26/performance-review-gender-bias (accessed November 17,
2017).

119 **Story of Ann Hopkins:** Ann Branigar Hopkins, *So Ordered:
Making Partner the Hard Way* (Amherst: University of

Massachusetts Press, 1996); Joseph L. Badaracco Jr. and Ilyse
Barkan, "Ann Hopkins (A)," Harvard Business School Case 391-
155, February 1991 (revised August 2001); Joseph L. Badaracco Jr.
and Ilyse Barkan, "Ann Hopkins (B)," Harvard Business School
Supplement 391–170, March 1991 (revised July 2001).

120 **good managers are typically male:** Arnie Cann and William D.
Siegfried, "Gender Stereotypes and Dimensions of Effective Leader
Behavior," *Sex Roles* 23, nos. 7–8 (1990): 413–419.

121 **the men get more credit:** Heather Sarsons, "Gender Differences in
Recognition for Group Work," working paper, November 4, 2017,
https://scholar.harvard.edu/files/sarsons/files/full_v6.pdf (accessed
November 17, 2017).

123 **not the case for women:** Victoria L. Brescoll, "Who Takes the
Floor and Why: Gender, Power, and Volubility in Organizations,"
Administrative Science Quarterly 56, no. 4 (2012): 622–641.

123 **incompetent and unworthy and are penalized:** Victoria L.
Brescoll and Eric Luis Uhlmann, "Can an Angry Woman Get
Ahead? Status Conferral, Gender, and Expression of Emotion in
the Workplace," *Psychological Science* 19, no. 3 (2008): 268–275.

123 **took the same test:** Steven J. Spencer, Christine Logel, and Paul
G. Davies, "Stereotype Threat," *Annual Review of Psychology* 67
(2016): 415–437; Steven J. Spencer, Claude M. Steele, and Diane
M. Quinn, "Stereotype Threat and Women's Math Performance,"
Journal of Experimental Social Psychology 35, no. 1 (1999): 4–28.

124 **leaders, negotiators, entrepreneurs, and competitors:** Laura J.
Kray and Aiwa Shirako, "Stereotype Threat in Organizations: An
Examination of Its Scope, Triggers, and Possible Interventions,"
in *Stereotype Threat: Theory, Process, and Applications*, ed. Michael
Inzlicht and Toni Schmader (New York: Oxford University Press,
2012), pp. 173–187.

124 **pain created by dental work:** Martina Amanzio and Fabrizio
Benedetti, "Neuropharmacological Dissection of Placebo
Analgesia: Expectation-Activated Opioid Systems versus
Conditioning-Activated Specific Subsystems," *Journal of
Neuroscience* 19, no. 1 (1999): 484–494.

126 **strides in their academic journey:** Robert Rosenthal and Lenore Jacobson, *Pygmalion in the Classroom: Teacher Expectation and Pupils' Intellectual Development* (New York: Holt, Rinehart and Winston, 1968).

126 **improves our performance:** Alison Wood Brooks, "Get Excited: Reappraising Pre-Performance Anxiety as Excitement," *Journal of Experimental Psychology: General* 143, no. 3 (June 2014): 1144–1158.

127 **Story of Bobbi Gibb:** Shanti Sosienski, *Women Who Run* (Berkeley, CA: Seal Press, 2006); Tom Derderian, *Boston Marathon: The History of the World's Premier Running Event* (Champaign, IL: Human Kinetics Publishers, 1996); Bobbi Gibb, *Wind in the Fire: A Personal Journey* (Boston: Institute of Natural Systems Press, 2012).

128 **devoted mothers than those who work:** Kathleen L. McGinn, Mayra Ruiz Castro, and Elizabeth Long Lingo, "Mums the Word! Cross-National Effects of Maternal Employment on Gender Inequalities at Work and at Home," Harvard Business School Working Paper, No. 15-094, June 2015 (revised July 2015).

128 **Weinstein had sexually assaulted multiple women:** Jia Tolentino, "Harvey Weinstein and the Impunity of Powerful Men," *New Yorker*, October 30, 2017.

129 **Story of Eileen Taylor of Deutsche Bank:** Interviews conducted with Deutsche Bank employees in February and March 2013.

129 **that reflects the U.S. equity market:** Cristian L. Dezsö and David Gaddis Ross, "Does Female Representation in Top Management Improve Firm Performance? A Panel Data Investigation," Robert H. Smith School Research Paper No. RHS 06-104, March 9, 2011, https://papers.ssrn.com/sol3/papers.cfm?abstract_id=1088182 (accessed November 17, 2017).

130 **a more stimulating workplace:** Work in progress in collaboration with Dan Ariely (of Duke University) and Evelyn Gosnell.

131 **organizations, nations, communities, and groups:** Adam D. Galinsky, Andrew R. Todd, Astrid C. Homan, et al., "Maximizing the Gains and Minimizing the Pains of Diversity: A Policy

Perspective," *Perspectives on Psychological Science* 10, no. 6 (2015): 742–748.

131 **and higher profits:** Cedric Herring, "Does Diversity Pay?: Race, Gender, and the Business Case for Diversity," *American Sociological Review* 74, no. 2 (2009): 208–224.

131 **products that were more innovative:** Katrin Talke, Søren Salomo, and Alexander Kock, "Top Management Team Diversity and Strategic Innovation Orientation: The Relationship and Consequences for Innovativeness and Performance," *Journal of Product Innovation Management* 28, no. 6 (2011): 819–832.

131 **travel and immigration:** Dean Keith Simonton, "Foreign Influence and National Achievement: The Impact of Open Milieus on Japanese Civilization," *Journal of Personality and Social Psychology* 72 (1997): 86–94.

131 **prosperity in a community:** Nathan Eagle, Michael Macy, and Rob Claxton, "Network Diversity and Economic Development," *Science* 328, no. 5981 (2010): 1029–1031.

131 **more financially solid:** Gianmarco I. P. Ottaviano and Giovanni Peri, "The Economic Value of Cultural Diversity: Evidence from US Cities," *Journal of Economic Geography* 6 (2006): 9–44.

131 **prevents price bubbles:** Sheen S. Levine, Evan P. Apfelbaum, Mark Bernard, et al., "Ethnic Diversity Deflates Price Bubbles," *Proceedings of the National Academy of Sciences* 111, no. 52 (2014): 18524–18529.

132 **fraternity and sorority members:** Katherine W. Phillips, Katie A. Liljenquist, and Margaret A. Neale, "Is the Pain Worth the Gain? The Advantages and Liabilities of Agreeing with Socially Distinct Newcomers," *Personality and Social Psychology Bulletin* 35, no. 3 (2009): 336–350.

133 **the fluency heuristic:** Ralph Hertwig, Stefan M. Herzog, Lael J. Schooler, and Torsten Reimer, "Fluency Heuristic: A Model of How the Mind Exploits a By-Product of Information Retrieval," *Journal of Experimental Psychology: Learning, Memory, and Cognition* 34, no. 5 (2008): 1191–1206.

133 **an organization's stance on diversity:** Geoffrey L. Cohen and Julio Garcia, "Identity, Belonging, and Achievement: A Model, Interventions, Implications," *Current Directions in Psychological Science* 17, no. 6 (2008): 365–369.

133 **they feel they do not belong:** Danielle Gaucher, Justin Friesen, and Aaron C. Kay, "Evidence That Gendered Wording in Job Advertisements Exists and Sustains Gender Inequality," *Journal of Personality and Social Psychology* 101, no. 1 (2011), 109–128.

134 **within the organization:** Valerie Purdie-Vaughns, Claude M. Steele, Paul G. Davies, et al., "Social Identity Contingencies: How Diversity Cues Signal Threat or Safety for African Americans in Mainstream Institutions," *Journal of Personality and Social Psychology* 94, no. 4 (2008): 615–630. See also Steven J. Spencer, Christine Logel, and Paul G. Davies, "Stereotype Threat," *Annual Review of Psychology* 67 (2016): 415–437.

134 **success for stereotyped individuals:** David M. Marx and Jasmin S. Roman, "Female Role Models: Protecting Women's Math Test Performance," *Personality and Social Psychology Bulletin* 28, no. 9 (2002): 1183–1193.

134 **additional resources to mixed-race groups:** Robert B. Lount Jr., Oliver J. Sheldon, Floor Rink, and Katherine W. Phillips, "Biased Perceptions of Racially Diverse Teams and Their Consequences for Resource Support," *Organization Science* 26, no. 5 (2015): 1351–1364.

134 **Story of the San Antonio Spurs:** María Triana, *Managing Diversity in Organizations: A Global Perspective* (New York: Routledge, 2017), p. 15; National Basketball Association, "NBA Tips Off 2013–2014 Season with Record International Player Presence," *NBA Global*, October 29, 2013, http://www.nba.com /global/nba_tips_off_201314_season_with_record_international _presence_2013_10_29.html (accessed November 29, 2017).

135 **the key to success:** Katherine W. Phillips, Gregory B. Northcraft, and Margaret A. Neale, "Surface-Level Diversity and Decision-Making in Groups: When Does Deep-Level Similarity Help?" *Group Processes & Intergroup Relations* 9, no. 4 (2006): 467–482.

136 who they thought committed the crime: Denise Lewin Loyd, Cynthia S. Wang, Katherine W. Phillips, and Robert B. Lount Jr., "Social Category Diversity Promotes Premeeting Elaboration: The Role of Relationship Focus," *Organization Science* 24, no. 3 (2013): 757–772.

136 more thorough in their preparation: Ibid. See also Samuel R. Sommers, Lindsey S. Warp, and Corrine C. Mahoney, "Cognitive Effects of Racial Diversity: White Individuals' Information Processing in Heterogeneous Groups," *Journal of Experimental Social Psychology* 44, no. 4 (2008): 1129–1136.

136 rather than as an opportunity: Research by Martin Davidson of the University of Virginia finds that organizations that rely on traditional approaches to manage diversity are generally ineffective, and that those that focus on leveraging differences are more successful in the long term. See Martin N. Davidson, *The End of Diversity as We Know It. Why Diversity Efforts Fail and How Leveraging Difference Can Succeed* (Oakland, CA: Berrett-Koehler Publishers, 2011).

137 she told *Time* magazine: Steve Lee, "Time Reveals 'Firsts: Women Who Are Changing the World,' a New Multimedia Project," *LGBT Weekly*, http://lgbtweekly.com/2017/09/07/time -reveals-firsts-women-who-are-changing-the-world-a-new -multimedia-project/ (accessed November 28, 2017).

6. COACH CHEEKS SINGS THE NATIONAL ANTHEM

139 Chapter 6 epigraph: Nathaniel Hawthorne, *The Scarlet Letter* (Cambridge, MA: Harvard University Press, 2009).

139 Story of Coach Cheeks: Ira Berkow, *Autumns in the Garden: The Coach of Camelot and Other Knicks Stories* (Chicago: Triumph Books, 2013). Video of the singing: https://www.youtube.com /watch?v=q4880PJnO2E.

141 a Good Samaritan: Ira Berkow, "Proper Praise for Cheeks's Saving Grace," *New York Times*, May 11, 2003, http://www.nytimes .com/2003/05/11/sports/sports-of-the-times-proper-praise-for -cheeks-s-saving-grace.html (accessed November 17, 2017).

141 **"guardian angel":** Elizabeth McGarr, "Natalie Gilbert," *Sports Illustrated*, August 2, 2010, https://www.si.com/vault /1969/12/31/105967059/natalie-gilbert (accessed November 17, 2017).

141 **Story of Patricia Fili-Krushel:** Kathleen L. McGinn, Deborah M. Kolb, and Cailin B. Hammer, "Traversing a Career Path: Pat Fili-Krushel (A)," Harvard Business School Case 909-009, September 2008 (revised June 2011); personal interview with Fili-Krushel, September 22, 2017.

142 **feel closer to us:** "Improving Relationships, Mental and Physical Health By Not Telling Lies," *Medical News Today*, August 7, 2012, http://www.medicalnewstoday.com/releases/248682.php (accessed November 17, 2017).

142 **paired them up for computer chats:** Li Jiang, Maryam Kouchaki, and Francesca Gino, F. (2017). "Attribution of authenticity: Powerful people benefit from self-disclosure of unfavorable information." Working paper (available from authors).

143 **"That's really embarrassing":** Lauren Sher, "Jennifer Lawrence Trips on Her Way to Collect Best Actress Award," ABC News, February 25, 2013, http://abcnews.go.com/Entertainment/oscars -2013-jennifer-lawrence-trips-on-her-way-to-collect-best-actress -award/blogEntry?id=18587011 (accessed November 17, 2017).

143 **"pratfall effect":** Elliot Aronson, Ben Willerman, and Joanne Floyd, "The Effect of a Pratfall on Increasing Interpersonal Attractiveness," *Psychonomic Science* 4, no. 6 (1966): 227–228. See also Robert Helmreich, Elliot Aronson, and James LeFan, "To Err Is Humanizing Sometimes: Effects of Self-Esteem, Competence, and a Pratfall on Interpersonal Attraction," *Journal of Personality and Social Psychology* 16, no. 2 (1970), 259–264.

143 **those who covered them up:** Joanne Silvester, Fiona Mary Anderson-Gough, Neil R. Anderson, and Afandi R. Mohamed, "Locus of Control, Attributions and Impression Management in the Selection Interview," *Journal of Occupational and Organizational Psychology* 75, no. 1 (2002): 59–76.

143 **Story of Scott Cook:** Personal interviews with Scott Cook in May 2014, May 2015, and October 2016.

145 evaluate this competitor: Karen Huang, Alison Wood Brooks, Brian Hall, et al., "Mitigating Envy: Why Successful Individuals Should Reveal Their Failures," Working paper, 2017 (available from authors).

145 results in higher grades: Xiaodong Lin-Siegler, Janet N. Ahn, Jondou Chen, et al., "Even Einstein Struggled: Effects of Learning About Great Scientists' Struggles on High School Students' Motivation to Learn Science," *Journal of Educational Psychology* 108, no. 3 (2016): 314–328. A 2012 study in Taiwan found similar results: When students read about scientists' struggles, they saw them as individuals (similar to them) who had to overcome obstacles; when they read about achievements, they saw scientists as special people with rare, innate talent. The students in this study who read about struggles performed better on a task in the laboratory. Huang-Yao Hong and Xiaodong Lin-Siegler, "How Learning About Scientists' Struggles Influences Students' Interest and Learning in Physics," *Journal of Educational Psychology* 104 (2012): 469–484.

146 there were no errors: Wendy Joung, Beryl Hesketh, and Andrew Neal, "Using 'War Stories' to Train for Adaptive Performance: Is it Better to Learn from Error or Success?," *Applied Psychology* 55, no. 2 (2006): 282–302.

146 reduced patient mortality: Diwas KC, Bradley R. Staats, and Francesca Gino, "Learning from My Success and from Others' Failure: Evidence from Minimally Invasive Cardiac Surgery," *Management Science* 59, no. 11 (2013): 2435–2449.

147 a simple explanation to the *Washington Post*: Ana Swanson, "Why It Feels So Good to Read About This Princeton Professor's Failures," *Washington Post*, April 28, 2016.

147 wanted to clean themselves: Francesca Gino, Maryam Kouchaki, and Adam D. Galinsky, "The Moral Virtue of Authenticity: How Inauthenticity Produces Feelings of Immorality and Impurity," *Psychological Science* 26, no. 7 (2015): 983–996.

149 questions about their self-esteem again: Murad S. Hussain and Ellen Langer, "A Cost of Pretending," *Journal of Adult Development* 10, no. 4 (2003): 261–270.

149 misrepresented themselves in interviews: Celia Moore, Sun Young Lee, Kawon Kim, and Dan Cable, "The Advantage of Being Oneself: The Role of Applicant Self-Verification in Organizational Hiring Decisions," *Journal of Applied Psychology* 102, no. 11 (2017): 1493–1513.

149 a fast-pitch competition: Francesca Gino, Ovul Sezer, Laura Huang, and Alison Wood Brooks, "To Be or Not to Be Your Authentic Self? Catering to Others' Expectations and Interests Hinders Performance," Working paper, 2017 (available from authors).

150 any Boston Red Sox fan: Francesca Gino and Maryam Kouchaki, "Feeling Authentic Serves as a Buffer Against Rejections," Working paper, 2016 (available from authors).

150 either authentic or inauthentic: Ibid.

150 when we're being inauthentic: Sebastian Korb, Stéphane With, Paula Niedenthal, et al., "The Perception and Mimicry of Facial Movements Predict Judgments of Smile Authenticity," *PLoS ONE* 9, no. 6 (2014): e99194.

150 a rise in blood pressure: Emily A. Butler, Boris Egloff, Frank H. Wilhelm, et al., "The Social Consequences of Expressive Suppression," *Emotion* 3, no. 1 (2003): 48–67.

150 even more than outright bragging: Ovul Sezer, Francesca Gino, and Michael I. Norton, "Humblebragging: A Distinct—and Ineffective—Self-Presentation Strategy," *Journal of Personality and Social Psychology*, 114, no. 1 (2018): 52–74.

151 candidates for a second date: Marian L. Houser, Sean M. Horan, and Lisa A. Furler, "Dating in the Fast Lane: How Communication Predicts Speed-Dating Success," *Journal of Social and Personal Relationships* 25, no. 5 (2008): 749–768.

152 inauthenticity exacts heavy costs: Ute R. Hülsheger and Anna F. Schewe, "On the Costs and Benefits of Emotional Labor: A Meta-Analysis of Three Decades of Research," *Journal of Occupational Health Psychology* 16, no. 3 (2011): 361–389.

152 before they went to bed: David T. Wagner, Christopher M. Barnes, and Brent A. Scott, "Driving It Home: How Workplace

Emotional Labor Harms Employee Home Life," *Personnel Psychology* 67, no. 2 (2014): 487–516.

152 **a large Australian hospital:** Alicia Grandey, Su Chuen Foo, Markus Groth, and Robyn E. Goodwin, "Free to Be You and Me: A Climate of Authenticity Alleviates Burnout From Emotional Labor," *Journal of Occupational Health Psychology* 17, no. 1 (2012) 1–14.

153 **the ideas behind the brushstrokes:** Personal interview with Davide di Fabio, July 26, 2016.

154 **ISPA Instituto Universitário:** Andreas Steimer and André Mata, "Motivated Implicit Theories of Personality: My Weaknesses Will Go Away, but My Strengths Are Here to Stay," *Personality and Social Psychology Bulletin* 42, no. 4 (2016): 415–429.

154 **our strengths over our weaknesses:** Albert Bandura, "Self-Efficacy Mechanism in Human Agency," *American Psychologist* 37, no. 2 (1982): 122–147.

154 **unintentionally proved this idea:** Donald O. Clifton and James K. Harter, "Investing in Strengths," http://media.gallup .com/documents/whitepaper--nvestinginstrengths.pdf (accessed November 17, 2017).

154 **Story of Deloitte:** Francesca Gino, Bradley R. Staats, and Paul Green Jr., "Reinventing Performance Management at Deloitte (A) & (B)," Harvard Business School Case 918-020 and 918-021, 2017; interviews conducted for the case throughout 2016 and 2017.

156 **performance by 36 percent:** Corporate Leadership Council, "Building the High-Performance Workforce: A Quantitative Analysis of the Effectiveness of Performance Management Strategies," 2002, http://marble-arch-online-courses.s3.amazonaws .com/CLC_Building_the_High_Performance_Workforce_A _Quantitative_Analysis_of_the_Effectiveness_of_Performance _Management_Strategies1.pdf (accessed November 17, 2017).

157 **focus on their strengths:** Susan Sorenson, "How Employees' Strengths Make Your Company Stronger," *Gallup News*,

February 20, 2014, http://news.gallup.com/business journal/167462/employees-strengths-company-stronger.aspx (accessed November 17, 2017).

157 **family members, friends, and coworkers:** Julia Lee, Francesca Gino, Daniel Cable, and Bradley R. Staats, "Preparing the Self for Team Entry: How Relational Affirmation Improves Team Performance," Working paper, 2017 (available from authors).

158 **I talked to the employees:** Daniel Cable, Francesca Gino, and Bradley R. Staats, "Breaking Them in or Eliciting Their Best? Reframing Socialization Around Newcomers' Authentic Self-Expression," *Administrative Science Quarterly* 58, no. 1 (2013): 1–36.

158 **lessons they had learned that day:** Giada DiStefano, Francesca Gino, Gary Pisano, and Bradley R. Staats, "Making Experience Count: The Role of Reflection in Individual Learning," Working paper, 2017 (available from authors).

159 **Story of Rachael Chong:** Personal interview with Rachael Chong, April 27, 2016.

160 **Story of Mellody Hobson:** Personal interviews with Mellody Hobson, November 4, 2014, December 8, 2014, and August 9, 2016.

7. THE SECRET OF STORY

163 **Chapter 7 epigraph:** Travis Bradberry and Jean Greaves, *Leadership 2.0* (San Diego, CA: TalentSmart, 2012).

166 **across industries and nations:** Gallup Organization, *First, Break All the Rules: What the World's Greatest Managers Do Differently* (New York: Gallup Press, 2016). Questions were simplified for younger participants. They included "At this school, I have the opportunity to do what I do best every day" and "I have a best friend at school."

168 **be themselves on the job:** Kevin Freiberg and Jackie Freiberg, *Nuts! Southwest Airlines' Crazy Recipe for Business and Personal Success* (New York: Broadway Books, 1996).

168 **Barrett has said:** Source of the quotation: "Southwest Airlines' Colleen Barrett Flies High on Fuel Hedging and 'Servant Leadership,'" http://knowledge.wharton.upenn.edu/article /southwest-airlines-colleen-barrett-flies-high-on-fuel-hedging-and -servant-leadership/ (accessed November 29, 2017).

169 **Story of Doug Conant at Campbell's:** Personal interview with Doug Conant, October 10, 2017; Douglas Conant and Mette Norgaard, *TouchPoints: Creating Powerful Leadership Connections in the Smallest of Moments* (San Francisco: Jossey-Bass, 2011); "Keeping Employees Engaged in Tough Times: An Interview with Douglas Conant, Former CEO of Campbell's Soup Company," *Harvard Business Review,* 2011, https://hbr.org/2011/10/keeping -employees-engaged-in-t (accessed November 29, 2017).

170 **"no longer competitive":** Robert Reiss, "Creating TouchPoints at Campbell Soup Company," *Forbes,* July 14, 2011, https://www.forbes .com/sites/robertreiss/2011/07/14/creating-touchpoints-at-campbell -soup-company/#72e2f2792c41 (accessed November 17, 2017).

170 **"a very toxic culture":** Conant and Norgaard, *TouchPoints: Creating Powerful Leadership Connections in the Smallest of Moments.*

173 **in the same period:** : CapitalIQ database, accessed November 20, 2017 (copy available from author).

173 **dedication, absorption, and vigor:** Engagement is a state that is broader and different from another state you may be familiar with: flow. Flow, a concept first described by psychologist Mihaly Csikszentmihalyi, is the holistic sensation we experience when we are completely absorbed in an activity, even with no promise of an external reward for doing so. Flow and engagement both are states of absorption, but conceptually, they are different. Flow is activity-specific, while engagement is more pervasive. Flow is often conceptualized as a peak experience. Engagement, instead, is a pattern that people carry over several domains. Those who are likely to experience engagement at work are also more likely to be engaged at home, research suggests.

173 **expression of gratitude, my research shows:** Adam Grant and
Francesca Gino, "A Little Thanks Goes a Long Way: Explaining
Why Gratitude Expressions Motivate Prosocial Behavior," *Journal
of Personality and Social Psychology* 98 no. 6 (2010), 946–955.

174 **after watching the video:** Productivity data was measured as
tons of tomatoes harvested per operating hour—calculated by
dividing the tons harvested by a harvesting team during the
shift by the number of hours the harvesting team operated that
shift. The number of shifts for which we captured data following
the intervention varied by harvester, as the harvest season end
is dictated primarily by the onset of fall temperatures and rain,
which varies across the state. Consequently, the number of post-
intervention records collected varied by harvester—from 1 to
26, with a mean of 13.06. The full paper is here: Paul Green
Jr., Francesca Gino, and Bradley R. Staats, "Seeking to Belong:
How the Words of Internal and External Beneficiaries Influence
Performance," Harvard Business School Working Paper 17-073
(2017). http://www.hbs.edu/faculty/Publication%20Files/17
-073_9e2b9c23-cac0-4dcc-86ae-aaa2d32698d1.pdf (accessed
November 17, 2017).

174 **pass their exams:** Wilmar B. Schaufeli, Isabel M. Martínez,
Alexandra Marques Pinto, et al., "Burnout and Engagement in
University Students: A Cross-National Study," *Journal of Cross-
Cultural Psychology* 33, no. 5 (2002): 464–481.

175 **Story of Pixar:** Personal interviews with with Ed Catmull,
Dan Scanlon, Jonas Rivera, Jamie Woolf, and Andrew Gordon
conducted during a visit at Pixar, March 31, 2017; personal
follow-up interview with Pete Docter, September 13, 2017; Ed
Catmull with Amy Wallace, *Creativity Inc.: Overcoming the Unseen
Forces That Stand in the Way of True Inspiration* (New York:
Random House, 2014); David A. Price, *The Pixar Touch: The
Making of a Company* (New York: Vintage, 2008); Lawrence Levy,
*To Pixar and Beyond: My Unlikely Journey with Steve Jobs to Make
Entertainment History* (Boston: Mariner Books, 2016).

184 **exploration of novel ideas:** Li Huang and Adam D. Galinsky, "Mind-Body Dissonance. Conflict Between the Senses Expands the Mind's Horizons," *Social Psychological and Personality Science* 2, no. 4 (2011): 351–359; Ella Miron-Spektor, Francesca Gino, and Linda Argote, "Paradoxical Frames and Creative Sparks: Enhancing Individual Creativity Through Conflict and Integration," *Organizational Behavior and Human Decision Processes* 116, no. 2 (2011): 229–240.

184 **learn novel information:** Travis Proulx and Steven J. Heine, "Connections from Kafka: Exposure to Meaning Threats Improves Implicit Learning of an Artificial Grammar," *Psychological Science* 20, no. 9 (2009): 1125–1131.

184 **a more cooperative mood:** Carsten K. W. De Dreu and Bernard A. Nijstad, "Mental Set and Creative Thought in Social Conflict: Threat Rigidity Versus Motivated Focus," *Journal of Personality and Social Psychology* 95, no. 3 (2008): 648–661.

184 **leads them to novel insights:** Bianca Beersma and Carsten K. W. De Dreu, "Conflict's Consequences: Effects of Social Motives on Postnegotiation Creative and Convergent Group Functioning and Performance," *Journal of Personality and Social Psychology* 89, no. 3 (2005): 358–374.

184 **appear to be at odds:** Ella Miron-Spektor, Francesca Gino, and Linda Argote, "Paradoxical Frames and Creative Sparks: Enhancing Individual Creativity Through Conflict and Integration," *Organizational Behavior and Human Decision Processes* 116, no. 2 (2011): 229–240.

185 **Story of *Toy Story*:** Ed Catmull, "How Pixar Fosters Collective Creativity," *Harvard Business Review*, September 2008, https://hbr.org/2008/09/how-pixar-fosters-collective-creativity (accessed November 28, 2017). Personal interview with Ed Catmull, March 31, 2017.

189 **greater employee effort than higher pay:** Duncan S. Gilchrist, Michael Luca, and Deepak Malhotra, "When 3+1:4: Gift Structure and Reciprocity in the Field," *Management Science* 62, no. 9 (2016): 2639–2650.

8. BECOMING A REBEL LEADER

191 **Chapter 8 epigraph:** John Reeve Carpenter, *Pirates: Scourge of the Seas* (New York: Sterling Publishing, 2008).

191 **the legendary Black Bart:** Within the span of his three-year-long career, he captured more than 400 ships. For comparison, Blackbeard captured about 120 of them in a two-year span. Articles like this one were quite common on pirate ships.

191 **Sources for the pirates' story:** Charles Johnson, *A General History of the Pyrates* (Seattle, WA: Loki's Publishing, 1724); Colin Woodard, *The Republic of Pirates: Being the True and Surprising Story of the Caribbean Pirates and the Man Who Brought Them Down* (Orlando, FL: Mariner Books, 2008); Marcus Rediker, *Villains of All Nations: Atlantic Pirates in the Golden Age* (Boston: Beacon Press, 2004); Peter T. Leeson, *The Invisible Hook: The Hidden Economics of Pirates* (Princeton, NJ: Princeton University Press, 2009); multiple conversations with Peter Leeson, spring 2017.

192 **a constitution drafted for each ship:** Peter T. Leeson, "An-*arrgh*-chy: The Law and Economics of Pirate Organization," *Journal of Political Economy* 115, no. 6 (2007): 1049–1094.

193 **Marcus Rediker:** Marcus Rediker, *Between the Devil and the Deep Blue Sea: Merchant Seamen, Pirates and the Anglo-American Maritime World, 1700–1750* (Cambridge, MA: Cambridge University Press, 1987), p. 267.

194 **three to seven members:** Robert Frees Bales, *Interaction Process Analysis: A Method for the Study of Small Groups* (Chicago: University of Chicago Press, 1950; reprinted 1976).

194 **see hierarchies develop:** Elizabeth Gellert, "Stability and Fluctuation in the Power Relationships of Young Children," *Journal of Abnormal and Social Psychology* 62 (1961): 8–15.

194 **they usually fail:** Harold J. Leavitt, *Top Down: Why Hierarchies Are Here to Stay and How to Manage Them More Effectively* (Cambridge, MA: Harvard Business Review Press, 2004).

195 **a less talkative colleague's same suggestion:** Henry W. Riecken, "The Effect of Talkativeness on the Ability to Influence Group Solutions of Problems," *Sociometry* 21 (1958): 309–331.

195 **the former an unfair sheen:** Muzafer Sherif, B. Jack White, and O. J. Harvey, "Status in Experimentally Produced Groups," *American Journal of Sociology* 60, no. 4 (1955): 370–379.

195 **poor decisions and performance:** Chester I. Barnard, *The Functions of the Executive* (Cambridge: Harvard University Press, 1968).

195 **more likely to die:** Eric M. Anicich, Roderick I. Swaab, and Adam D. Galinsky, "Hierarchical Cultural Values Predict Success and Mortality in High-Stakes Teams," *PNAS* 112, no. 5 (2015): 1338–1343.

196 **according to its website:** Cheese Board Collective, "The Cheese Board: A Worker-Owned Collective Since 1971," http://cheeseboardcollective.coop/about-us/about-main/ (accessed November 17, 2017).

196 **Story of Valve Software:** Ethan Bernstein, Francesca Gino, and Bradley R. Staats, "Opening the Valve: From Software to Hardware (A)," Harvard Business School Case 415-015, August 2014.

197 **committed, satisfied, and productive:** Linn Van Dyne and Jon L. Pierce, "Psychological Ownership and Feelings of Possession: Three Field Studies Predicting Employee Attitudes and Organizational Citizenship Behavior," *Journal of Organizational Behavior* 25, no. 4 (2004): 439–459.

197 **think about their current job:** Maryam Kouchaki, Francesca Gino, and Ata Jami, "It's Mine, But I'll Help You: How Psychological Ownership Increases Prosocial Behavior," Working paper, 2017 (available from authors).

200 **Formula One racing:** Martin Williamson, "Monaco Grand Prix 1950: Fangio Escapes the Pile-Up," ESPN, http://en.espn.co.uk /f1/motorsport/story/12022.html (accessed September 25, 2017); Gerald Donaldson, "Monaco Smart Win for Fangio—1950," http://www.f1speedwriter.com/2012/05/grand-prix-de-monaco -1950-juan-manuel.html (accessed September 25, 2017).

201 **the front of his car:** Sources for the story: Robert F. Kennedy, *Thirteen Days: A Memoir of the Cuban Missile Crisis* (Boston: W. W.

Norton & Company, 1971); Ernest R. May and Philip D. Zelikow, eds., *The Kennedy Tapes: Inside the White House During the Cuban Missile Crisis* (New York: W. W. Norton & Company, 2002); Arthur M. Schlesinger Jr., *A Thousand Days: John F. Kennedy in the White House* (Boston: Houghton Mifflin Company, 1965).

202 **quieting dissent and suppressing alternatives:** Irving L. Janis, *Victims of Groupthink: A Psychological Study of Foreign-Policy Decisions and Fiascoes* (New York: Houghton Mifflin, 1972).

202 **Robert Kennedy would comment:** Kennedy, *Thirteen Days*, p. 36.

203 **disagreement in private meetings:** Tony L. Simons and Randall S. Peterson, "Task Conflict and Relationship Conflict in Top Management Teams: The Pivotal Role of Intragroup Trust," *Journal of Applied Psychology* 85, no. 1 (2000): 102–111.

203 **"what the decision is all about":** Tim Hindle, *Guide to Management Ideas and Gurus* (New York: Bloomberg Press, 2008); "Alfred Sloan," *The Economist*, January 30, 2009, http://www .economist.com/node/13047099 (accessed November 29, 2017).

203 **a technique they call "plussing":** Personal interview with Ed Catmull during a visit at Pixar, March 31, 2017.

204 **anything-goes listening sessions:** Boris Groysberg and Michael Slind, "Leadership Is a Conversation," *Harvard Business Review*, June 2012.

204 **what I do, and much more:** Personal interview with Doug Conant, October 10, 2017.

205 **in Silicon Valley, all men:** Kathleen L. McGinn, Deborah M. Kolb, and Cailin B. Hammer, "Traversing a Career Path: Pat Fili-Krushel (A)," Harvard Business School Case 909-009, September 2008 (revised June 2011); personal interview, September 22, 2017.

206 **lacing their shoes:** Andrew Hill with John Wooden, *Be Quick— But Don't Hurry: Finding Success in the Teachings of a Lifetime* (New York: Simon & Schuster, 2001).

205 **can span 6 months:** Gary P. Pisano, Francesca Gino, and Bradley R. Staats, "Pal's Sudden Service—Scaling an Organizational Model to Drive Growth," Harvard Business School Case 916-052, May 2016 (revised March 2017).

206 with this goal in mind: Francesca Gino and Bradley R. Staats, "Samasource: Give Work, Not Aid," Harvard Business School Case 912-011, December 2011 (revised June 2012).

206 "five different textures and temperatures": Personal interviews during visit at Osteria Francescana, July 26–27, 2016.

207 the moon mission of Apollo 13: William David Compton, *Where No Man Has Gone Before: A History of Apollo Lunar Exploration Missions* (Washington, D.C.: U.S. Government Printing Office, 1989).

208 surpass expectations—or better: Irene Scopelliti, Paola Cillo, Bruno Busacca, and David Mazursky, "How Do Financial Constraints Affect Creativity?" *Journal of Product Innovation Management* 31, no. 5 (2014): 880–893.

208 Forbes's list of highest-earning pirates: Kris E. Lane, *Blood and Silver: A History of Piracy in the Caribbean and Central America* (Oxford, Eng.: Signal Books, 1999).

208 Yes, Forbes made a list of top-earning pirates: "Top-Earning Pirates," *Forbes*, September 19, 2008, https://www.forbes.com /2008/09/18/top-earning-pirates-biz-logistics-cx_mw_0919piracy .html#521a37307263 (accessed November 29, 2017).

208 lead to better solutions: See: Irene Scopelliti, Paola Cillo, Bruno Busacca, and David Mazursky, "How Do Financial Constraints Affect Creativity?" Ravi Mehta and Meng Zhu, "Creating When You Have Less: The Impact of Resource Scarcity on Product Use Creativity," *Journal of Consumer Research* 42, no. 5 (2016): 767–782.

210 their three closest friends: Leon Festinger, Kurt W. Back, and Stanley Schachter, *Social Pressures in Informal Groups: A Study of Human Factors in Housing* (Stanford, CA: Stanford University Press, 1950).

210 Del Monte canning factory: Personal interviews during a visit at Pixar, March 31, 2017.

210 team did as a whole: Jennifer L. Berdahl and Cameron Anderson, "Men, Women, and Leadership Centralization in Groups Over Time," *Group Dynamics: Theory, Research, and Practice* 9, no. 1 (2005): 45–57.

CONCLUSION

213 **Conclusion epigraph:** Jeff Gordinier, "Massimo Bottura, the Chef Behind the World's Best Restaurant," *New York Times Style Magazine*, October 17, 2016, https://www.nytimes.com/2016/10/17/t-magazine/massimo-bottura-chef-osteria-francescana.html (accessed November 29, 2017).

213 **Sources for the earthquake story:** Nick Squires, "Earthquake Strikes Northern Italy Killing Six," *Telegraph*, May 20, 2012; Elisabetta Povoledo, "Thousands Are Homeless in Deadly Quake in Italy," *New York Times*, May 21, 2012; "Another Earthquake in Italy Hits Almost Same Spot as Previous One," *Tripoli Post*, May 29, 2012; Andrea Vogt and Tom Kington, "Earthquake in Italy Kills Five and Razes Centuries of History," *Guardian*, May 21, 2012; Tom Kington, "Wheels of Misfortune: Race to Save Parmesan Toppled by Earthquake," *Guardian*, May 23, 2012; interviews with locals, July 2016 and May 2017.

219 **less time-constrained:** Cassie Mogilner, Zoe Chance, and Mike Norton, "Giving Time Gives You Time," *Psychological Science* 23, no. 10 (2012): 1233–1238.

EPILOGUE

221 **Epilogue epigraph:** Jayson DeMers, "51 Quotes to Inspire Success in Your Life and Business," *Inc.com*, November 3, 2014, https://www.inc.com/jayson-demers/51-quotes-to-inspire-success-in-your-life-and-business.html (accessed November 29, 2017).

INDEX

extracts reading groups
competitions books new
discounts extracts
competitions
books
new
events
books
extracts
new titles reading groups
interviews
discounts
new books events
events new
discounts extracts discounts
www.panmacmillan.com
extracts events reading groups
competitions books extracts new